MAY GIBBS
MORE THAN A FAIRY TALE

AN ARTISTIC LIFE

ROBERT HOLDEN
& JANE BRUMMITT

hardie grant books
MELBOURNE · LONDON

Published in 2011 by Hardie Grant Books

Hardie Grant Books (Australia)
Ground Floor, Building 1
658 Church Street
Richmond, Victoria 3121
www.hardiegrant.com.au

Hardie Grant Books (UK)
Dudley House, North Suite
34–35 Southampton Street
London WC2E 7HF
www.hardiegrant.co.uk

All rights reserved. No part of this publication may be reproduced, stored in a retrieval system or transmitted in any form by any means, electronic, mechanical, photocopying, recording or otherwise, without the prior written permission of the publishers and copyright holders.

The moral rights of the authors have been asserted.

Copyright text © Robert Holden and Jane Brummitt 2011
Copyright May Gibbs © The Northcott Society and Cerebral Palsy Alliance 2011

Cataloguing-in-Publication data

Holden, Robert.
   May Gibbs: More than a fairytale/ Robert Holden ; Jane Brummitt.
   ISBN 9781742701509 (hbk.)
   Subjects: Gibbs, May, 1977-1969. Women authors, Australian - 20th century - Biography. Authors, Australian - 20th century - Biography. Illustrators – Australia - Biography.
   Other Authors/Contributors: Brummitt, Jane.

A823.2

Publisher: Pam Brewster
Cover and text design: Trisha Garner
Page layout and typesetting: Kerry Klinner
Colour reproduction by Splitting Image Colour Studio
Printed in China by 1010 Printing International Limited

INTRODUCTION:	
'Without the details there could be no larger picture'	vii
1 'The roughness of the life'	1
2 'Western Australia is England over the water'	13
3 May Gibbs on show	27
4 A 'remarkable little lady'	39
5 The wide world beckons	55
6 'I find my work my greatest pleasure'	73
7 May—the emancipated woman	93
8 Women on the march	105
9 'Cut away from home'	123
10 'Gum-Nut Brownies'	135
11 The gumnut corps go to war	143
12 'Sister Susies Sewing Shirts for Soldiers'	153
13 'Humans Please be kind to all Bush Creatures'	169
14 Conquering a nation	179
15 Australia's Beatrix Potter?	195
POSTSCRIPT	209
A NOTE FROM THE AUTHORS	216
ILLUSTRATIONS	220
BIBLIOGRAPHY	224
INDEX	229

WITHOUT THE DETAILS THERE COULD BE NO LARGER PICTURE

INTRODUCTION

It is a familiar nursery image, one which has endeared itself to generations of children worldwide. It has been made popular in picture books, legends and fairytales. It is the image of a stork delivering a newborn baby—a sentimental and nostalgic illustration, certainly, but one that is evocative and charming. One example, among many, is a celebrated Australian interpretation. It held an iconic status in Australian nurseries from the 1920s until the mid-twentieth century.

This particular image first appeared as a poster. Later, it was reduced in size and printed (and reprinted) countless times on the cover of a handbook for baby health clinics in New South Wales. The sustained appeal that this local version achieved is easily explained. To the customary image of the harassed stork delivering a swaddled bundle, something inspired and original was added: a gumleaf border and a kookaburra. These additions made it unmistakably Australian. So, too, did the caption, a snippet of advice from the stork to the kookaburra. 'I hardly like delivering the Goods Mrs Kookaburra,' the stork complains, 'them Humans is so Gum careless of 'em.' This combination of folklore and humour in an Australian setting made the traditional image endearingly specific to yet another culture.

Self portrait in pencil by May Gibbs, completed while living in Neutral Bay, Sydney c. 1917.

Poster commissioned by the Department of Public Health, Division of Maternal & Baby Welfare, first produced in 1920 to encourage mothers to attend baby clinics that were being established for the first time across New South Wales.

Not surprisingly, this became the scenario which the creator of the image consistently used to begin her repeated attempts at an autobiography (unpublished). That artist was Cecilia May Gibbs. She entitled her memories *That (or This) Other Fairytale* and depicted herself as one of the stork's deliveries. Even as late as 1968, in the last full year of May's life, her last words in the rambling reminiscences she recorded for the National Library of Australia invoked such imagery: 'As far as I can remember, it was just a fairytale all the time'. By conflating these fragmentary accounts into a composite, we can hear May's inimitable voice introducing us to her fantasy world.

According to May's fairytale, her mother-to-be, who was also called Cecilia, was playing the piano and singing at a family birthday party in 1877 in rural England when the festivities were interrupted by one of those sudden dramas that occur so frequently in such stories:

> Dr. Stork alighted by the chimney ... 'House a blaze of light,' he muttered, 'laughter and singing! Oddy Dod! Must be some mistake.' He slid down the slate roof and pulled the door bell. The door opened and a small maid in black with white apron & cap stared at him.
> 'Mrs. Gibbs here?'
> 'Yes sir, that's her singing.'
> 'Powerful voice!' said Dr. Stork, cocking his head to listen, 'smooth, round, rich & mellow.'
> 'Yes sir.'
> 'Tell her I'm come,' said Dr. Stork, putting his umberella [sic] in the hall stand and hanging up his coat & hat. He looked in his little black bag.
> 'Warm and snuggled,' he said, 'but a little restless ...'

In quick succession, as May recorded it, 'Dr. Stork came, I came and the party left'. Thereafter, the traditional fairytale expectation is amusingly overthrown by an unexpected pronouncement: "Looks like a frog, sir,' gasped the maid, 'just like her Ma!"

This, then, was the way May Gibbs chose to introduce herself to the world—by borrowing elements from fairytales. In one sense this was singularly appropriate. After all, this same fairytale child would later create a whole new folklore for children halfway across the world. She would become Australia's first professionally trained book illustrator, devoting herself to writing and illustrating children's books. And she would do all this when inspired by something magical—the unique flora and fauna of her adopted country, Australia.

May's detailed studies of wild flowers provided the botanical inspiration for the successful wild-flower babies books.

Unfortunately, major parts of May Gibbs' story have been sacrificed in the telling of this fairytale, put aside in order to concentrate on the celebration of another 'birth'—that of the gumnut babies. May's childhood and her early adult life have been accorded only a relatively brief overview. Almost 120 years after the stork delivered May, George Seddon asserted in his book *Swan Song* that her 'character is obscure' and that 'it scarcely emerges from her only full biography'.

Some minor evaluations have focused on May's early life, including Jean Lang's *Pathway to Magic* and Chris Sharkey's *May and Herbert Gibbs*. But they reveal little of the diversity and experience of those years. They fail to describe the full and sustained extent of her contribution to the evolving theatrical and artistic life of Perth from the 1890s into the early twentieth century. Nor has that experience been properly assessed as a formative influence and as seminal inspiration for her illustrative work. For these reasons, much of May Gibbs' long life has remained hidden. The one notable exception to this lacuna was the fortuitous unearthing of over sixty pieces of work previously unknown to the public and which had been held by the Gibbs family for generations. The resulting exhibition in Perth in 2001 was a revelation. Its impact and significance in revealing two lost decades of May's work (1891 to 1910) were best conveyed by the curator, Chris Sharkey:

> It reveals a long experimental period before her creative drive became focused on children's literature. It shows a range of her interests and talents and we can see her competence develop as she tackles very different sorts of subjects and media.

Nevertheless, it is substantially true to say that May Gibbs' early life has historically been condensed, and certainly undervalued. In the rush to arrive at the fairytale 'birth' of the gumnut babies, it has been tempting to gloss over what were actually the most formative years of May's life. If ever there was convincing proof that, as Wordsworth said, 'the child is father of the man', then May's experiences and training in these years provide it.

May Gibbs' sensational popularity, achieved almost overnight after her arrival in Sydney in 1913, has also been seen as a fairytale. In one of the earliest items of extended biography, a 1917 article entitled 'Queen of the gum-nuts', she was described as 'the brown-eyed, curly-haired sprite at whose bidding the gum-nut babies and wattle blossom elves and the

x

xii

creatures of the bush come tripping from fairy land for our delight'. Aspects of this fairytale outlook were undoubtedly fostered by the private, even reclusive lifestyle which the artist led. And, admittedly, this almost certainly helped to give May the privacy and quiet space in which she could think, write and illustrate.

During May Gibbs' lifetime, it became commonplace for commentators to describe her as if she were a princess locked away in a castle. As early as 1916, when her illustrations were buoying the spirits of adults and children alike in wartime Australia, the *Bulletin* complained that 'she's almost a stranger in our midst'. Six years later, in one of the first major interviews that May gave after becoming a household name in Australia, the fairytale bias was still being reinforced. She was described in a *Woman's World* piece as 'a woman as shy and elusive as her own gum nut babies, shrinking from the glare of personal publicity and the fierce light that beats upon a throne'.

In 1947, that same image was reworked for a full-page interview for *Woman*, which described May 'as timid and reluctant of curiosity as one of her own Gumnut Babies'. And almost a half-century later, May's celebrity status was still being described in otherworldly terms. In Seddon's *The Birth of Snugglepot* she was likened to Pallas Athena, the Greek goddess of wisdom, who was said to have sprung fully formed from the head of Zeus—though this comparison was rightly acknowledged as only existing 'because we lack a credible background'.

Now, however, this is to be redressed. Hidden away in brief newspaper snippets, shipping records and exhibition and concert catalogues, programs and reviews are the first thirty-six years of May Gibbs' life. In the process of uncovering these, we discern not only the genesis of the inspired creativity that followed, but also a completely different human being to the reclusive and studio-bound Sydney artist. What we see for the very first time, in fact, is the child, the girl and the young woman leading a life of vibrant opportunity, social engagement and considerable variety.

In many respects, May Gibbs' early life followed a similar trajectory to that of her fellow Australian writer and contemporary Miles Franklin, who was born in 1879, just two years later than May. At virtually the same time, both

Watercolour study of May's English friend Rene Heames. May often used friends and family as models for her sketches and portraits.

women were travelling overseas gaining formative experiences, as well as involving themselves in the suffrage movement. Unlike May, however, Franklin left much more detailed written documentation of her life, which proved invaluable in the compilation of Jill Roe's biography *Stella Miles Franklin*, as well as in providing the context for Franklin's considerable correspondence, published in two volumes.

This is not, of course, to say that May Gibbs and her contribution to Australian children's literature, let alone to Australia's self-image and national consciousness, have been overlooked. She has, after all, received the same iconic status as England's Beatrix Potter. And that is a context that is illuminating. The first major biography of Potter, Margaret Lane's *The Tale of Beatrix Potter*, which appeared in 1946, presented her as a solitary child who treated her pets as substitutes for human affection and companionship. Twenty years later, however, when Potter's journals were deciphered by Leslie Linder, a much more vigorous and determined character emerged. Something similar is surely happening now as May Gibbs the child, the adolescent and the young adult are finally revealed. In this comparative context we see that both these illustrators enjoyed and were inspired by visits to zoos, and that both were united in their admiration of the work of the nineteenth-century British illustrator Randolph Caldecott.

In the following pages, the early experiences of the young May Gibbs, including the formative artistic and cultural opportunities presented to her, are revealed. A new history emerges from a neglected past as what was previously unknown or considered irrelevant is gleaned and savoured as contributions to a reassessment. Each of us is the child of the historical, cultural and social milieus which we inhabit, and May Gibbs proves not to be immune to these influences. From her earliest years on into her cosmopolitan travels as a young adult, we trace the experiences and influences which clearly fashioned the unique artistic vision of this remarkable woman.

The research for this biography followed a variety of paths; some of these have been well trodden by previous researchers, while others required pioneering enterprise. In the course of this research, the authors discovered how easily anyone can disappear from history. Perhaps women are more susceptible to being erased or dismissed than men; after all, even someone as well known in her own day as May Gibbs has proved elusive. It has

therefore seemed reasonable, at times, to draw attention to the problems encountered in the writing of this book. Ultimately, there can be no seamless narrative because there are always gaps, silences and omissions in the text of a life story. May Gibbs is no exception.

For these reasons, a telling quote from Ian McEwan's moving 2001 novel *Atonement* has been used to preface this book. The injunction 'Without the details there could be no larger picture' was a succinct and constant reminder of the priorities throughout the writing. The authors believe that this 'larger picture' finally restores May Gibbs as a more complete human being, yet not at the expense of the fairytale. This is because her early years, from her birth in 1877 to 1913, when her gumnut babies first appeared, can now be seen to have been filled with the magic of theatre and performance and public acclaim.

CHAPTER 1

'THE ROUGHNESS OF THE LIFE'

So what is the reality behind the fairytale version of May Gibbs' birth? Although May always claimed that she was born at her grandparents' home in Ganders Green Lane, Cheam Fields in Surrey, her birth certificate, which was signed by her mother, states that Cecilia May Gibbs' birthplace was Lower Sydenham, Kent on 17 January 1877. What is beyond challenge is that she was born into a family where art and culture were celebrated yet woven into a work ethic that would take them halfway across the world.

May's paternal grandfather, William Gibbs, studied at Bonn University in Germany in the 1820s. At about the age of twenty-one he arranged 'a runaway marriage' with Eliza Emery at St Dunstan's, West London, and upon the providential arrival of an inheritance the couple moved to England's south coast, near Portsmouth. There, William Gibbs bought out a small-time ship owner and merchant in the town of Hardway and commenced a life of some standing: as an officer of the Hants' Yeomanry and a member of the Royal Victoria Yacht Club of Cowes on the Isle of Wight. For a number of years the Gibbs household was affluent enough to employ a groom, a cook, a housemaid, a nursemaid and a house boy, and to sail their own yacht.

Watercolour painted by May Gibbs of Gander Green Lane in Surrey, where May's grandparents, Ishmael and Jennett Rogers lived.

Interestingly, by the mid-1890s, May's father Herbert also owned yachts—*Pysche* and *The Gadfly*—and had helped found the Perth Sailing Club. Herbert Gibbs took this inherited love of life under sail still further: his depictions of late-Victorian pastimes on the Swan River and along the Perth coastline were recognised, even in his own day, as valuable early records of West Australian history. Eventually, he became so noted for these pioneering depictions of Western Australia that, in 1895, two such works—*Cottesloe Beach* and *North Beach*—were acquired by the Art Gallery of Western Australia. The tradition of sailing in the Gibbs family was maintained by May herself, surfacing in her frequent depictions of the gumnuts' escapades aboard 'yachts' made from kurrajong pods.

Herbert and his brother George were both competent sailors and the idea of sailing across the seas to the other side of the world with the opportunity to own their own farm was very appealing.

By the early 1860s, the lifestyle enjoyed by William Gibbs and his family had collapsed in debt. Later in life, Herbert's mother told him that his father had no business training and that, while indulging his passions for yachting, shooting, hunting and fishing, he had left the operation of his business to a manager). Fortunately, a yachting friend came to the rescue. Francis Palmer Astley, a wealthy land and coalmine owner, settled the Gibbs family on his estate in Singleton, Sussex, and engaged William as a tutor to his son, ten-year-old Frank. While Frank was eventually sent to Eton, however, Herbert Gibbs, the eldest of William's seven children, had to be content with the nearby grammar school.

At fifteen, Herbert was already showing a talent for drawing, but it was a talent that could have been disastrously curtailed when, with ill-timed curiosity, he stepped out from behind a tree during a game of archery and was blinded in one eye. He was sent to convalesce with his grandparents in Brighton, where he was able to attend the Eye Institute as an outpatient, but it would be two years before he could read again.

In 1868, when Herbert Gibbs was sixteen, his family moved to London where his father sought to re-establish himself, this time as an employee in the Records and Accounts Department of the General Post Office. The upheaval came as a stark contrast to Herbert's former life. His family was now compelled to live near the Queen's Road Station—in Herbert's words, 'a hateful place' after 'the freedom and luxury' of the Sussex countryside. Nevertheless, metropolitan life had at least one advantage. Herbert was able to enrol in the Royal College of Art in South Kensington and later attend the Slade School of Art. During these years of training, he began working

as a clerk in the same department as his father. And then, in 1872, after the Slade had begun admitting women to its art classes for the first time, Herbert met a fellow student while travelling there by train.

Cecilia ('Cecie') Rogers was the ninth of twelve children born to musical and artistic parents, Ishmael and Jennett Rogers. This particular daughter seemed to have inherited the combined talent of both her parents—the leading roles which Cecie took in a variety of choral and operatic productions after emigrating to Australia provided clear evidence of a sound musical education. However, it was the art world that claimed her first, with twenty-one-year-old Cecie and her older sister, Emily, both enrolling at the Slade.

On 24 October 1874, within two years of meeting, Cecie and Herbert Gibbs were married. The couple moved to Surrey to be near Cecie's parents and it was there that their first child, Herbert Mordaunt ('Bertie') Gibbs, was born on 3 July 1875. Two years later the renowned stork delivered a sister for little Bertie—Cecilia May, who thereafter, within the family, was always called Mamie.

A lifetime later, May Gibbs claimed to recall an extremely early experience. Her memories of her 'baby days' were captured in vignettes in *That Other Fairytale* that were like the flickering images in a primitive newsreel:

> In dark despair, left by my mother—the first time—an aunt I did not know heard my passionate crys [sic] of misery—she wrapped me in her arms & I was lifted into a new world—spanking along in a high dogcart. I saw the hedges and fields rushing away & the flowers in the roadside grass. The shiny hind quarters of the huge animal that took us behind him. Aunty tucked the rug more closely round me. 'Comfy darling?'

It seems singularly appropriate that these descriptions are so visually precise. As May herself concluded in her autobiography, 'I was to remember that little picture all my life'.

May Gibbs' maternal grandparents, her aunts and cousins from this large family, all had a profound influence on her throughout the first four years of her life, during which time her father continued to work as a clerk in the General Post Office. Then, in 1881, the Gibbs family resolved to follow the example of so many of their fellow countrymen by emigrating to the colonies.

Their decision was encouraged by a story of good fortune. A friend of theirs had a relative who had taken up land in South Australia and praised its

For May's parents, too, the move was radical and energising. Her father at last met fellow artists, and almost overnight his life and his opportunities were enhanced. One such artist was the professionally trained Henry Charles Prinsep, who came from a highly cultured English family. The immediate affinity forged between the two resulted in a partnership that launched Perth's first comic and satirical paper, *The 'Possum*. Their close friendship also saw them produce stage sets for local productions. In short, they became cultural catalysts in the life of the colony.

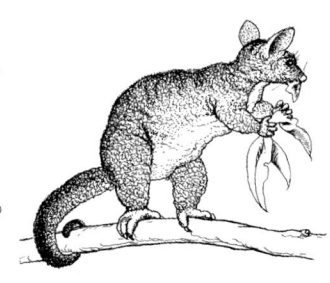

The cover of their brave, all-too-brief literary attempt, which at first appeared fortnightly, then weekly, comprised a ring-tailed opossum looking down from his gum tree at Perth's Government House. The premise of the paper was that, from this vantage point, the animal could see and report on the entertaining foibles and misdeeds of the local citizens. This purpose is proclaimed in *The 'Possum*'s debut edition, published on 30 July 1887:

> … to 'shoot' the public and hit them on their funny bones—their comical sides so to speak but he will insert his claws if necessary, into any obnoxious bills … and he hopes his claws will be a chef d'oeuvre to temper the wind from any shorn lambs and trusting all will twig his meaning, he begs respectfully to make his bow to the public.

Over the six months of *The 'Possum*'s struggling existence, after which it transformed into the *W. A. Bulletin*, Herbert relished the chance to pillory corrupt landowners, mock politicians, snub Britain and embrace a new patriotism. Undoubtedly, the wordplay, comic invention and pictorial humour which May's father created for each issue helped establish her own pictorial vocabulary and her skill as an episodic storyteller. The paper's pictorial character sketches and cartoons played a fundamental part in moulding her own imaginative world.

In June 1890, within a few years of Herbert Gibbs' debut as an illustrator, the *West Australian* reported that he was regarded as one of Perth's most 'skilful wielders of the pencil and brush'. May's father understandably followed the prevailing cartoon style of his era, one popularised by such British luminaries as Phil May and Livingston Hopkins, though he eventually became a landscape artist noted for his depictions of the metropolitan beaches and rivers of Perth—so much so that he was credited with helping to shape Western Australia's self-image.

It was surely inevitable that, with such an accomplished paternal example, May's early work took on many of the characteristics of her father's style.

At times, both of them favoured a collage style of layout with overlapping images—a crowded, if not fussy, debt to Victorian taste. It was May's personal achievement to move beyond this, realigning the scattered format into a more sequential narrative and producing a more orderly layout.

Two other fundamental changes in the Gibbs family's fortunes occurred in 1887. The first of these was when Cecie Gibbs' eldest brother Ishmael Rogers, his wife Fanny and some of their large family arrived in Western Australia as emigrants, disembarking from the SS *Australind* on 11 February; eventually, all eight of their daughters joined them. Suddenly, May found herself within a greatly enlarged family circle, one which contributed significantly to her cultural development. Then, on 3 October, another brother for May arrived: Harold Emery Gibbs.

By now, May was ten years old and a more formal education was at last possible. Among that year's intake at the popular local Bishop's Girls' College were two members of the Gibbs household. When the school advertised the commencement of the new term in September 1887, Herbert Gibbs was listed as its drawing master; he remained there for almost a year. Although May was enrolled at the school, it seems likely that she received additional tuition, either formally or informally, from the Rogers family—in mid-1887, May's aunt and cousins opened their own school, which taught music, singing, painting and drawing for over a decade.

Eighty years later, while being recorded by the National Library of Australia, May recalled those early schooldays with obvious pride and nostalgia. Her reminiscences offer an intriguing insight into the embryonic years of the young artist. 'I was a very silly, stupid student at school', May said, 'but I did the maps so beautifully that my mistress wouldn't put them in with the others.' She also declared: 'I could draw almost as soon as I could walk. And I loved everything … I used to lie down in the grass so that my eyes were on the same level amongst the grass stalks as the ants … And I loved drawing.'

Equally significant were May's fond recollections of her parents and the highly formative examples they set. She described her father sitting on his 'little three-cornered stool, in front of an easel with a big board on it … painting something and mother sitting beside him in a more comfortable chair, reading some interesting book'. May would 'come round and perch somewhere', making this a charmed family circle.

May's baby brother, Harold Emery Gibbs, was the family's first Australian-born child.

Herbert built two boats, *The Gadfly* and later *Psyche*, while living in South Perth. The family was 'always on the water' according to May.

opportunities. Furthermore, Herbert's younger unmarried brother, George Gordon Gibbs, was eager to accompany them and seek his own fortune. It seemed that May was not the only family member susceptible to the allure of fairytales! Perhaps the idea of regaining some of the standing lost when their father's business had failed was a lure for them. When May recorded her reminiscences for the National Library of Australia in 1968, however, she gave an alternative explanation for her family's antipodean move: Herbert Gibbs had left England because, there, 'he'd have to be working in an office in a false light, artificial light, and that would be so bad for the eyes'.

At that time, South Australia seemed to be the Elysian Fields of the colonies, offering the tempting prospect of a new beginning on the land. German migrants had established the Barossa vine-growing area in the 1840s and 1850s, and the area had become the granary for the rest of the continent. There was no hint of the recession to come in the mid-1880s, or of the depression that would follow in the 1890s. South Australia was wealthy and optimistic enough to be immersed in plans for an international exhibition, to be held in mid-1881. In anticipation of unprecedented publicity, the colony had published a handbook for prospective emigrants and had issued it to the Emigration Agent for South Australia in Westminster for gratuitous distribution.

The promises contained in *South Australia: a brief account of its progress and resources* would have been lure enough for Herbert Gibbs. 'With very little capital,' the handbook declared to the world, 'a selector might with safety start farming in South Australia'. Its detailed statistics were so encouraging that it seemed the wilderness had not only been conquered but was blossoming. 'No British colony in the world', it assured potential selectors like Gibbs, 'can boast of a better rate of individual progress than can South Australia'. And, of course, this destination had one other overriding attraction—it had been founded as a free, rather than a convict, colony.

Even so, at the very beginning this particular dream received a setback. On the eve of departure, May developed measles. Together with her mother and older brother, May stayed behind while her father and uncle went on ahead. Herbert and George, aged twenty-eight and twenty-two respectively, sailed from Plymouth on the Orient Line steamer SS *Chimborazo* on 14 April 1881 and arrived in Port Adelaide at the beginning of June.

Herbert and George set off from Plymouth, bound for Adelaide, with 250 other passengers.

By this time May had recovered, and so on 22 July the rest of the family, including a pregnant Cecie Gibbs, embarked on the SS *Hesperus*. Cecie must have expected, or at least hoped, to be able to deliver the baby in Adelaide. But after rounding the Cape of Good Hope, their ship was becalmed for some weeks—before setting off, they surely would never have imagined enduring such a protracted voyage. Then, exactly a week before the ship was to dock, on 24 October, Cecie Gibbs gave birth to another child—Ivan. This gave Ivan the opportunity, later in life, to refer to himself as the wreck of the *Hesperus*!

Once again, May's autobiographical scraps can be relied on to provide amusing and colourful anecdotes from the voyage. Her lively interest in social interaction was evident even at this early age. Her naturally retentive mind remembered the sea shanties she heard on board and she insisted on 'entertaining' her fellow passengers with her own renditions. A decade later, her applauded performances on stage in Perth, singing at concerts in company with her mother, validated her written assessment of her precocious debut on board the *Hesperus*: 'I was a star performer and took it quite seriously'.

May's autobiographical attempts repeatedly recalled the antics and the characters aboard the *Hesperus* that helped her and her brother pass the time:

> Tom McKinley … a lovely [sailor], minded us when off duty—always loved him … listening outside cabin door—hear strange noise.
> 'What's that?' I am asked.
> 'A cock crowing,' I said.
> It was my baby brother just born.

These early memories are delivered with an engrossing coda, a humorous reaction from May's older brother to the latest 'bird' in the family nest: 'We'll make a pigeon pie of it,' said Bertie.

Whatever the impetus for their emigration, the Gibbs family had set out with little idea of what they were to confront as 'new chums' (British immigrants) in 1880s Australia. Herbert and George had envisaged themselves as gentlemen farmers in a new world of golden opportunity. But the stark reality of the final landfall at Cowell on Franklin Harbour was sobering. As Herbert related almost fifty years later in his *Arrival in South Australia*, they had been led to picture 'a most attractive place and life' but instead were confronted with 'a scene of dirt, disorder and discomfort'.

Herbert travelled everywhere with his paints and sketchbook.

The family found itself in a two-room slab hut in the Australian bush. Life here had dangers that were unheard of back in England. Only six months earlier, the South Australian Register had published a dreadful story: a local mother and her six children had burned to death in a bushfire. After a life of some gentility and comfort in provincial England, Herbert and his wife had arrived to all this, not only with May and Bertie, but also with a newborn child.

This was not the pastoral idyll they had imagined. The Australian countryside was utterly different from England's—it had to be subjugated. But in spite of stake fences, the Gibbs were besieged by hordes of wallabies that ate the crops. Wild bullocks trampled down the fences to get to the wheat, and dingoes were always on the prowl for sheep. Then there was the menace of bushfires and other natural disasters that wreaked their worst upon the area—severe hailstorms and flooding rains swept the Eyre Peninsula in December 1881.

With two gulfs separating the isolated outpost from Adelaide, the settlers were a world away from assistance. Communications were intermittent, mail was sporadic and although the overland telegraph line ran to within only a few kilometres of Cowell, there was no connection—visible nearby, the wires mocked the family's isolated existence.

May's first biographer, Maureen Walsh, succinctly pointed out the radical dislocation of the family: 'Gone were the halcyon days of Cheam Fields where servants took care of menial tasks and a regiment of grandparents and aunts fought to spoil the children'. There was, however, one outstanding blessing: 'it was a strange kindergarten for a little four-year-old girl ... [but] to a budding artist whose skills must include the powers of observation it was a great schoolroom'.

Decades later, May remembered that her father had tried to soften the harsh welcome with the only means available—a bunch of wild flowers. Nothing, however, could have ameliorated the discomfort and grim reality of the family's new home. Their dream of a pastoral utopia was shattered. Cecie and the children returned to Adelaide on the first available paddle steamer, three gruelling months after having disembarked. Herbert later wrote that 'Cecie could not stand the roughness of the life' and that 'all crops in Franklin Harbour failed and we had to leave'.

As a child of four arriving in the colonies, May Gibbs had exchanged the cuckoo and the nightingale for new serenaders—the kookaburra and

To reach their new home, the family travelled six miles by cart through the mallee scrub to where Herbert had built a two-room log hut.

the bellbird. Change seemed to be the order of the day. By the beginning of the next decade, native-born Australians finally outnumbered immigrants and they began to celebrate and value their own landscape. Australia's flora and fauna started to become icons of national pride and, as part of the new generation entering the twentieth century, May Gibbs was influenced by this evolving consciousness. A growing appreciation of nature education, outdoor recreation and even conservation was emerging.

As May entered her adult years, her adopted country was eager to find national symbols to fulfil its quest for self-definition and pride. Her role in creating this national pictorial vocabulary would make her a household name.

CHAPTER 2

After the abortive attempt at establishing a new life at Franklin Harbour, Herbert Gibbs abandoned his ambition to settle on the land and returned to Adelaide. Unemployment was high, but the Crown Lands office was seeking experienced draftsmen and by 1882 Herbert was once again behind a drafting board. The Gibbs family first settled in the suburb of Norwood—although it had only been declared a municipality in 1853, Norwood was entering a period of development and made a welcome contrast to the family's previous home on the Eyre Peninsula.

In the year of their arrival in Norwood, a foundation stone was laid for a new town hall. What was obviously becoming one of Adelaide's most desirable areas was enthusiastically described in the *South Australian Register* that September: 'In all directions, lordly halls, neat villas, and humble cottages are occupying former vacant lots'. The newspaper piece attributed the popularity of the suburb as a place of residence 'to the laying-down of

In summer the children swam in the Harvey River waterholes—the biggest is still known as Gibbs Pool.

May Gibbs reading Dickens' *Bleak House*, painted in oils by Herbert Gibbs at their home in Murray Street, Perth, in 1889.

water-mains … the supply of gas, and, above all, to the establishment of the [horse] tramway'. Municipal advances were also evident in the laying and upgrading of roads, the planting of trees and the installation of street lamps. For a time, it appeared that May and her family could settle into a more genteel life, even when they moved to nearby Knightsbridge in 1883.

Then, in August 1885, history repeated itself. Once more enticed by the lure of golden opportunities, Herbert Gibbs relocated his family near to Bunbury in the southwestern corner of Western Australia. Only a few years later, that colony was extravagantly praised in terms that could well have inspired the nursery-rhyme illustrations May Gibbs went on to produce in the 1890s and 1900s. The encyclopedic *West Australian Settler's Guide and Farmer's Handbook* likened the region to 'a huge pie, the crust of which has only, as yet, been nibbled round the edges'. This tempting feast only awaited the arrival of 'Jack Horners … to pull out the plums'. At the time, however, Herbert could well have been tempted to move west by a pamphlet produced by British shipping lines and emigrant outfitters, extolling Western Australia above all the other colonies.

Western Australia: a short sketch of the climate, products, population and prospects of the colony asserted that 'Western Australia is England over the water, with the advantage of a practically unlimited amount of unoccupied land'. It promised 'ample room for all, and a hearty welcome from old Colonists awaits those who arrive'. Its ultimate enticement was surely a recent quote from the governor: 'Each little township resembled an English village rather than the colonial assortment of stray atoms one is familiar with elsewhere'.

Once more, Herbert and George journeyed first. The again-pregnant Cecie and her three children, now aged ten, eight and three, sailed later in the saloon cabin of the *South Australian*. After a 2400-kilometre voyage, they made landfall at Bunbury. From there it was a short journey north by coach to the homestead of the Harvey River Cattle Station, which had been built in 1830 as a hunting lodge for Western Australia's first governor, Captain James Stirling.

The Gibbs family's arrival at Harvey River was not, at least, as disappointing as their initial visit to South Australia. Indeed, when in her nineties, May recalled that 'my happiest time ever was during the 2 years my father managed at Harvey with Uncle George to help'. She explored the

neighbourhood on her pony, 'Brownie', enjoyed picnics in the bush with her brothers and spent days cooling off in the few precious waterholes that were all that remained of the river throughout the summer—she undressed behind trees to then dash into the pools, and used galvanised-iron bathtubs as boats. It was there that she developed a passion for the close observation of the Australian bush and its creatures, guided by her father's keen eye as an amateur naturalist. It is easy to imagine how these memories might have later inspired her illustration of the gumnuts bathing in a diving pool.

George Grey had explored the area in January 1839 and the idyllic scene which he described in his published journals had not changed by the 1880s. In his words, the Harvey River 'bore the appearance of a mountain trout-stream … whilst on the banks of the river good forage abounded'. Towards the end of the nineteenth century, the 'remarkable picturesqueness' of this location was still being praised. The *Settler's Guide and Farmer's Handbook* noted that 'tall red gums here and there darken the sky with their heavy foliage, and battalions of blackboys are drawn up in picturesque array'. These blackboys, or spear-grass trees, became such a formative memory for May that she incorporated them into illustrations throughout her life.

There was one particular attraction of the Harvey River district that inspired May and helped her find her first artistic niche—that of botanical artist. The area's wild flowers were so varied and so abundant that, again in the words of the handbook, they 'make even the roughest scrub paddocks at a little distance resemble a conservatory, and supply beautiful displays at the competitive shows which are held throughout the season'.

Sadly, despite all this natural beauty and inspiration, not all of May's memories of Harvey River were to be happy ones. On 13 December 1885, Cecie gave birth to a stillborn baby. Christmas that year must have been a somewhat muted affair, although an event on New Year's Eve brought new joy to the family: George Gibbs married Ellen Holden in nearby Bunbury. Among those accompanying the bride was her sister, Winifred. She not only became a new aunt for May but, in later life, her stalwart supporter.

Although it has been claimed that May and her brothers were educated at Harvey River by their parents, an advertisement in the 17 September 1885 edition of the *West Australian* indicates that the children may have benefited from more than their parents' guidance: 'Governess wanted: English and

An illustration by May Gibbs for an unpublished book, *Mimie and Wag*.

The wicked Banksia Man drew on the unusual botanical shapes formed by dried banksia flower spikes.

Music, three children. Address Mrs. H. W. Gibbs, Harvey River, Bunbury'. If the family did manage to procure the services of an acceptable teacher, it would have taken much pressure off the beleaguered parents, who found their new undertaking no easier than the last. Years later, May recalled her father's weary existence there: '[He] nearly killed himself trying to keep order—book keeping at night, stock hunting by day—never having had previous experience of any of it'.

The following November, the *West Australian* carried an advertisement for another addition to the Gibbs' household: 'Wanted—A good General Maid Servant'. These notices surely indicate how seriously the family attempted to settle in at Harvey River.

For May, besides her stillborn sibling, there was only one cloud on her childhood horizon here: this was where the idea of the Big Bad Banksia Man was generated. In her autobiography, May jotted down a sketchy account of a traumatic incident that happened when she was about eight years old:

> The day parents went to visit the Smiths—we were left at home, the long shed—Isaac held the little girl (8 years?) she snatches his pocket knife from the bench and threatens to stab his hand—he releases her and she fled, small brother throws stones at shed.

This describes some kind of confrontation with an old carpenter called Isaac who was employed on the property. Whether Isaac had tried to assault the child or simply frightened her with inappropriate or misunderstood behaviour, we will never know. He was dismissed by May's parents, but the memory of his grizzled face and threatening presence remained. 'Sitting on almost every branch' of the native banksia trees, her fertile imagination pictured 'ugly little, wicked little men' with faces like Isaac's. May eventually turned her belief that she had escaped the clutches of a real-life Banksia Man into the central dramatic conflict which haunted the miniature world of the gumnut babies.

The Gibbs' brothers and their families struggled to make a living. For all its apparent fertility, Harvey River Cattle Station was literally a world away from their own experiences. Before any Europeans could establish themselves as farmers there, they needed to acquire knowledge of the local conditions. But how were crops to be grown and stock nurtured in geographical and economic conditions where farming had never been attempted before?

Eventually, the Gibbs' brothers realised that they were simply not suited to working this radically different land, with its unpredictable seasons and setbacks.

After eighteen months at Harvey River, George Gibbs took a job as mine manager for a tin-mining company further south. Ten-year-old May and her family moved closer to Perth, looking to settle into a lifestyle more suited to their natures and abilities. It was a move from rural isolation to suburban life, one that offered the social and cultural opportunities that had been so lacking and were so missed in their lives. Furthermore, Herbert had become intent on distancing himself from his failed pastoral attempts and earning a living from what he knew best—his art.

The family leased an old cottage on a small parcel of land at Lake Claremont, formerly known as Butler's Swamp. They were about halfway between Perth and Fremantle and close to Butler's Siding, which was on the railway line between the two towns. Their neighbours were Francis and Maud Bird and their six children. Here at last was some cultured companionship for Herbert and Cecie and playmates for May and her brothers. The immediate affinity between the two families was evident in the watercolour card that May painted as a New Year's greeting, an offering the Birds treasured for a lifetime. This card, created by May just before her tenth birthday to welcome in the year 1887, is believed to be her earliest work still in existence.

Eleven-year-old Mary Bird became May's particular friend. Her diary (unpublished), written after she became Mary Cowle, contains what is almost certainly the first known description of May by someone outside the family circle:

> Claremont. The Gibbs came to live across the line. The Gibbs were English people—very cultivated and artistic. Later when the Operatic Club was formed they were the leading lights in it. May Gibbs used to come over and play with me. She was only a child but she painted quite well.

For the rest of her life, May thought of this as an idyllic time when she had companionship other than that of her brothers—all in a comfortable home set in a picturesque landscape. And the frogs! May always remembered the swamp for its abundance of frogs. Years later they appeared as the inspired musical corps in her Gum Blossom Ballet illustrations in *Tales of Snugglepot and Cuddlepie*.

The card that nine-year-old May Gibbs created and gave to life-long friend Mary Cowle to celebrate the beginning of 1887.

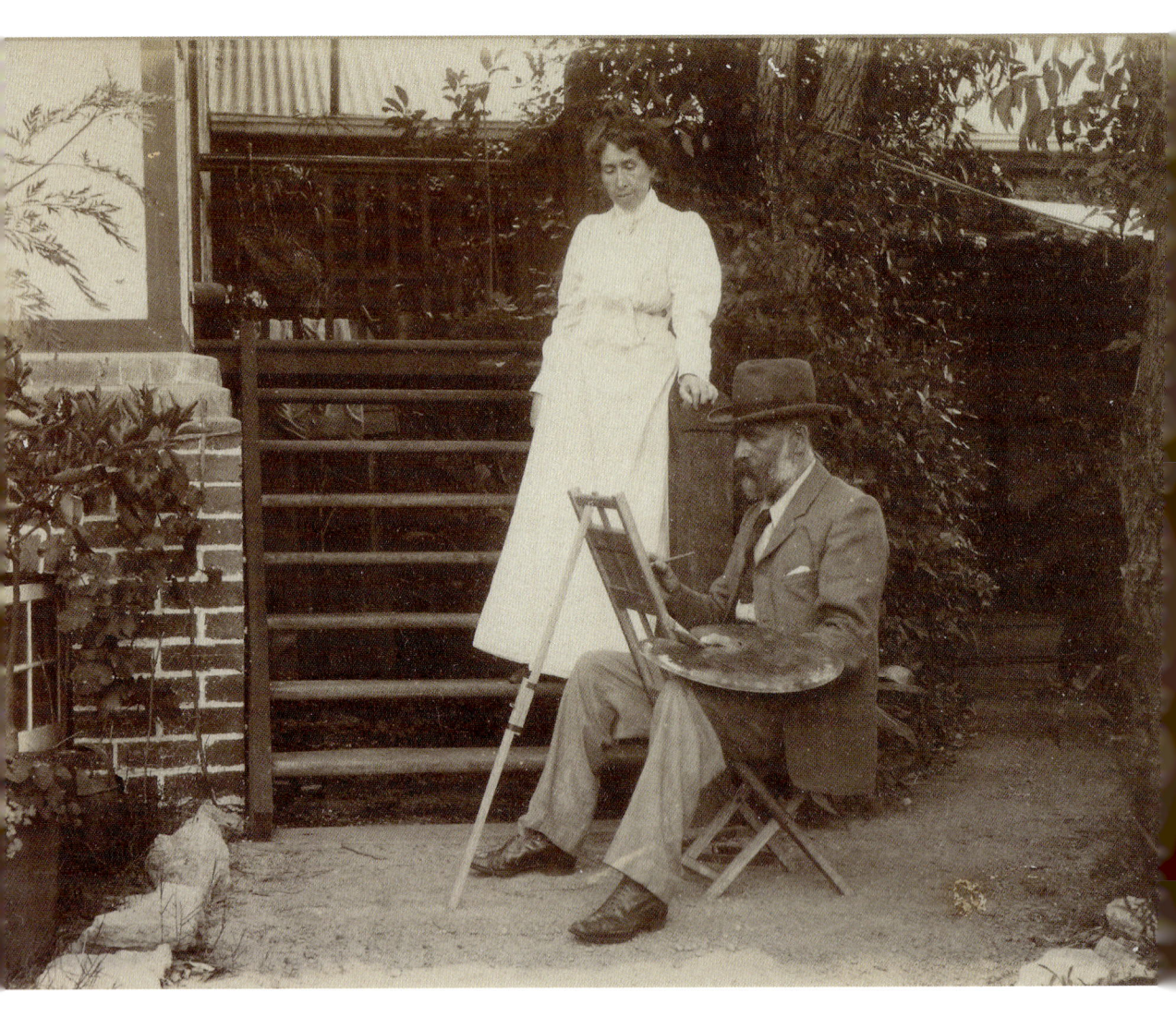

Herbert and Cecie Gibbs in the garden of 'The Dune'—the rambling family home of red brick and stucco, built over three levels. Upstairs were the music room and studio.

The Gibbs family home, 'The Dune', in South Perth.

FACING PAGE: May's father, Herbert was a 'naturally wonderful' father, who 'was so good he could teach me,' said May. He was the mentor and role model who encouraged her as an artist, cartoonist and satirist.

Many of Perth's founding families sent their daughters to Bishop's Girl's College. Their faith in the school was validated by a significant social commentator, the journalist Richard Twopeny (Richard Nowell), who visited the Australian colonies in the 1880s. In his resulting book, *Town Life in Australia*, Twopeny criticised most schools for girls in the eastern states but then lauded Bishop's for its combination of 'social and intellectual qualifications'. May was, of course, only one of a number of girls who benefited from this teaching. Also attending the school in those years was Janet Nanson, who became Western Australia's first full-time female journalist—as 'Sigma', she joined May as a contributor to the *Western Mail*.

After only a year in Claremont, the Gibbs family moved to Murray Street in Perth. They had as neighbours the influential Forrest family—John was to become Western Australia's colonial treasurer (he was given the courtesy title of 'premier') in December 1890—as well as Bernard Woodward, who was appointed the first curator of the West Australian Museum in 1892, and fellow artist Florence Fuller.

By now, Herbert's work with the *W. A. Bulletin* had petered out and once again he was forced to take up teaching—for a brief time he was the drawing master of Perth Grammar School. Then, in 1889, Herbert returned to his former occupation: he was appointed to the Western Australian Lands & Survey Department as a draftsman and clerk, a professional position that he held until his retirement in December 1917.

In confirmation of the fact that the family was finally consolidating its opportunities, 1889 was also the year in which they made one more move across the Swan River to South Perth—to 'The Dune', which remained the Gibbs family home for a generation.

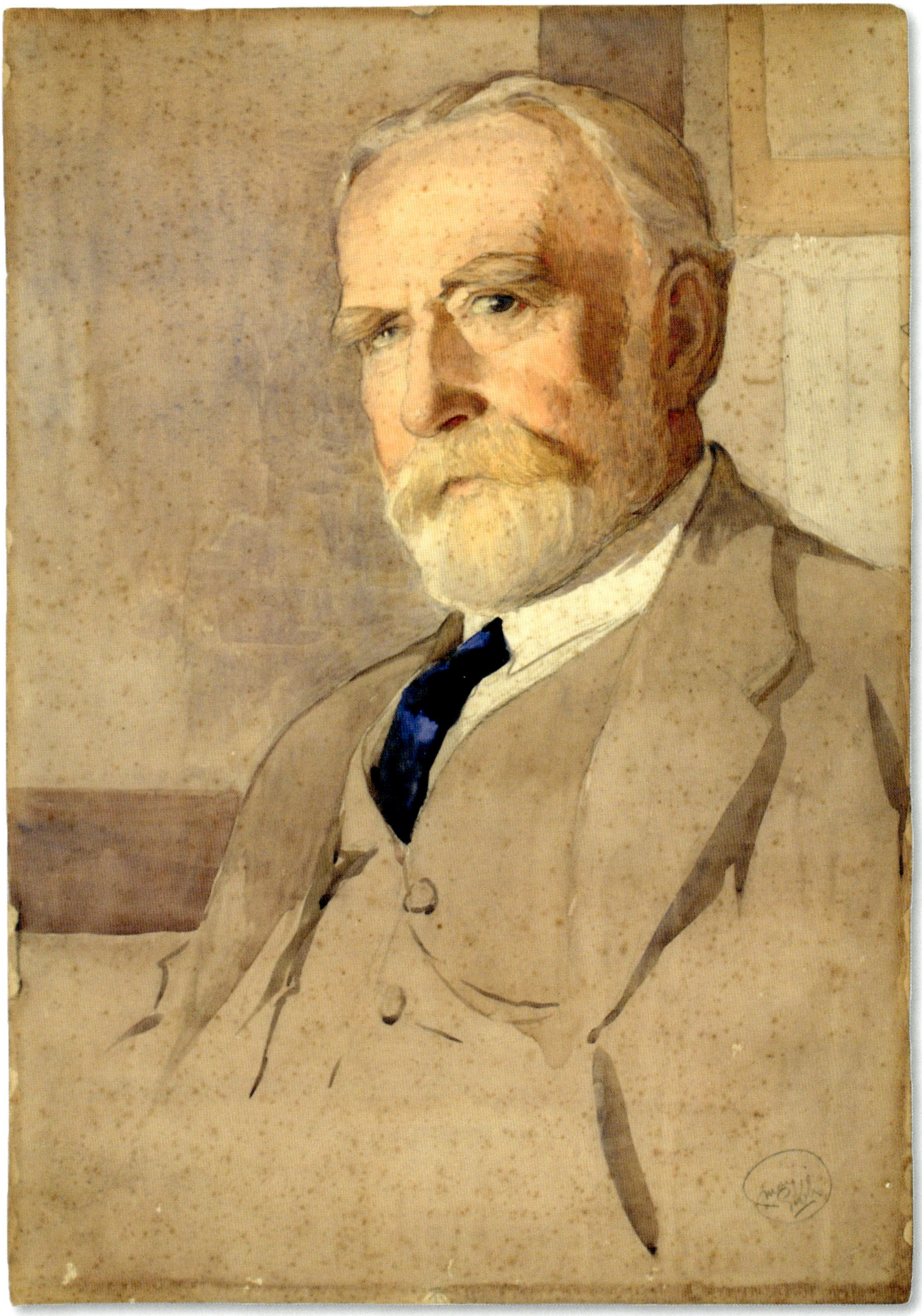

The Gumblossom Ballet

Frontispiece

CHAPTER 3

MAY GIBBS ON SHOW

By the time the Australian census of 1891 had been compiled, May Gibbs was fourteen years old. In the newly self-governing region of Western Australia, where May was growing up, she was shielded from the dire effect that the early-1890s depression had on the eastern states. Geographically, Perth may have been held to ransom by the Indian Ocean on one side and the Nullarbor Plain on the other, but this very isolation seemed to encourage an independent outlook in its citizens. Economically, also, the state was prospering. Its gold discoveries over the coming decade would see its population increase fourfold.

In comparison, therefore, with so many young Australians of her generation, May Gibbs was a privileged fourteen-year-old. For her, and indeed for her entire family, the move from South Australia to Western Australia had been a move from rural and cultural isolation to a small but close-knit suburban elite on the outskirts of a capital city that was entering a decade of unprecedented wealth and self-realisation.

Once the Gibbs family had arrived, they welcomed all the social and cultural opportunities Perth was just beginning to offer. Not only that, but

May Gibbs' experience as both a member of the audience and a performer would later inspire the illustration, 'The Gum Blossom Ballet' in *Tales of Snugglepot and Cuddlepie.*

Feb. 9th -03.

Myself.

May's parents began to take an active role in initiating cultural developments themselves. After 1887, the family's resettlement ultimately immersed them into some semblance of the cultured, provincial life they had left behind in England. Although they must have pined for these social and cultural contacts, could they ever have imagined what a formative influence these new-found opportunities would be on their young daughter?

When the Gibbs family moved to 'The Dune' in South Perth in 1889, they found an ideal haven. The intellectual backgrounds, social adaptability and cultural aspirations which Herbert and Cecie shared served them well in integrating into a welcome and comfortable clique quickly—almost overnight, in fact. May's parents completely reinvigorated their lives. Within a very short period of time, they were assimilated into new and varied milieus: community cultural efforts (musical, choral and operatic, and artistic and fancy-dress occasions) in which they served as performers, committee members and exhibitors. The couple also gave their support to charitable ventures, including fundraising for their local church, the Dorcas Society, the Perth Temperance Cricket Club, the St George's Boys Brigade and the Perth Home of the Good Shepherd.

Furthermore, May's parents separately engaged in other pursuits. Herbert Gibbs became one of three founding members of the Wilgie Sketching Club (along with Bernard Woodward and Henry Charles Prinsep), a scenery painter for the Perth Amateur Operatic Society's Gilbert and Sullivan productions, and a supporter of the South Perth Mechanics' Institute. Cecie Gibbs, in turn, became a solo performer in oratorios and operas, and served as a committee member of the newly founded Karrakatta Women's Club. This was one of the first women's clubs formed in Australia. It gave women the opportunity to be active and vocal in public affairs. The club was involved in the push for women's suffrage, which was achieved in Western Australia in 1899, earlier than most of the rest of the world.

Not surprisingly, this individual and combined community involvement resulted in May's parents being integrated into Perth society at its most elite level. In August 1894, for example, they were invited to dine at Government House, and four years later they attended a civic reception for the governor of South Australia. But equally significant was the fact that May eagerly embraced and followed her parent's example—the whole future of May Gibbs was in the making.

The Gibbs family picnicking.

FACING PAGE: A self-portrait completed shortly after May returned from her first experience of art school in London.

May's botanical work, possesses both scientific accuracy and artistic charm.

FACING PAGE: The door to the studio, in oils by Herbert Gibbs. Art was a part of everyday life at 'The Dune'. Herbert Gibbs was a founding member of the Wilgie Sketching Club, to which May, Cecie and Herbert were all contributors.

In 1887, when the Gibbs family first moved to Perth, virtually none of these cultural and social blessings were possible. To appreciate the cultural wasteland which this pioneering family encountered, one has only to consider the bleak editorial 'Vigilans et Audax' that appeared in Perth's leading newspaper, the *West Australian*, shortly after their arrival. 'Nothing', the paper declared emphatically in May 1888, 'strikes a stranger more … in Perth, than its dullness'. To illustrate the city's mediocrity, the paper itemised all that was lacking: 'there is no good public library … A picture gallery there is not'. Then, apart from one exception, it lamented that there were 'absolutely no periodical or regular entertainments in the shape of concerts or dramatic performances'. The piece ended with the most despairing of summations: 'Perth is like a city of the dead'.

Thankfully, the redeeming exception pointed out by the newspaper offered the Gibbs some hope for the future. This was the Perth Musical Union, which was already notable for its excellent concerts. Herbert Gibbs became its honorary secretary, while Cecie played a central role in its choral productions. She performed with it for the first time on 24 July 1888, in its presentation of Mendelssohn's *Athalie* in the Perth Town Hall. In October the following year, Cecie performed in another oratorio, before revealing her full ability in a Christmas presentation of *The Messiah*. The *West Australian*'s knowledgeable critique singled her out for high praise: 'The alto work all devolved on Mrs. Gibbs' very competent hands'. It continued enthusiastically: 'Her sympathetic and exquisitely finished' renditions 'were not surpassed by the efforts of any'.

The year 1889 was a turning point for Perth's cultural scene. Just as it had been enlivened by the formation of a single musical society, it took only one art exhibition to begin further enrichment. Late in the year, the renowned Australian wild-flower painter Ellis Rowan, in company with Margaret Forrest wife of John Forrest, embarked on a painting expedition in the northwest of the state. These two intrepid women travelled by horse and carriage in search of rare and unusual specimens—the art of flower painting and illustration was considered by some a highly fashionable practice, but to this pair it was a serious scientific and artistic pursuit. The unprecedented result was a joint exhibition that opened on 5 November 1889 in Perth's Railway Station Reading Room, and is believed to be the first art exhibition ever held in Western Australia. And there are three other distinctions that added status to this event: the exhibition was solely comprised of the work of women

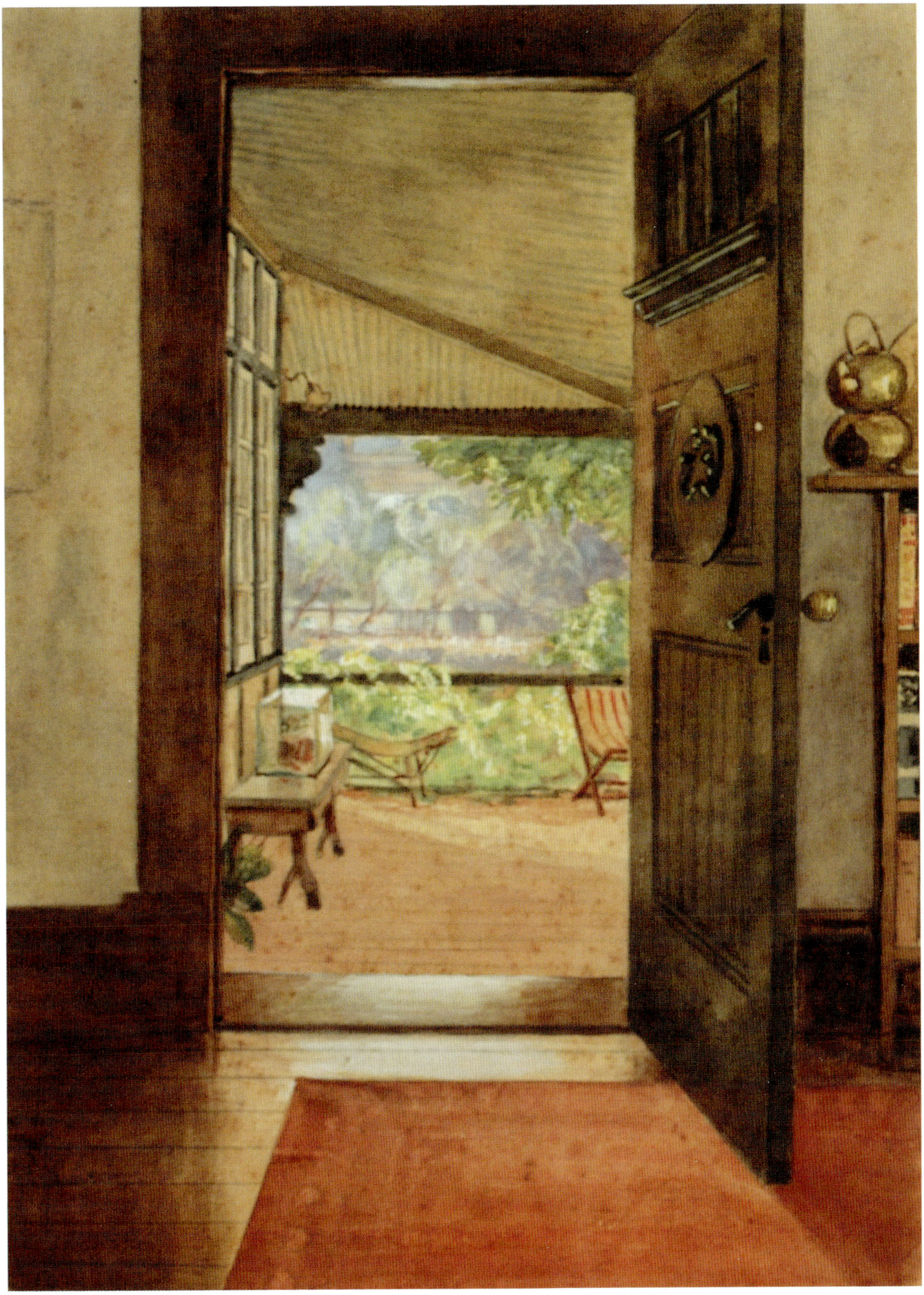

The decorative art of flower painting and the amateur study of botany was seen as an acceptable occupation for young ladies

artists; they ventured into remote and largely unexplored terrain in search of inspiration; and as botanical artists they reaffirmed the genre of flower painting as a particular area of female endeavour.

Ellis Rowan had achieved extraordinary distinction over the previous decade. At the Melbourne International Exhibition of 1880, Rowan had been one of only two artists to be awarded a gold medal. The fact that a woman who was also a botanical artist had usurped the popularity of landscape painting caused widespread consternation in Australian art circles. Even so, the distinction was reconfirmed at the 1888 Centennial Exhibition (also held in Melbourne), when Rowan again was singled out as the only Australian artist to receive a gold medal. Throughout the 1880s, she reaped a score of medals on the international stage. Rowan carved a distinguished niche in what formerly had been a male-dominated realm, delivering a welcome example to May Gibbs and her sisters in the art world.

Ever since the earliest days of settlement, the wild flowers of Western Australia had been extravagantly praised. The wife of an early governor of the colony, Lady Anne Broome, spoke for countless others when she voiced her astonishment at the botanical profusion in the colony's north in her 1885 book *Letters to Guy*:

> The first wonder is that they are there at all, for the little bushes on which they grow seem just to sit lightly on the top of the sand; and there they are, blooming away without a drop of water, and under a fierce sun.

Julian Ashton, a British artist who made an influential contribution to Australian art, was similarly enthusiastic. In his autobiography, *Now Came Still Evening On*, he described how, in Albany, he made 'many drawings, including specimens of wild flowers' which he found there 'in great profusion and beauty'. Indeed, his visit was enough to convince him that this bounty was 'more beautiful than any … seen elsewhere in Australia'.

Throughout the 1890s, May consistently exhibited and won prizes for her botanical studies. As reported in the *West Australian* on 23 September 1897, the prevailing taste at an exhibition where May won first prize clearly endorsed her choice of subject:

> To speak of Western Australia is almost the same as to mention its rich growth of wild flowers, justly regarded as being one of its leading features. Long before its position as a gold-bearing country was established, or even

Light Green and black paw, but warm; very vivid effect

And this hand of p- be lives the The one R.

too long

Every bit of stem black haired, but not as dark as lips of flowers little black hairs even lightest part of flowers all branches even length

printable leaf, scarcely visible

Western Australian Kangaroo Paw. (district?) think rare

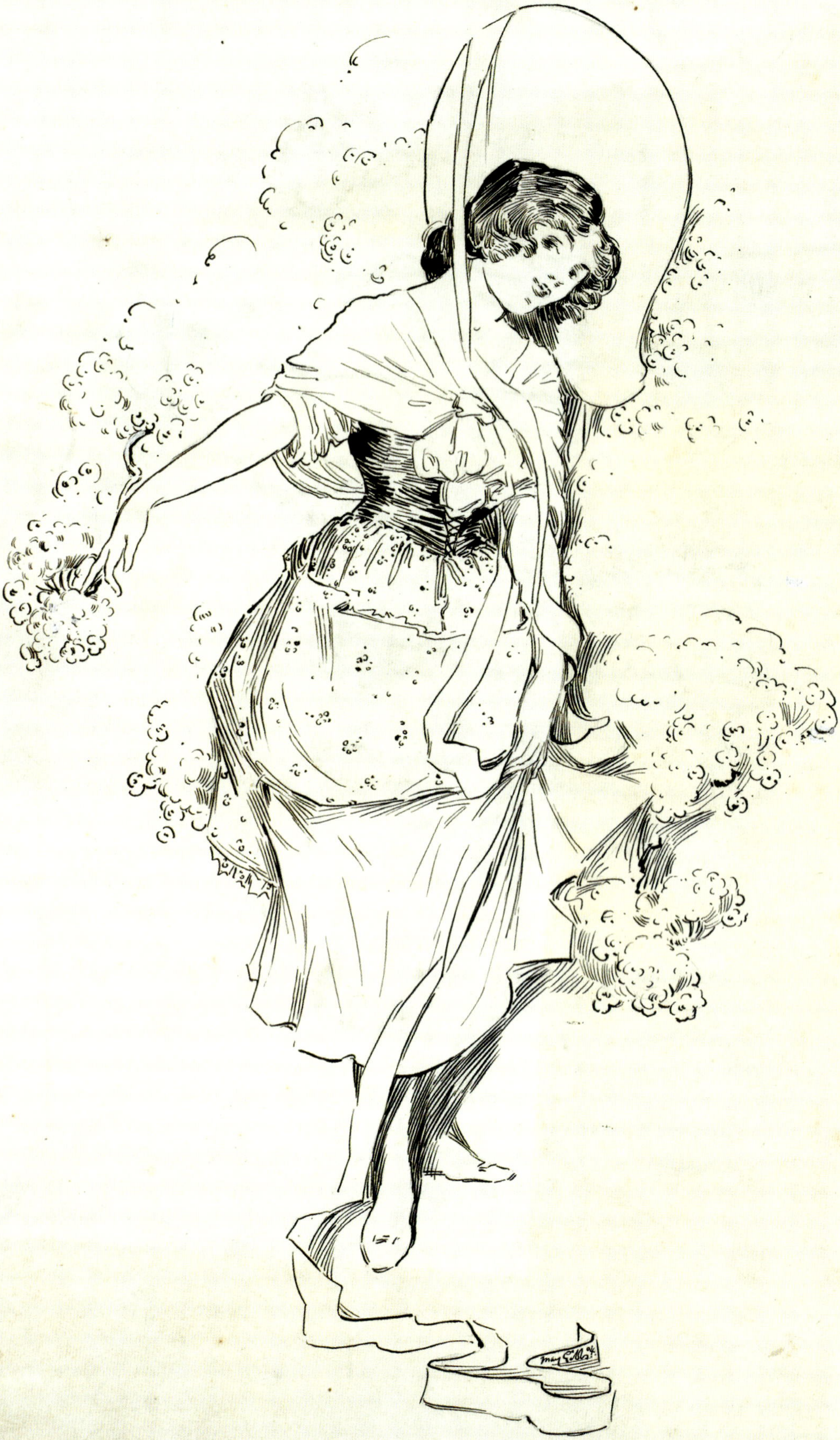
May Gibbs 04

conjectured, its reputation as the flower garden of the Australian continent was known, and if travellers spoke of the monotony of its bush they always found a great compensation in the luxuriance, the beauty, and the variety of the wild flowers.

It might easily have been expected that May Gibbs would remain a dilettante botanical artist, safely ensconced in a woman's genre and a social niche. And perhaps at this stage, May herself had no grander ambitions than to paint botanical subjects. But with her father's example as a satirical cartoonist before her, these limitations were always unlikely.

The Rowan–Forrest joint exhibition energised the small community. Within days, the Wilgie Sketching Club was founded, providing something quite new and surely welcome: the formal opportunity for members to submit sketches which the club committee then appraised. It is highly likely that May Gibbs submitted examples of her work, perhaps one entitled 'Little Folks'.

On 21 December 1889, a month before May's thirteenth birthday, a double-page spread of her 'Little Folks' appeared in the *W. A. Bulletin*, and it is from this date that we can begin to trace her emerging talent as an illustrator. As could reasonably be expected, this illustrative debut by a child who was still twelve years old showed its derivation, as May paid homage to the classic illustrations of childhood by the British artist Kate Greenaway.

The impact of the Kate Greenaway style on May's whole era was immense. In 1891, for example, at one of the many fancy-dress balls which May attended in costume, there was not only one entrant actually dressed as Kate herself, but also twin girls in Greenaway dresses. The appeal and sentiment which fancy dress held for May's generation is something easily overlooked today, but its enduring significance continually surfaced in her illustrations and cartoons. Gumnut babies dressing up in and satirising adult modes became a standard part of May's pictorial repertoire later in her life.

In 1890, May Gibbs made debuts on two fronts: in the exhibition room and on the stage. When the Wilgie Sketching Club opened its first (and only) exhibition on 4 June, not only was there a significant representation by women artists, but botanical subjects were their most popular choice. The pioneering example of this club, believed to be the first artists' society in Western Australia, was clearly appreciated by the local newspapers. The *Western Mail* pointed out that most of the other 'principal cities of Australia can now boast of several exhibitions of pictures during the year'.

ABOVE: An early watercolour by May Gibbs, painted in 1891. BELOW: Kate Greenaway's style affected a generation of young women.

FACING PAGE: A far more sophisticated illustration in pen and ink from May's time in London.

It then acknowledged that, while Western Australia had not yet been able to share in these advantages, it was now being given 'a beginning'.

And it was a substantial beginning, not merely that of a Cinderella colony overvaluing its new status. Almost 300 works of art were shown, including, according to an advertisement for the exhibition, some 'sent specifically from England … [some] lent by residents in the colony, and contributions from the Wilgie Club'. Among the artists taking part in this group exhibition were Ellis Rowan, Margaret Forrest and May, Herbert and Cecie Gibbs. Between them, in fact, the Gibbs family contributed a substantial twenty-nine of their own efforts. Furthermore, on 9 June, mother and daughter sung together in the concert that closed the exhibition.

This artistic stimulus was not allowed to falter. In October 1892, the first of what was to become an annual series of exhibitions was held. The Perth Wild Flower Show was an exhibition of native specimens and floral arrangements complemented by a competitive showing of botanical illustrations. The extensive press coverage that the show attracted was quick to praise the Wilgie Sketching Club for its impetus. The *West Australian* commented that the collection was 'of considerable merit, giving ample evidence that the "Wilgie" Club is exercising a good influence over the local artists'.

When we realise that May Gibbs was only fifteen years old at the time, it is clear that the preeminent attention which her work was accorded was testimony to her precocious ability. The press enthused that 'the first picture that claimed attention amongst those for competition is that of Miss Gibbs'. And it revealed a most appropriate choice of subject: 'Altogether it is a truly artistic picture, the light and shade being skilfully effected, while the composition is excellent.' It was hardly surprising, then, that *Australian May* took out the first prize in oils in this inaugural wild-flower exhibition.

This forgotten fact appears to mark the debut of May Gibbs as a competitive exhibiting artist. Her highly competent showing might cause us to ask just who had guided and trained May's developing artistry. The answer is simple: her parents were her principal mentors. They gave her the benefit of the professional art training which they had enjoyed before they emigrated.

This debt was fondly acknowledged in May's later books. Published in 1918, the first edition of *Tales of Snugglepot and Cuddlepie* included a

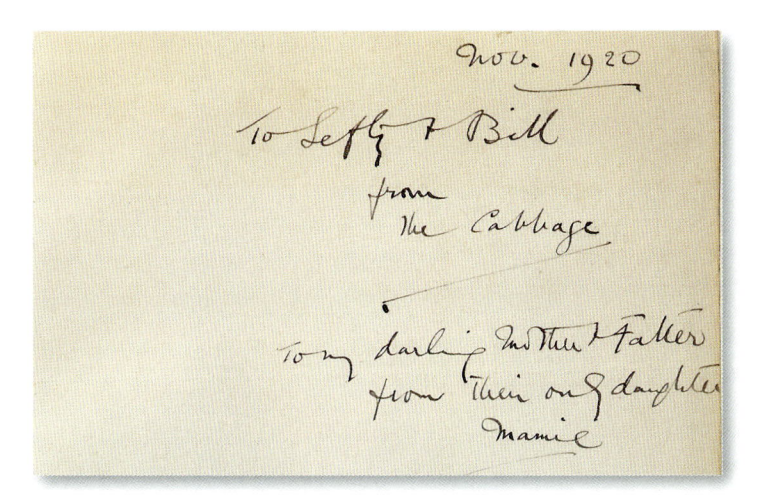

May's inscription to her parents in *Little Ragged Blossom*.

printed dedication: 'To the Two Dearest children in the World, Lefty and Bill'. The wide world would have been left wondering at this gesture, ignorant of the fact that the proud recipients 'Lefty and Bill' were May's parents. A decade later, she inscribed their copy of *The Further Adventures of Bib and Bub* as follows: 'To me very own beloved Blocks from their Chip'. Here, in the vernacular humour of the day, was a grateful acknowledgement from May—that she was 'a chip off the old block'.

Displaying tenacity and a penchant for hard work, May soon demonstrated to her parents that her artistic debut in 1892 was not to be an isolated triumph. In 1893, at the Perth Wild Flower Show's second annual exhibition, she was awarded the special prize for a study of West Australian wild flowers. The work achieved further renown when it was purchased by the colony's governor. Concurrent with this exhibition was the Floral Fete, which was staged in the Fremantle Town Hall. Once again, May Gibbs' industry and maturity were rewarded—she received two prizes, for both oil and watercolour painting.

Thereafter, throughout the rest of the 1890s, May Gibbs not only maintained but increased her profile as a botanical artist. From the inception of these wild-flower exhibitions in 1892 until she left for London in 1900, May continued to exhibit in the annual series. Significantly, she won either a first or a second prize almost every year. With such success, she was best evaluated as a botanical artist making a name for herself in the context of such luminaries as Margaret Forrest and Ellis Rowan. May's dedication would attract sustained and growing acclaim throughout this productive era.

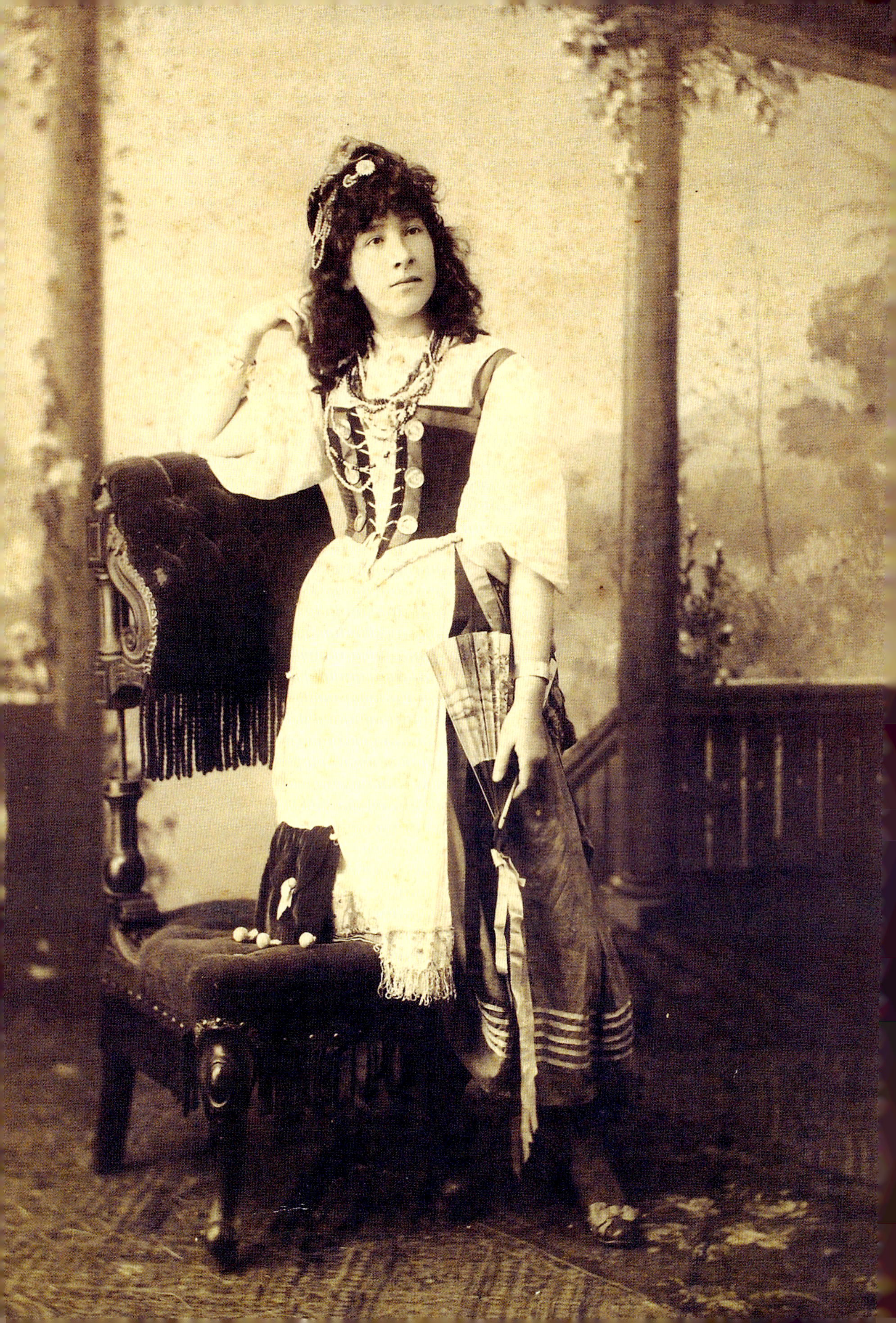

CHAPTER 4

A 'REMARKABLE LITTLE LADY'

The arrival in Fremantle on 11 February 1887 of the family of Ishmael Rogers, the eldest brother of Cecilia Gibbs, came at the very beginning of the year in which the Gibbs family largely renounced any pastoral ambitions and settled in Perth. Such a consolidation of a far-flung family could not have come at a more auspicious time. May and her family had just faced the hardest, most disillusioning and isolated six years of their lives. This reunion reintroduced some highly formative influences—social, psychological and artistic—to May's upbringing.

Within six months of her arrival, Fanny Rogers had opened a girls' school—Mrs. Rogers & Daughters, Mulgrave House School—which taught French, German, music and singing. She was assisted by one of her daughters, who gave classes in painting and drawing; presumably this was Daisy Rogers, who later accompanied her cousin May on two trips to London. Unfortunately, very little is known about the formal schooling that May Gibbs was given. This has contributed to the idea that May's ability was a sudden efflorescence. We have, however, seen that her mother advertised for a governess as early as 1885, when May was eight years old and living

A teenage May Gibbs dressed in costume for a theatrical performance of 'The Gondoliers' in 1892. May also played the piano and was considered a promising violinist.

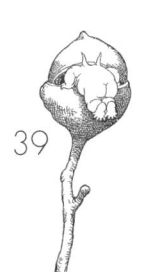

'The Dune' in South Perth remained the centre of May's life until the turn of the century.

FACING PAGE: May's mother, Cecie, was fortunate that her parents were among the vanguard of their time, allowing their daughters to have a good education and encouraging artistic pursuits. Cecie brought the same love of the arts to family life in Perth.

in isolation in the bush. Surely the family, and May herself, would have embraced the opportunity of an aunt and cousins opening a girls' school. Although there is no record of May attending classes at this school, either formally or informally, the timing and the benefits make it inconceivable that the Gibbs family did not take advantage of it.

May always acknowledged her father's expert artistic guidance and encouragement of her art. Indeed, it is easy to see his influence in her animated and comic character sketches. As Ted Snell pointed out in *Cinderella on the Beach*, Herbert's 'wit and sophisticated graphic ability' are also evident in his daughter.

In August 1889 came specific evidence that Fanny Rogers' school and the Gibbs family were intimately involved. They combined in noteworthy support of a charity concert in which Cecie was the leading performer. Fanny's young pupils opened the program with a song, then delivered three additional numbers as well as an encore. A review in the *West Australian* said they appeared 'dressed as fairies', leaving us to wonder if twelve-year-old May Gibbs was one of their number.

The earliest extant photograph of May Gibbs as a performer was probably taken the very next year. She appeared in costume for a concert performance as a character in *The Pirates of Penzance*. This was almost certainly the Gaiety Theatre Company's production of excerpts from the work, which was staged in Fremantle on 17 May 1890 and included May's mother in its cast. Five days later, the first description of May Gibbs performing in public was published in the *West Australian*. It told of how May and her mother appeared as members of a company performing William Bennett's cantata *The May Queen* on 21 May. It was reported that 'Miss Gibbs, though evidently suffering slightly from the effects of the prevailing influenza, sang very creditably'.

Later on the same program, as if to confirm that performing in public was not too daunting for her, May made another appearance, contributing 'a most amusing recitation, in character, and in response to a demand for its repetition, this remarkable little lady and her brother, Master Ivan Gibbs, gave a funny dialogue, which in its turn was encored'. May showed a maturity beyond her years, as well as revealing how much she was the daughter of two trained, versatile and experienced performers.

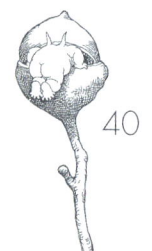

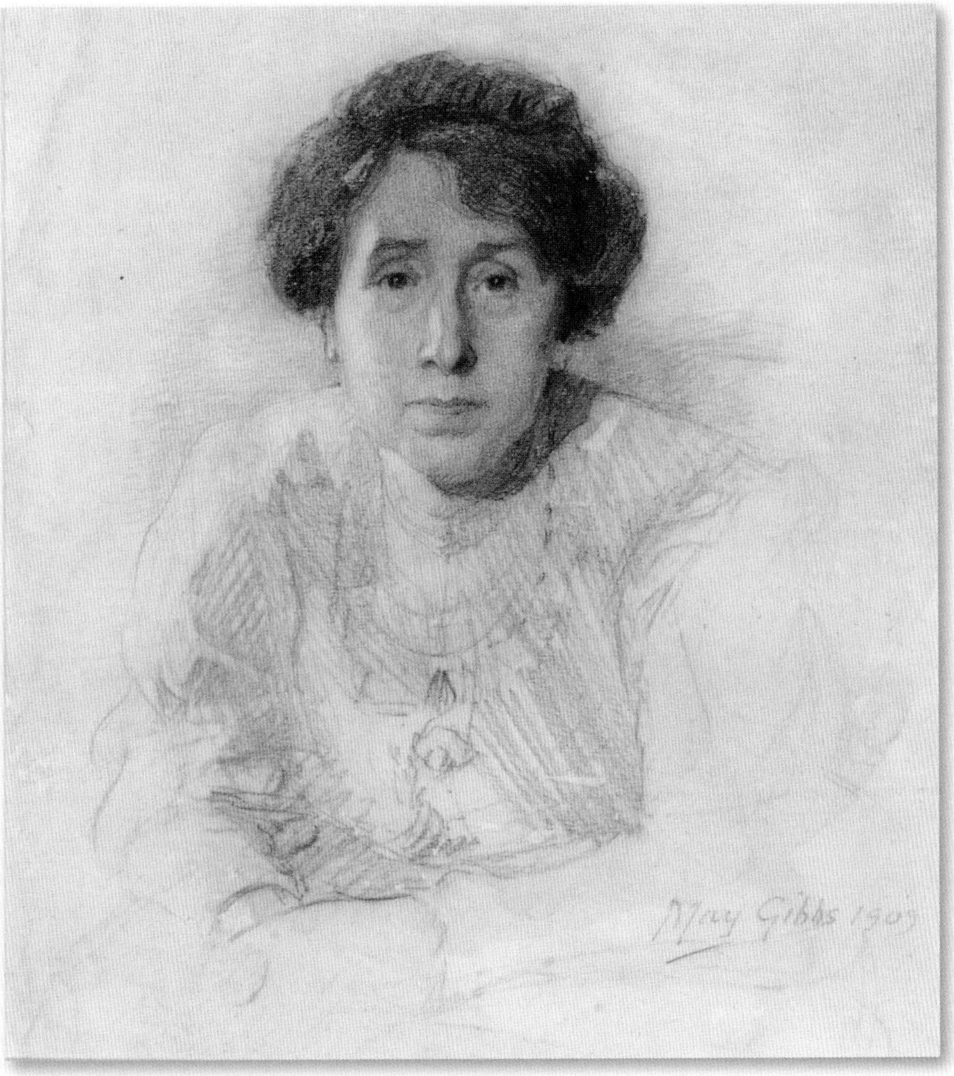
May Gibbs

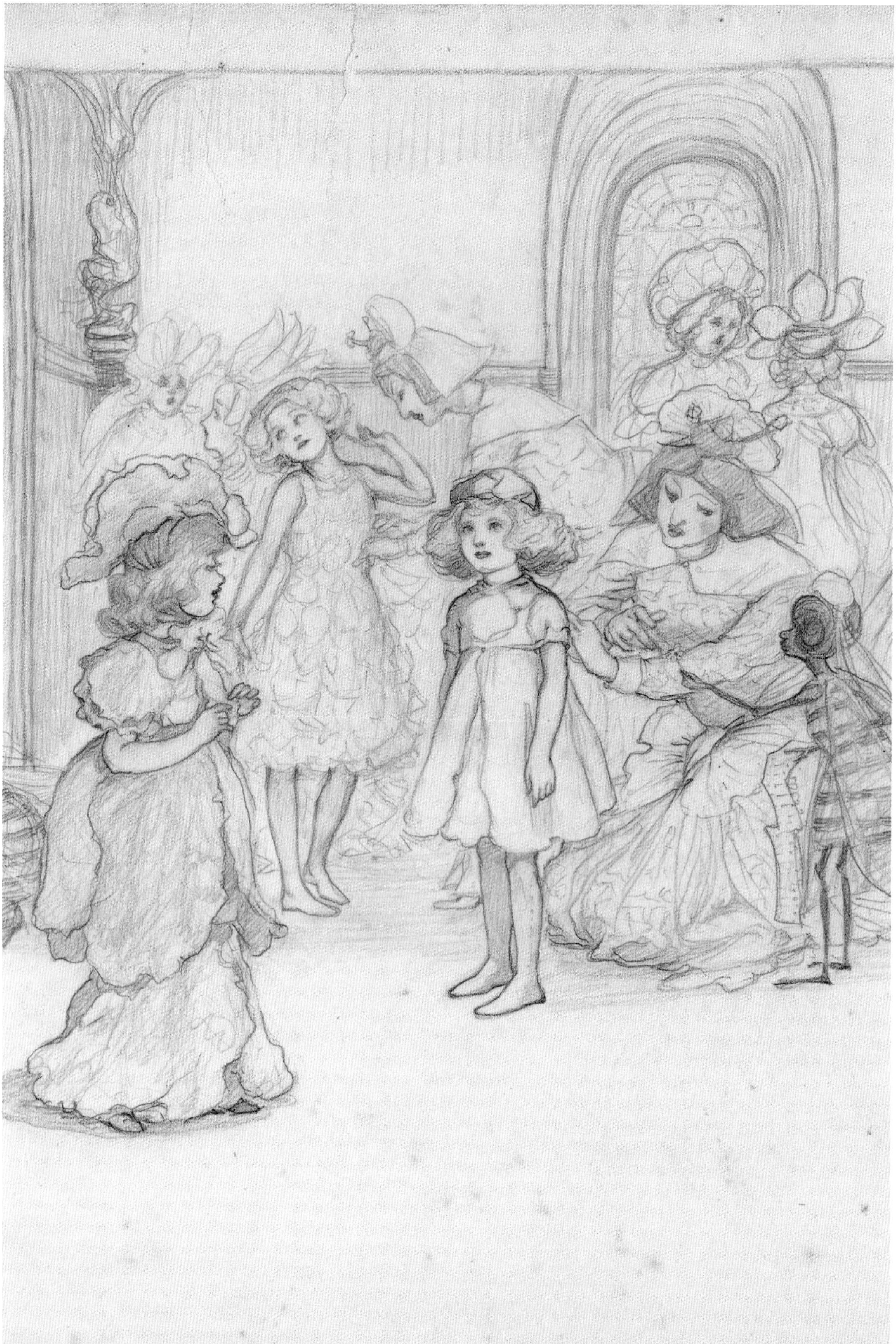

In September 1890, May made several appearances in Gilbert and Sullivan productions alongside her mother, first in *Patience* and then in *The Sorcerer*. It appears that once May set foot upon the stage, her ability was matched by her zeal to perform. That year, the indefatigable thirteen-year-old sang on three other public, though more modest, occasions in Perth.

These public performances continued throughout the 1890s. They were given laudatory mention in the newspapers of the day, with May herself sometimes singled out for praise or comment. One of her triumphs occurred in 1892, when she was only fifteen years old. As if to show that Western Australia was not a cultural backwater, the Perth Amateur Operatic Company mounted a production of *The Gondoliers* within eighteen months of its London premiere. On the performance night, 20 June, Herbert Gibbs played viola in the orchestra, having also designed the cover for the evening's program, while young Ivan Gibbs appeared as a drummer and May and her mother both sang. It was reported in the *West Australian* piece that 'Miss Gibbs, as the ancient nurse, Inez, was really marvellously made up, and looked, and … played the part of the Spanish duenna to perfection'. What was a memorable family event as well as a cultural accomplishment was captured in a Henry Prinsep photograph of May in costume.

The year 1892 was a milestone in the musical life of Perth. The unexpected arrival of a single international visitor energised the community. The newcomer was Herr Adalbert Francik, a virtuoso violin player who had come to Australia from Prague in 1881. After a celebrated decade in Sydney spent giving recitals and teaching, Francik arrived in Perth in August 1892. He stayed for almost seven years, and in that time he transformed the city's music scene and encouraged the local talent. Foremost among these local supporters were May Gibbs and her parents. From Herr Francik's first recital in Perth (under vice-regal patronage) on 17 August 1892 until he left for Vienna in April 1899, they regularly performed in his concerts.

The immediate patronage of Herr Francik by the colony's new governor and his wife, Sir William and Lady Robinson, was enough of a cultural stimulus to cause the local newspaper to wax lyrical: 'the presence of our distinguished Governor makes Perth an altogether different city to live in'. The occasion which attracted this praise was the performance of the musical *At Home* at Government House in August 1892. In its wake, the *West Australian*

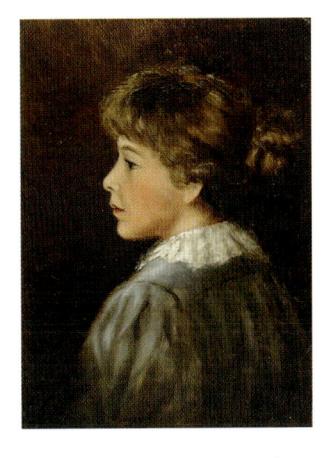

In 1893, when May was sixteen, her older brother 'Bertie' died. The year after Bertie's death, May painted these portraits of her younger brothers Ivan (top) and Harold.

FACING PAGE: An illustration by May Gibbs that recalls her backstage experiences as a child.

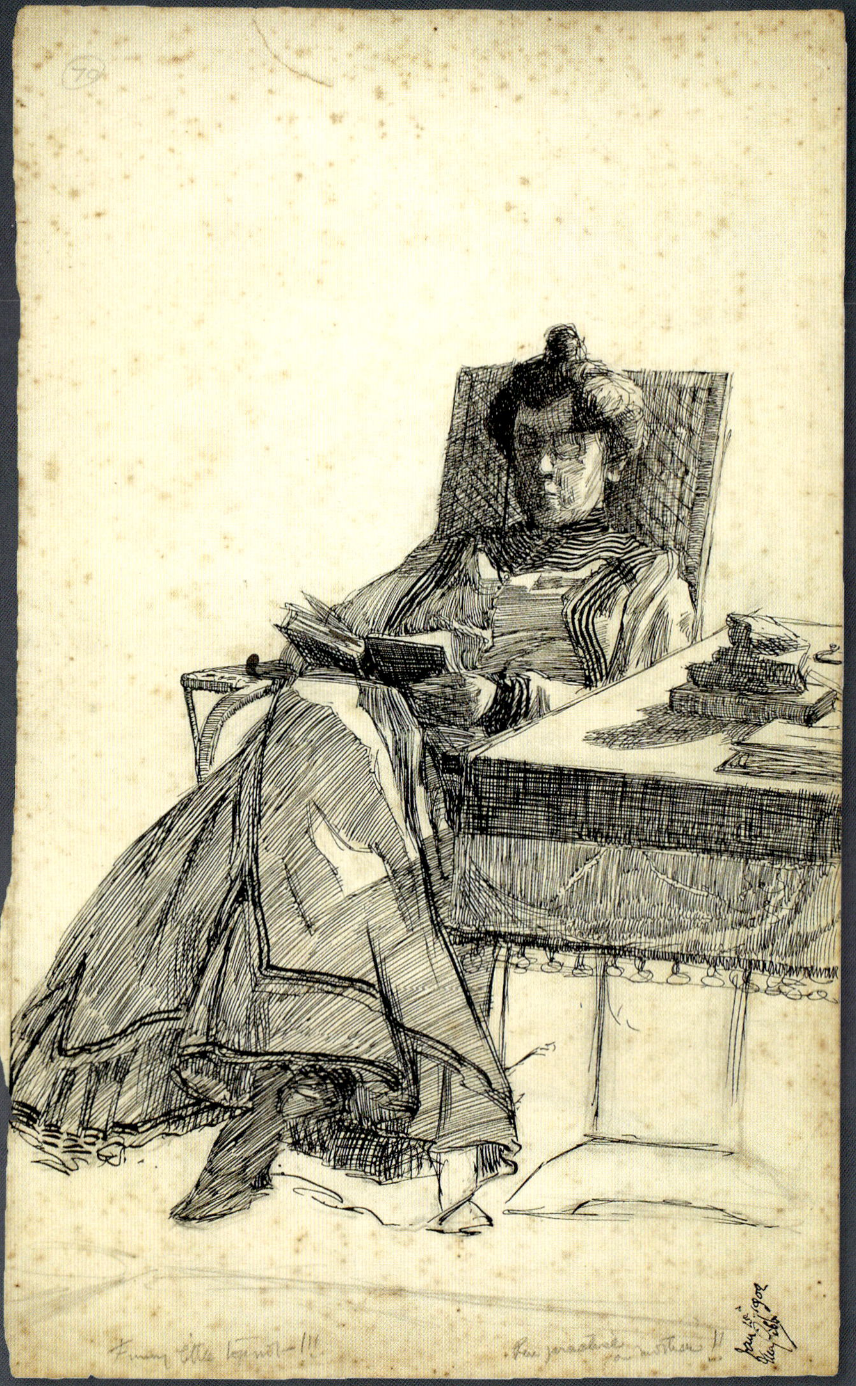

boasted that 'although only a small city [Perth] is musically miles ahead of other places with much larger populations'.

It seems that May Gibbs was taught singing by Francik, and that her parents might also have received singing and instrumental lessons from him. The highlight of the Gibbs family appearances at his concerts came on 22 August 1894 at the Perth Town Hall, when May and both her parents featured in more than one item. Herbert and Cecie performed on newly learned instruments in a Mozart quartet: he on viola and she on cello. Cecie and May both sang, but it was the seventeen-year-old who was particularly praised for her performance in the review of 'Herr Francik's concert': 'Miss Gibbs has a very sweet and promising "mezzo soprano" voice'.

Through all these opportunities and varied presentations before the public, we can see the young May Gibbs searching for a creative role—putting aside the bigger issues of a genre, a medium and an individual style—before she finally chooses a career as an artist. And what a time and place in which to be conducting such a search. Of all the colonies which the Gibbs family might have chosen at that particular time, Western Australia could not have been surpassed. Their arrival in Perth coincided with the beginning of a real-estate boom, while entrepreneurial schemes for railway construction were also attracting much interest—thankfully, this increasing speculation was to have none of the dire results which the eastern colonies experienced during the financial crash of 1893.

In the late 1890s, the immensely large colony in which they lived was trying to decide whether or not to be a part of the federated states of Australia. In sentiment and in loyalty, its inhabitants felt much closer to the Crown than to their eastern neighbours. And although they were isolated, gold made them the focus of international interest, with the mining boom reaching its climax between the years 1897 and 1903. At a time when other Australian colonies were only slowly recovering from financial and unemployment crises, Western Australia was progressing at an unparalleled rate. One new gold discovery followed another, and a dramatic inflow of population and prosperity completely transformed the colony's economy. Western Australia eventually became a significant part of the economy of the whole of Australia.

Its unique position is best described by an analogy that brings to mind the fairytale that May Gibbs later used to explain her own birth—that of the 1880s being the colony's 'Cinderella' period. This word was used by Lady

A photograph of May Gibbs in 1900.

FACING PAGE: The household run by May's mother, Cecie, was vibrant and unconventional. Among May's childhood recollections was the joy of listening to her mother read aloud. She remembered one holiday when 'she read all day, only stopping for meals'.

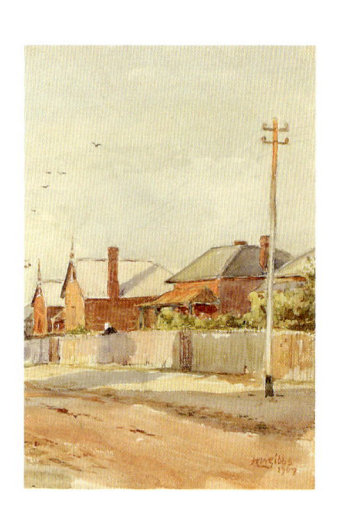

Western Australia became known as the Golden West and bypassed the 1890s depression. Its population trebled in that decade.

Anne Broome in her book *Colonial Memories* to describe the colony's magical reversal, a time when 'Cinderella's shoes … turned out to be made of gold'. By the following decade, Western Australia's wealth from mining, timber milling and pearling had set it above all the other colonies. And as its economy became more diversified, merchants, agents and other professional men achieved greater prominence in the community. According to Lady Anne Broome, the result, to continue the fairytale analogy, was that this good fortune ushered in 'the Fairy Prince' of 'Responsible Government'.

This 'magic' was abundantly clear in May's own neighbourhood. Although the population of South Perth did not reach 1000 until the end of the century, it included an overwhelming proportion of the colony's most substantial citizens: the registrar-general, the assistant surveyor-general, the curator of the Perth Museum, the chief justice and prominent politicians and businessmen all resided there. Herbert and May Gibbs became part of a coterie of Western Australia's pioneering artists, which included James WR Linton and Frederick Matthews Williams. All this, along with South Perth's abundance of native flora, including banksias, and its tranquil isolation, created a somewhat elite suburb.

In 1897, when she was only twenty years old, May must have thought that she had reached the very pinnacle of success. Her artwork achieved a great distinction—it reached an international audience. When Sir John and Lady Margaret Forrest were invited to attend the London celebrations for Queen Victoria's Diamond Jubilee, it was decided that they would take with them two congratulatory illuminated and illustrated addresses, which were a particular fashion of the day. One of them was to be from the women of Western Australia. On 6 May, only days before the Forrests' departure, this address was proudly exhibited in Perth. Imagine the pride which the Gibbs family must have felt when they read the newspaper announcement:

> The congratulatory address from the ladies of Western Australia, to be presented to Her Majesty … will be on view … this morning … The address … is enriched with a beautifully executed emblematic design in water colours, from the brush of a local artist, Miss Gibbs.

Six months later, on 30 November, the family's pride was further elevated when a report of the presentation appeared in the *West Australian*. Among the numerous addresses presented from subjects worldwide, Lady Forrest considered that their 'women's address was one of the handsomest'.

Furthermore, upon handing it to the Queen, she noted that Her Majesty 'seemed to be pleased'.

Within two years, this patriotic zeal had turned into bellicose support as the Australian colonies vied with one another to send individual contingents off to South Africa to fight in the Boer War. Perth was aroused by inflamed sentiment, and as 1899 drew to a dramatic close, even the city's stores and shopfronts were displaying signs of British allegiance. At the beginning of November, Bon Marche, the largest store in town, added a militant touch to its advertising: 'we claim that for discipline, training, organisation, and true grit, our forces in the field are invincible [and] we have won the proud distinction in many a hard-fought field and will maintain it to the end'.

On 4 November, the West Australian contingent paraded through Perth before embarking for South Africa. Although there is no extant confirmation, we can imagine that the Gibbs family was present at that proud farewell. A newspaper report stated that Perth's 'citizens were taken at a disadvantage in the matter of time to enable them to decorate the premises along the route of [the] march'. Despite the hasty arrangements, however, 'strong efforts were made to add colour to what eventually proved a remarkable scene—one of wild enthusiasm'.

The local paper, which devoted no fewer than three pages to this departure, took particular note of the displays mounted along the route. It enthused over 'the display of bunting' at one store and 'the more elaborate decorations' which 'appeared at intervals [in] masses of fluttering colour'. Predictably, the most elaborate of these displays was mounted by Bon Marche. It was singled out for the 'considerable trouble [which] had been gone to in the brief time at the disposal of the proprietors'.

As the Boer War contingent marched past Bon Marche, some of its thunder was almost stolen by one of the store's large and eye-catching window displays. This had appeared overnight, as if by magic. And the creators of this magic were none other than May Gibbs and her mother.

May and Cecie had approached Perth's 'leading oldest store' and offered to dress a window for the parade. Their offer was accepted and Cecie had made life-size dummies while May painted a backdrop. Then, after the store had closed, May's sense of adventure surfaced. 'Under cover of dark', she admitted in her autobiographical 'Notes', 'we stole over with our props [and]

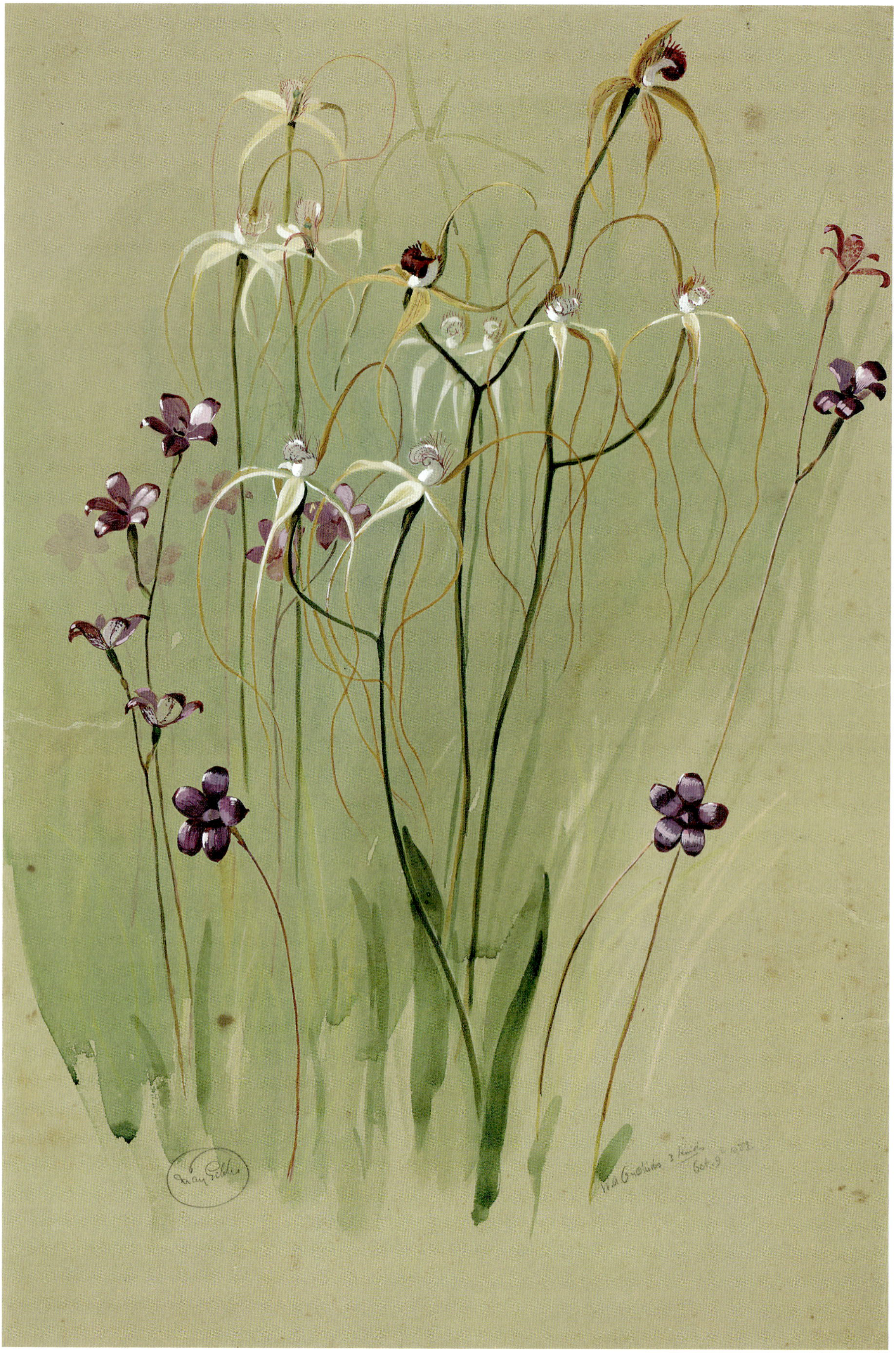
May Gibbs
W.A. Orchids 3 kinds
Oct. 9th

with blind down we fixed the stage'. The result was so novel that the next day a policeman 'stood by to move the crowd on'.

What was this clandestine window-dressing that stopped their Perth neighbours in their tracks? Nothing less than a dramatic tableau of John Bull, a caricature of the British forces, pointing a gun at the head of the South African president Paul Kruger. It was a collaboration that netted the enterprising pair a fee that made a considerable addition to their savings.

The year 1899 was also memorable for one last accolade. Western Australia submitted the only Australian contribution to the Fine Arts section of the 1900 Paris Exhibition. Its monumental entry highlighted wild-flower painting as the dominant artistic genre in the soon-to-be-federated state. To achieve this, in late 1899 the Western Australian Paris Exhibition Commission conducted a competition for wild-flower painting, attracting fifteen competitors. These entries became a late addition to that year's exhibition by the West Australian Society of Arts, and the first prize of five guineas was awarded to May Gibbs, now twenty-two years old. Her work won high praise in the *West Australian* for its 'freedom of brushwork, strength of colour, and natural taste in arrangement, combined with a by no means incorrect rendering of the subject botanically'.

Unfortunately, by the time the official British catalogue was issued, only Mildred Creeth and Lady Forrest had been accorded individual mention as independently exhibiting botanical artists. Space restrictions presumably limited the commission's entry to being listed as an undifferentiated group of 'seventy wildflower paintings'.

By the end of the nineteenth century there were four jetties at South Perth, and ferries provided a regular connection with the city. Pleasure steamers plied their trade and picnic, bathing and picturesque sketching points had also become popular, adding further distinctions to the area. In October 1898, when Perth's Zoological Gardens opened there, the Gibbs family was among the official guests. The gardens quickly became a major attraction, particularly with families. One early visitor, May Vivienne, attributed this popularity to the fact that 'many Western Australian children have never seen wild animals elsewhere, except in picture-books'. May Gibbs was certainly one of those visitors, and it is more than likely that she went to the Saturday-evening concerts which were held there during the summer.

May's wild-flower paintings had received many accolades prior to her selection to participate in the Western Australian contribution to the Paris Exhibition of 1900.

At The Zoo

Blob — 1903

The variety of the zoo's attractions was evident in its regularly placed newspaper advertisements: 'Fine collection of WILD ANIMALS, Lions, Tigers, Bears, Llama, Huanaco, Deer, Buffalo, Pythons, etc'. To supplement this exotic array, the zoo often accompanied this tempting notice with a significant plea: 'Wanted, Native Animals and Birds'. This was an engrossing visual resource on May's very doorstep. At the same time, a world away, Beatrix Potter was similarly entranced and inspired by visits to a zoo.

In June 1903, May contributed a half-page cartoon called 'At the Zoo' to a local paper, the *Spectator*, under the pseudonym 'Blob'. Six years later, the Zoological Gardens inspired a full page of cartoon vignettes in the *Western Mail* called 'Zoo Notes'. In it, May drew people alongside their lookalikes in the animal world. The accompanying verse explained it all:

> Have you ever seen the people in the cages
> And the animals awalking round the Zoo
> I've noticed this phenomenon for ages
> I feel quite sure you must have seen it too.

If we look closely enough, we can see personal touches—May's father, with his leonine profile and mane of hair, confronting a lion while May's mother looks down her hooked nose at a beaky cockatoo! Surely it is the memory of that zoo that inspired May in later life, whenever she had frequent need of animal models for her drawings.

Like the cartoonists who came before and after her, May Gibbs was known to carry a sketchbook everywhere she went. The autobiographical words of Phil May, the celebrated British cartoonist who inspired her father's style, could easily have described May's working methods:

> My types are all individuals. I am constantly on the look-out for the individual who embodies a type. When I am drawing a picture with several figures in it I often go out into the street to look for types. But I am collecting them at all times and in all places, more particularly in trains and omnibuses ... they will all come in useful some day.

In August 1899, a year after the zoo had opened in South Perth, the suburb welcomed another cultural addition. The colony's premier and one-time neighbour to the Gibbs family, Sir John Forrest, proudly unveiled the South Perth Mechanics' Institute Hall. A local resident himself, he boasted in his opening speech that his suburb had built the hall from public subscriptions. He praised South Perth as 'a very rising suburb, though it was an absolute

Following in her father's footsteps but using a pseudonym, 'Blob', May Gibbs contributed to the *Spectator* newspaper as a satirist and social observer in 1903.

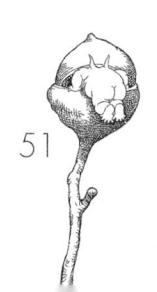

Newspaper work was an excellent opportunity for May to develop storytelling techniques and illustrative skills.

FACING PAGE: May's newspaper contributions led to opportunities in commercial illustration.

waste a few years ago, with scarcely a house upon it'. Forrest saw it becoming 'like Toorak in Melbourne or Potts' Point in Sydney'. All in all, he 'did not suppose that such a great change had come over any colony in so short a time as in Western Australia'.

Forrest's pride was certainly shared by other residents of the suburb. After his speech, a concert gave that pride a community voice—a voice that was strengthened by 22-year-old May Gibbs, appearing in a solo singing role.

Not surprisingly, some of South Perth's local attractions began to appear in May's newspaper cartoons. At this stage, her illustrative work, whether it was a botanical study or a passing event, was firmly based on the close and personal observation of her everyday world; during these formative years, she drew inspiration from daily life. Later, this training in selecting the most pertinent and amusing details, the most animated occasions, would be used for a transition into fantasy work.

In 1897, May had drawn a group of vignette illustrations which depicted the varied holiday attractions of the Swan River. Although this was not to be published until December 1907, it showed May's willingness to enlarge her repertoire and move beyond botanical art and into commercial illustration. Even more noteworthy was the pair of full-page illustrations which were published in the *Western Mail* in 1908: 'On the beach at Cottesloe' and 'Sketches at the Royal Agricultural Show'. Together, they showed a great advance in ability and in the inventive positioning of her characters within a picture frame.

These outdoor sketches were ideal training for May's eyes and hands. They developed her ability to depict character and personality, to convey humour in faces and in situations, which stood her in good stead through decades of bread-and-butter cartoon work. Significantly, these sketches increasingly depicted children and the world of childhood, a choice of subject matter which eventually became her forte. During the first decade of the twentieth century, May's published work concentrated on everyday scenes of local life, only occasionally enlivened with a touch of fantasy. It was as if she was still earthbound, not yet ready to take flight into the fully imaginative realm of fantasy.

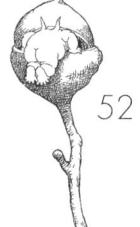

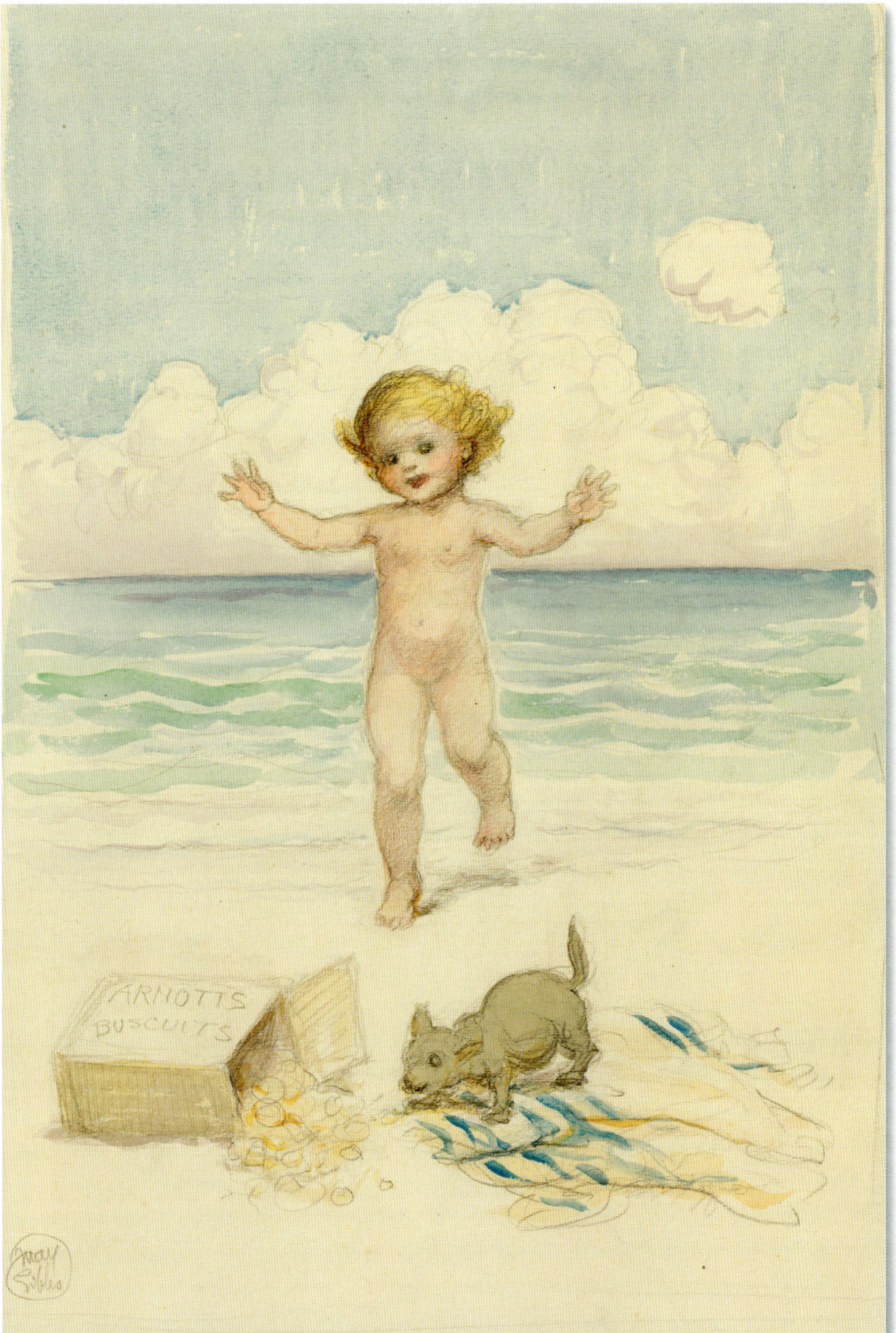
ARNOTTS
BUSCUITS
May Gibbs

From Betsie

CHAPTER 5

THE WIDE WORLD BECKONS

The last decade of the nineteenth century saw rapid change in Australia's social climate, which continued into the dawn of the next century. Not only did Australia become an independent nation in 1901, but by 1903 it was the only country where women could both vote and stand for national parliament. There was much discussion and reassessment of the role and possible future of women, which was epitomised in the feminist ideal of the New Woman.

We know that May Gibbs was greatly encouraged by the example set by her parents' cultured and liberal views and lifestyle, and in some ways she embodied aspects of this New Woman. However, just how much of this advanced thinking was a personal inspiration to her is the subject of conjecture. What May did have in common with this new entity was that she, too, wanted the independence, the absolute freedom to choose her own occupations and interests.

In the 1890s, as a woman-oriented culture gained both a visible presence and a voice throughout the colonies, there was a growing market for journals devoted to women readers and their interests. Henry Lawson's

Cecie used some of her small inheritance to give May the opportunity to attend art school in London as she and Herbert had done.

From life (from mother)
May Gibbs. 1898
(Before I had any Artwork)

mother, Louisa Lawson, created one such forum in Sydney, *The Dawn*, while the suffrage movement was represented there by the short-lived *Woman's Voice*. Together, these pioneering efforts in eastern Australia paved the way for more populist journals. This growing chorus extended the presence of women beyond the realm of the Australian home.

In late 1892, the American social reformer Jessie Ackerman visited Western Australia, where the indefatigable world traveller advocated woman's suffrage and the ideals of the Woman's Christian Temperance Union. The formation of allied groups throughout the colonies thereafter made the union the largest women's reform organisation in Australia. It was only a short step from here to demanding the vote, although it was not until April 1899 that a Woman's Franchise League was formed. That same year, Western Australia enfranchised women, five years after South Australia had been the first colony to do so. (In 1907, a return visit by Ackerman inspired a small cartoon of May's that appeared in the 6 July edition of the *Western Mail*.)

As a young woman in Western Australia, therefore, May Gibbs might have been encouraged by the example of middle-class women entering the public arena. These were social activists who campaigned for education, the vote and participation in politics. Their efforts, inevitably, were particularly directed towards social reforms that affected their gender—child welfare, women's working conditions, temperance, prostitution and divorce. These women may have provided energising examples for the aspiring young artist, who was searching for her own identity and career. But there were other role models, women who had literally set their sights on a more distant horizon.

By the turn of the century, it had become a markedly popular rite of passage for young Australians of both sexes to seek their fortunes in London, or at least to seek cultural opportunities, careers, adventures and professional and educational advantages in that metropolis—opportunities that had been largely denied to them back in Australia. For them, London was the heart of the Empire. Because it offered the most renowned art schools, publishers and critics, it had become a mecca where creative or professional success could be bestowed. Into this heady mix was added the chance of freedom from family, as well as the possibility of sheer adventure. For May Gibbs, the journey was to be an assertion of independence and a bid for self-discovery.

May attended the Cope and Nicol Art School in South Kensington and the Chelsea Polytechnic Institute as well as 'lots of night schools, which were rather fun'.

The opening of the Suez Canal in 1869 and the advances in steamship technology that occurred throughout the late nineteenth century encouraged tourism between Australia and Britain. However, up until 1934, when commercial air travel between the two countries began, a month-long sea trip was the only option. For single women like May, the very act of adventurously committing to this voyage was itself an act of self-assertion. The more well-to-do adventurous spirits were routinely accorded a farewell concert or benefit dinner. Then, on their return, they might expect a comparable homecoming welcome and proudly patriotic press notices. This bestowed an imprimatur of considerable cachet on the returned traveller.

Beatrix Tracy was an aspiring Australian journalist who made the voyage in the 1900s. Among her many articles is one, 'London', which captures the spirit that certainly animated May Gibbs to become an expatriate:

> London! the very word has the lure of a siren's song. It whispers of wonderful adventure in the ears of five continents. But it never sounds more full of promise, more irresistible in attraction, than when it speaks to Australia … When you sailed for England, did you not detect, with some complacency, that your friends considered you were attaining to the far limit of good fortune? If you had been setting off by P & O for Paradise you could not have aroused more poignant envy in those dear stay-at-homes who overwhelmed you with 'bon voyage' wishes and armfuls of pungent boronia and wattle blossom.

The epitome of the successful colonial expatriate was, of course, Nellie Melba. Her achievements are unique among Australian artists in any medium and she was the country's best-known cultural 'export' for decades. In 1901, though, when Melba was conquering the world stage, other Australian artists and singers could still find themselves 'lost in the maelstrom of [London's] great dinginess [where] … all come, and all are swallowed up'—as Maude Wheeler said in *The Lights O' London*. Yet, even if it was true at the time that Melba was the only Australian who did 'any real good' abroad, this bleak assessment did not deter others from trying their own luck.

Up until this time, any travel, both historically and culturally, had been defined as a male prerogative. But now it had become an assertion of female modernity; for some, it was a striving for the freedoms which militant suffragists were fighting for. Some women who undertook the voyage to England were, like May, not simply travellers. They were transforming their lives and their very selves. They were claiming a right to work, to be seen

May and her mother sailed for London reaching Europe in time for the 1900 Paris Exhibition, an exposition that promised to be a review of the great developments in the modern world as well as the arts.

May's portrayal of herself in 'Some Impressions of the Ball' in the *Western Mail*.

FACING PAGE: A photograph of May in the same fancy dress for the ball.

in the public domain, to have professional careers and recognition, and to be paid, while all the time retaining complete public respectability.

Once they arrived in London, these venturesome Australian women found education and employment in a wonderfully modern mix of trades and professions: journalism, voice production, singing and acting, art and illustration. Some, rare birds of passage indeed, even enrolled at the Fabian Society's socially democratic London School of Economics. All of these Australians were as much in search of teachers and publishers as they were of inspiration, experience, variety and adventure. And some, like May Gibbs, were not disappointed.

Whatever their reaction, these expatriates still often yearned for Australia. Their solution was another federation, of sorts—one of social and cultural groups. These offered identity in an otherwise anonymous existence in London and included the Austral Club, which held weekly 'At Home' meetings; the Pioneer Club, set up specifically for Australian women; and the offices of the *British-Australasian* magazine, which was launched in 1909. The *British-Australasian* even went so far as to establish a permanent gallery for the Australian artists in their midst, although these same artists could also strive for a place on the walls of esteemed British art institutions such as the Royal Academy, the New English Art Club, the Royal Society of Oil Painters and the Modern Society of Portrait Painters. So great, in fact, was the sense of artistic brotherhood in London that, from 1905, a series of Australasian Artists' Dinners were held there annually.

This influx of Australians into London was so observable that it provided a ready source of witty comment for more than one amused journalist. Typical of these reactions was a full column by Montague Grover in the Melbourne *Argus* in 1904, which exclaimed: 'At first sight, London seems to a newly-arrived visitor to consist principally of … Australians trying to raise the price of a fare back to their own country'. Narrowing its gaze to a specific clique, it continued: 'there appear to be enough Australian artists to carry out the much wanted work of painting the vault of heaven blue'. The column then went on, tantalisingly, to detail the names and careers of expatriates who had made a significant addition to the life of the great city. All this, of course, was guaranteed to be a lure for hopeful Australians casting their eyes and their aspirations back to what many still called 'home'.

61

Shipping in Fremantle Harbour

This journalistic barrage was echoed in the popular novels of the day. In their pages, the overseas experience of Australian women as writers, journalists, actors, singers, artists and illustrators became a significant and enduring theme. In 1907, for example, the Australian-born writer Winifred James fictionalised her travel experiences in *Bachelor Betty*. With perhaps only slight exaggeration, she recounted how her conduct in London was a 'disappointment' to the British. 'They had read books about Australia', she explained, 'and I was not acting up to form at all'.

In the following entertaining anecdote, James inverts the usual tale of rosy colonial expectations into one of equally distorted English attitudes:

> I did not stroll down Piccadilly in a scarlet shirt cracking a stock whip and shouting 'Cooee' light-heartedly and cheerily … nor did I come to loggerheads with the police through attempting to boil my billy under the trees in Hyde Park.

James, like other Australians at the time, was embracing the cosmopolitan experience while still valuing and acknowledging her formative Australian upbringing.

Winifred James was part of a virtual exodus of ambitious Australasian women to London in the first decade of the twentieth century. She was in the company of writers like Barbara Baynton, Katherine Mansfield, Katharine Susannah Prichard and Henry Handel (Ethel) Richardson; singers like Amy Castles, Ada Crossley and Nellie Melba; artists like Margaret Preston, Thea Proctor and Dora Meeson; illustrators like Norman Lindsay's sister, Rose; actresses like Carrie Moore; musicians like Daisy Kennedy and Una Bourne; sculptors like Margaret Baskerville; and journalists like Ada Holman. Their names, their contributions to London's cultural life and their achievements were noted in that capital's newspapers and magazines, and this cachet was a guarantee of further comment in the Australian press. All of these women could have served as an example to the aspiring artist May Gibbs, and it was inevitable that she would eventually choose to pursue the same path to overseas fame and fortune. Throughout that decade, in fact, she was to make not one but three journeys to London.

In her cultured enclave of South Perth, May Gibbs' talents had been recognised and nurtured. But not all of her artistic peers enjoyed the same opportunities. One has only to compare her life with that of her exact contemporary, Kathleen O'Connor, to see the contrasting effect of geographical and cultural isolation. Although the social and economic

'Shipping in Fremantle Harbour', a newspaper illustration that recalls May's departure from Fremantle to London in 1900.

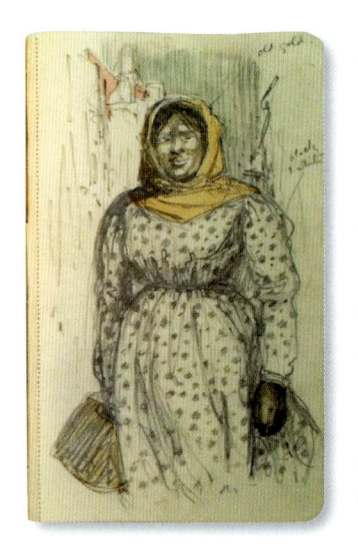

May's sketchbooks are a lively reminder of the exotic ports of call on her voyage across the world.

standing of O'Connor's family were easily the equal of May Gibbs', and although O'Connor ultimately led the most cosmopolitan life of any Western Australian artist of the time, in the 1890s she was marooned in Fremantle. She endured an upbringing in what was then a cultural backwater until 1902, when she moved to Perth. O'Connor finally left for Europe in 1906, by which time May Gibbs had already benefited from two such study trips abroad.

The 1891 Australian census pointed to a sorry future for any aspiring young woman, its statistics offering no indication of the great change to come. It revealed that the majority of women in employment in Western Australia had found work in dress-making and domestic service; less than ten per cent could claim the professional status of schoolteachers, governesses and music teachers. When May travelled to London for the first time almost a decade later, in February 1900, the number of women in employment had increased more than fourfold. But even so, their prospects for employment beyond menial roles were still disappointing. Surely May Gibbs was urged on by the insignificant role which women were being given in the economic life of the country. More pertinent still, what were the local opportunities for an aspiring artist? Even with her successes in the annual wild-flower shows, May was sufficiently self-critical to see that the pursuit of a career as a botanical artist offered no real prospects. Furthermore, the provincial limitations of Perth (and Australia) loomed larger as the 1890s unwound.

Even in 1897, the year of May's Diamond Jubilee triumph, her disappointing prospects were made clear by the sobering verdict of the *Western Mail*. That significant voice proclaimed: 'It may be doubted whether the time has yet come when an artist could live by his profession in Western Australia'. This opinion was delivered after a viewing of the latest brave Society of Arts exhibition. The newspaper elaborated further:

> [An artist] might, of course, paint in Western Australia and exhibit and sell in London or elsewhere, but it must be admitted that neither from a commercial point of view ... nor from others which appeal to the artistic mind perhaps even more profoundly, can it be said that Western Australia is yet a country which a painter would instinctively choose as his home.

May understandably chose London. She sailed from Fremantle on 21 February 1900 aboard the German mail steamer the *Konigin Luise*. She arrived in Southampton, after travelling via Colombo, Aden, Suez, Port Said,

65

"Persie" Southern Indian Ocean. Nov. 19th 1909.

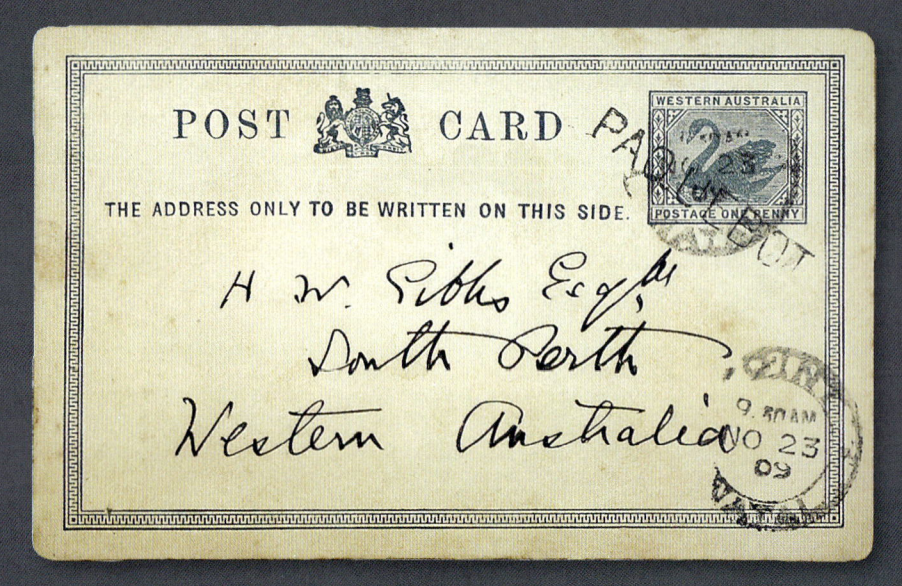

The hush of night.

Love May

POST CARD

THE ADDRESS ONLY TO BE WRITTEN ON THIS SIDE.

H. W. Pibbs Esq
South Perth
Western Australia

Naples and Genoa, on 26 March, a good five days ahead of schedule. In the early 1900s, unmarried women like May were regarded as being inexperienced in the ways of the world, and travel was only considered possible when accompanied by a parent or a guardian. On this voyage, May was chaperoned by her mother as well as by her cousin, Daisy Rogers. Although she was living at the start of a new century, May found that old Victorian mores were still limiting her freedoms.

Even so, she was an excited young traveller and began a diary immediately upon embarking. Significantly, in view of the reclusive lifestyle which May later embraced, it revealed that she eagerly joined in shipboard life and pastimes. On her first morning aboard she wrote that 'when I scrambled up on deck in a loose wrapper … the sea was running high and a stiff wind was blowing—and also my hair'. She exhibited a keen desire to experience all that this voyage, all that this escape, had to offer.

With rare self-confession, May also recorded a personal insight into her emotions: 'I had … quite given up all idea of an even scamped toilet—even the vainest girl forgets personal appearances the first two or three days on board'. And then there was the reality of a sea crossing begun at the height of an Australian summer:

> the cabin was so smelly and hot that after forcing myself to stay in my bunk for a few moments, I came to the conclusion that no one but a helpless fool would, could endure it and tumbled out, staggered along the passage dragging on my dressing gown as I went regardless and indifferent to everything but the one mad desire to get out of such an inferno.

For all May's genteel upbringing, she was not a slave to convention. Was this an early example of her rebellious, or at least her independent, nature? Certainly, this forthright attitude was maintained:

> On Friday Feb. 23rd mother and I spent the night on deck in preference to the small hell, I mean the cabin. We had rugs & cushions and made a hard but deliciously cool & fresh bed on the top of a large hatchway.

Within days, May was writing of a shipboard 'circle of friends' and had actively initiated a role in her new social milieu. But, for all this sociability, there was also a touch of the reserved (perhaps withdrawn) personality that she later exhibited: 'People talk rather too much for my pleasure but that is ever the same wherever one goes'.

Like her father, May enjoyed sending amusing illustrated messages home by post.

Soon, May reverted to recording her shipboard life in the one format she knew best—not words, but drawings. Her diary became a sketchbook as she recorded in telling detail the faces and personalities of her fellow travellers, as well as the exotic life glimpsed at such ports of call as Colombo, Aden and Genoa. Undoubtedly, these vignette drawings helped to relieve the inevitable boredom of idle days at sea. And already May's forte for close observation of character and of comic possibilities was emerging. This developing skill of deftly capturing the personalities of her fellow travellers in a quick sketch would stand her in good stead throughout the long career that was now evolving.

It was in these and later sketchbooks that May's true self was secretly being hoarded and quietly accumulating. She was never to lose the childhood pleasure that came from seeing her pages covered with drawings. For May, the very act of drawing itself became her reason for being. It was what she had always done. It maintained her thread of continuity with all that was most precious to her in life and in the imagination.

In 1904, a fellow voyager from Western Australia, titling herself 'A Correspondent', sent three lengthy reports of her journey to the *Western Mail*. Although she described a different trip, her words provide the perfect text to accompany and give a voice to May's drawings. They allow us to imagine the small dramas of life at sea, the 'ship flirtations, little comedies and tragedies, that relieve the monotony of the voyage'. May's pictorial observations complement that other traveller's words. They illustrate that, 'beneath the social veneer', there existed 'endless little intrigues and intricacies, heart-burnings and jealousies, for the ship is like a little village or a town, and human nature is the same there as everywhere else in this funny planet'. Our retrospective vision can see such insights as grist to the mill for May's later, seemingly endless series of comic strips portraying the foibles of the personalities who inhabited Gumnut Town.

Upon arriving in England, May and Daisy stayed with family members in rural Surrey, where the contrast between the Australian bush and English fields was dramatic: the travellers had exchanged exotic West Australian flora for wild violets and bluebells. The impact of London on the young artist was greater still. May had arrived from a small city and a provincial society to the largest city in the world—almost twice the size of Paris. In a population of over six million, she found a thriving cultural scene bustling

The genteel English countryside
portrayed in May's watercolours.

with artists and their societies, with dealers and exhibitions, with unimagined opportunities and distractions. And although we lack a sizeable cache of May's letters, a detailed diary or even a scrapbook from her stay of two years in London, we can still imagine the impact it might have made on her by unearthing some of London's attractions during that time.

Only weeks after May had arrived, the main exhibition of the year at the Royal Academy opened. It is impossible not to imagine that May was an eager presence in the crowds which flocked there. She may, however, have been disappointed in the showing by her fellow Australians—as a journalist for the *British-Australasian* lamented, 'Australasians make but a poor show in this year's Royal Academy'. Without doubt, the most frequently heard Australian name on everyone's lips was not that of an artist but that of a singer—in May, Nellie Melba opened at Covent Garden in *Faust*.

These London attractions, however, were not the only wonders on offer to the young traveller. The French capital was not only across the Channel, but the seven-month-long Paris Exhibition opened on 15 April 1900, less than a month after May arrived in England. Furthermore, as the premier exhibiting artist representing the Western Australian Commission in that exhibition, May's name headed the French catalogue listing the seventy works submitted by her home colony. These works were part of the largest world fair to date: over half the countries of Europe were represented, along with forty other nations. Its varied attractions celebrated the accumulated industrial and artistic triumphs of civilisation and, incredibly, it attracted over 50 million paying visitors.

Because May's personal papers from this period have only survived in fragmentary and frustratingly incomplete form, there is no extant documentation to prove that she visited the Paris Exhibition. However, it seems almost inconceivable that she would not have crossed to France. May's earlier success with the 1897 Diamond Jubilee album was being resoundingly reaffirmed. Indeed, one cannot resist speculating that this major international exposure and accolade from Paris was the final impetus that sent May Gibbs abroad. And once she had reached London, surely the allure of this exhibition, now on her very doorstep, was irresistible.

Among the many gaps in the records of May's life, the lack of specific comment on the Paris Exhibition, both at a personal level as well as at a wider public level, is one of the most frustrating. This frustration is further

The Paris Exhibition of 1900 was one of the most successful world exhibitions ever organised. With over fifty million visitors and forty-three countries participating, it was an amazing exposition of technology, the arts and the sciences. May's wild-flower paintings featured in the West Australian Court.

exacerbated in light of the fact that a rare, firsthand account of the Western Australian Court in the Paris exhibition boasted of its popularity. In the 4 August 1900 edition of the *West Australian*, Henry W Venn, the president of the Western Australian Commission for the Exhibition, reported: 'Our court continues to excite the warm admiration of the large crowd visiting the Exhibition, whose spontaneous testimony is conveyed to us daily'. Surely much of this 'warm admiration' was excited by the exotic allure and impact of 'seventy wildflower paintings' from a far corner of the world, an exhibition in which May Gibbs' work held pride of place.

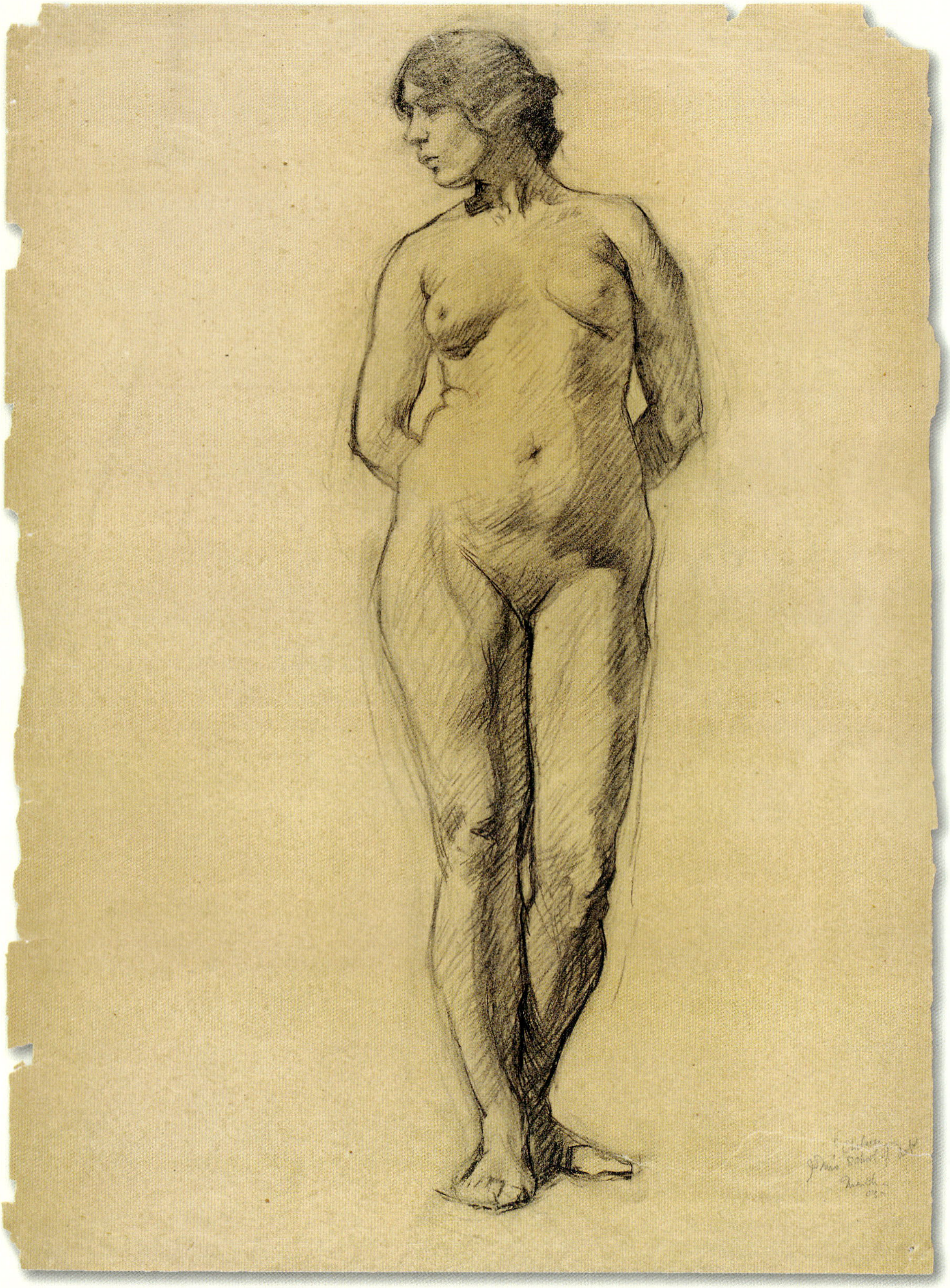

CHAPTER 6

'I FIND MY WORK MY GREATEST PLEASURE'

Regrettably, for all the pictorial material that has survived from these first years in London, there is virtually nothing of May's reactions and thoughts in writing. One rare exception, a mere fragment of a letter to her parents, preserved in *That Other Fairytale*, was most probably written in 1901. It contains a unique glimpse of her days at the Cope & Nicol Art School.

'I have had some praise for my work ... from Mr. Nichol [sic]', May boasted. He said, she continued, that 'I was "alright" and that I was getting on "very well, very well"'. Then, perhaps thinking that this might sound like faint praise, May went on to reassure her family that although her teacher's visit 'was short [it] means that you are getting on favourably & do not need his help'. More reassuring words followed in a cautionary note: 'Do not worry about me Father'. Finally, although still at an early stage of her training and her artistic life, May showed that she had already achieved great maturity and personal insight. 'I shall get on', she insisted. 'I have all faith in myself but no conceit, just simply that I feel sure of what I shall be able to do with earnest hard work.'

Only one generation earlier, May's mother was among the first women to be permitted to attend art school.

Art Nouveau, especially in the decorative arts, evolved out of the Paris Exhibition in 1900, which presented an overview of 'modern' style. Art Nouveau was most popular from 1890 to 1905 and was characterised by organic flowing curvilinear lines.

FACING PAGE: May's gumnut stories often mimicked real life with art school depicted in *Little Ragged Blossom*

She concluded with a characteristic statement of her work ethic: 'I find my work my greatest pleasure & Sundays are very tedious. I am always glad when Monday comes again.'

May obviously revelled in the intense and demanding training that she was given—six days a week at the Cope & Nicol Art School and night classes at the Chelsea Polytechnic Institute. The range of training provided was formidable. Besides the technical challenges of learning to work in the different mediums of pencil, charcoal and pen, May also had the welcome opportunity to attend classes where professional models posed for the students. These life classes diversified May's repertoire still further into costume drawing, character sketching and even nude studies.

By the end of 1901, May Gibbs was back in Perth. Her return to the city's provincial circle was clearly appreciated. In May 1902, she was the most acclaimed exhibitor at the Eighth Annual Exhibition held by the West Australian Society of Arts. She not only contributed eleven works, but one of them was used as the cover design for the society's catalogue. This design attracted one of the three first prizes that May secured for these efforts, and it imported a firsthand experience of Art Nouveau graphics into Western Australia.

Its sinuous lines were complemented by its lettering which eschewed heavy Victorian typography in favour of stylistically integrated calligraphy. With an economy of line, the design showed a young woman in a flowing Grecian robe not kneeling before a temple of art but rather before a campfire in the Australian bush. She was fanning the tentative flames of artistic endeavour in the furthest reaches of Britain's colonies. This was a juxtaposition in which May's own ambitious determination was strikingly illustrated.

The next most significant of the three prizes May secured was for the best oil painting of flowers. That said, she amply demonstrated her newly heightened versatility—prizes were conferred for her work across two different mediums: both for oil and for black-and-white work. She was also commended in the local press for the depictions of her cosmopolitan travels: watercolours of the Isle of Wight and Port Said. Altogether, May's highly impressive return to the fold acknowledged her overseas training.

Unfortunately, there was little opportunity for May to continue to display the training and experience she had gained in London. In the second half of

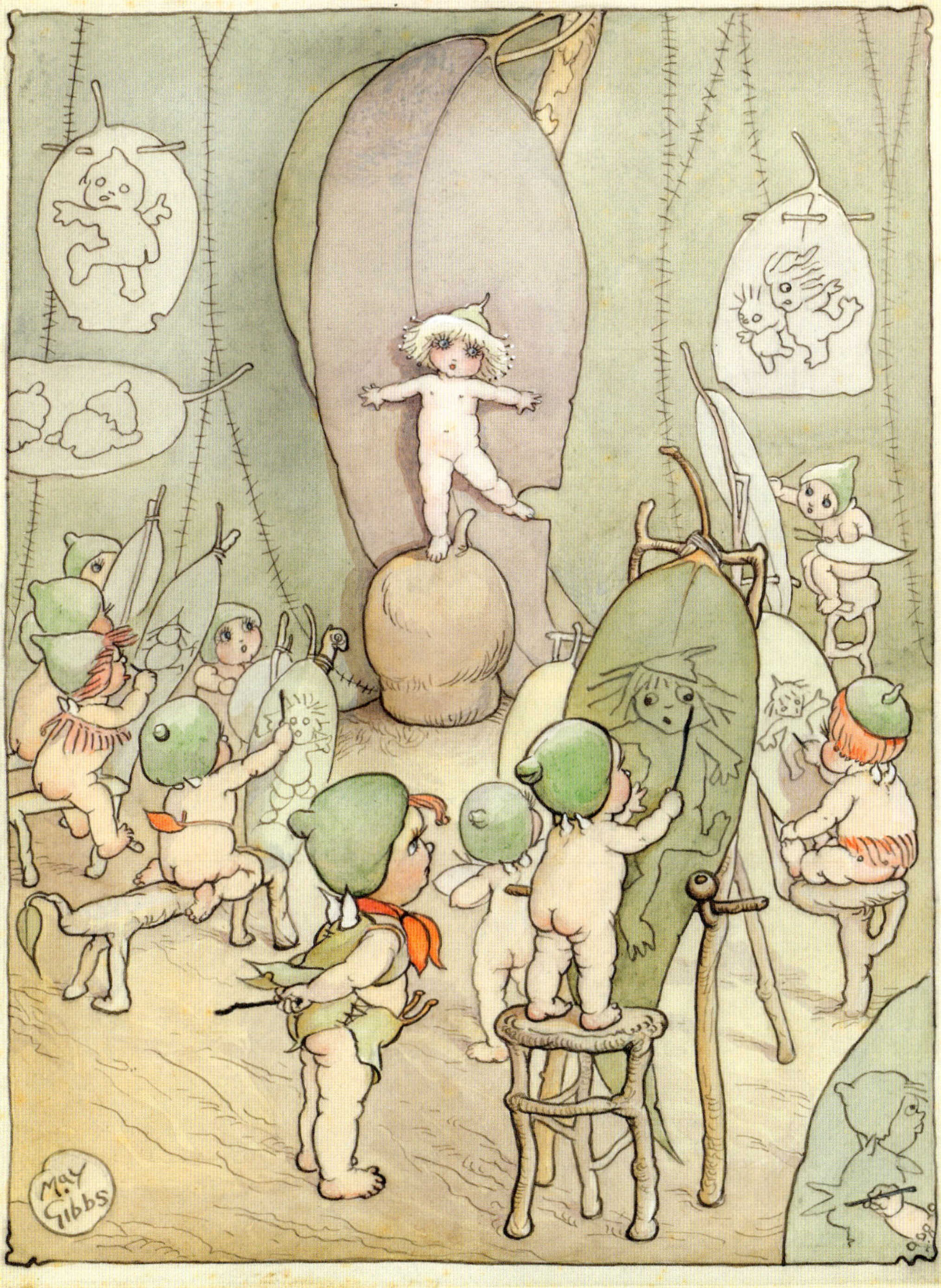
May Gibbs

Commercial illustration was bread-and-butter work for many artists of the time. May's fashion illustrations often appeared in West Australian newspapers.

1902, she finally secured ongoing commissions, but these were merely to create fashion advertisements for a Perth store. The most significant of these illustrations appeared intermittently in the daily newspaper the *Morning Herald* until mid-1903.

Hack work like this had become a staple for illustrators the world over as technical advances in the printing industry changed newspaper layouts from unending columns of text to increasingly enlivened pages carrying topical illustrations and enticing visual advertisements. It was energised by a demand from department and other merchandise stores, which saw it as a modern way of offering the public new visual temptations. While such work hardly stretched the capabilities of the aspiring illustrator, its demand for depicting changing poses and close detail was not to be wasted on May. Within months, she was also caricaturing fashion and its accessories in much livelier work.

This workaday artwork advertising a store's finery also contained evidence of May's real graphic interest—children and the world of childhood. Among the illustrations for adults depicting diaphanous, Edwardian fashions, May welcomed the chance to add charming vignettes of little girls. The contrast between these advertisements and her schoolgirl efforts of a decade earlier clearly revealed the disciplined art training that had given May both assurance and versatility.

In June 1902 May was also commissioned to create political cartoons for *The Social Kodak*, a paper published 'to assist in the improvement and diversion of womankind'. It was the first 'woman's paper' to be published in Western Australia. May's first cartoon on the cover was 'Women's Franchise' leading light. May concealed the fact that she was a woman and used her pseudonym, 'Blob'. May's caricatures and political cartoons continued to appear throughout 1902 and 1903, always under this pseudonym.

By the end of 1903, however, May had realised that Perth could not offer her the same stimulation or professional challenges which she had experienced in London. And so she travelled to that city once more, sailing from Albany on 7 December aboard the White Star liner SS *Afric*. On this voyage, she was one of thirty passengers who embarked in Western Australia to join the 300 others already aboard.

Once again she was chaperoned by her mother, and throughout this second period of study she was entrusted to the care of relatives. One of her mother's sisters, Emily Hadfield (nee Rogers) had married and was living in Merton Park, Wimbledon. This family home became May's haven throughout 1904, and since her cousin Alice Hadfield was also an eager art student, the two young women were able to attend art classes together. The close relationship which May formed with Alice was fondly recorded in a charming pastel portrait. Less well known was a lively series of caricatures and verses that May created while spending Christmas 1904 with the Hadfields.

May attended Henry Blackburn's School for Black & White Artists in the daytime and Chelsea Polytechnic at night. At the evening school she was taught by Augustus John. Although he was to become famous for his unique style of portraiture, this exposure to more modernist teachings failed to impress May. Her diligence was rewarded, however, and she graduated at the end of 1904. Her certificate from the South Kensington Board of Education proclaimed that she had achieved a 'First Class in Drawing from Life'.

In mid-1905 May's parents arrived in England, bringing their youngest son Harold with them: he was to attend boarding school while May, it was decided, was to accompany her parents back home. After she had returned, May established herself as a regular contributor to the state's leading newspaper, the *Western Mail*, starting with its colour Christmas cover. Then, in September the following year, her work for the newspaper suddenly took off in a new direction. She created full pages of drawings of local tennis players, the first in a long-term series of seven large sporting cartoons that challenged her ability to adroitly capture frozen moments in women's tennis, domestic cricket and lawn bowls. These apparently out-of-character vignettes were significant for a number of reasons. Firstly, they showed that May was willing to try her hand at new illustrative opportunities. Furthermore, they showed that her art studies in London had developed her eye for depicting personality and humour with deft and economical pen strokes. Her newly adopted style used an elegant, assured line to convey all the balletic style and poise (or the lack of them) of the various players.

May obviously relished these commissions, which were surely a welcome challenge after her earlier series of static fashion drawings for Perth's rival

May's cousin and fellow art student Alice Hadfield portrayed at her easel.

Sketches from a Perth Sketch Book

paper, the *Morning Herald*. They were also, importantly, a recognition of her versatility in regard to pen work. May delighted in the comic possibilities inherent in both ungainly and sinuous body lines and in swirling costumes caught in action. And she remained objective, even producing an unflattering caricature of herself, for a piece published on 20 October 1906, as surely the most frumpy tennis player of all!

In 1905, lawn tennis courts had been attached to the Zoological Gardens near the Gibbs family's house in South Perth. Like the zoo, this new addition to the neighbourhood provided a source of inspiration for the eager illustrator. Ivan Gibbs became a regular sight on the new courts, his developing prowess in local matches as well as in the annual national championships cheered on by May and the rest of his family. May's keen eyes could not resist the comic opportunities inherent in the sport, and she caricatured Ivan in his tennis garb at least three times between September 1906 and April 1913. On this last occasion, Ivan was given a credit: a caption acknowledged that he had provided 'good copy' for his sister's talent.

The footnote to this was that, by his late thirties, Ivan Gibbs had achieved some distinction as a tennis player, particularly in the mixed-doubles matches he played with Violet Mather. Their partnership won the Open State Championships four times between 1919 and 1923. At Ivan's peak, he represented Western Australia in interstate matches.

The most celebrated of May's sporting cartoons appeared on 30 March 1907. In this contribution, May caught the personality and the fluid motion of one particularly famous local cricket player with a dextrous line. This was during a match between New South Wales and Western Australia, and she depicted Bobbie Selk in 'Some Variations of a Prominent Cricketer'. May's sequential type of cartoon was perfectly suited to conveying an eye-catching and appealing series of snapshots of a game in progress. By way of contrast, she surrounded Selk with recognisable vignettes of some of his teammates—'a few other brilliant players'.

It seemed that not even the presence of vice-regal guests and over 4000 spectators had been enough to daunt the ready pen of the confident illustrator. And so May's editor commissioned another page of graphic 'impressions' for the following year's interstate match. Five years later, in April 1913, by way of a variant, and giving clear evidence of even further artistic

May's brother Ivan was a successful local tennis player and at a time when May's caricatures of sportsmen were appearing in the *Western Mail*.

FACING PAGE: 'Sketches from a Perth Sketch Book', published in the *Western Mail* show May's maturing ability as an artist and observer.

May's caricatures of sportsmen were skillfully drawn with an economy of line.

expertise, May contributed impressions of Perth's bowling carnival. When the players assumed their hierophantic poses unique to this sport, it was once again May's quick eye for telling gesticulation and comic pose that came to the fore.

Before all this, in 1906, May's developing skill as a caricaturist had been recognised and given major exposure. At a fete held in aid of the Home of Peace on 9 March, the local press had enthused over the entertainment arranged by May and her mother. 'Every one expected to be thoroughly amused,' wrote the *West Australian*, 'knowing the talent of the organisers of this artistic portion of the programme, and they were not disappointed'. The novelty of the entertainment offered clearly allowed May full rein to express her varied talents: 'The picture gallery, a series of caricatures painted by Miss Gibbs, was very clever and provocative of mirth as one after another recognised their friends portrayed with that extraordinary streak of likeness which is only produced by the skilful pen of the caricaturist'. In particular, the newspaper praised 'the picture of the South Perth people catching their ferry'. What could have been a disjointed presentation was held together by May's ability as a stage manager: 'Not the least enjoyable part of the evening's amusement were the original tableaux, in which Mrs Gibbs took part, Miss Gibbs explaining in her inimitable way one comic picture after another'.

In the period between May's second and third trips to London (late 1905 to late 1909), there was one particular year which stood out for its sustained productivity and acknowledged achievement—1907. In that year, for the *Western Mail* alone, May contributed seven full-page black-and-white and two full-page colour plates as well as vignette work. May also produced two extraordinary illustrations for the *Western Mail*—one at the beginning of the year and the other at the end. While one was charmingly decorative and the other dramatically descriptive, both of them were endowed with more than passing newsworthy appeal. The significance of these images was strikingly acknowledged when they were reproduced, in a reduced format, as postcards.

The first of these illustrations was presented as a half-page sketch and depicted a real-life event: a diver braving a flooded mine to bring light and, ultimately, salvation to a trapped miner.

At the height of the West Australian mining boom of the time, any incident in the gold mines was newsworthy. The year before, on 9 January 1906, it had been reported that three men had been killed in a mining accident at Bonnievale near Coolgardie. Then, on 19 March 1907, a massive downpour flooded another mine there. While there was no initial loss of life, one miner was trapped underground. For nine full days, until his rescue on 28 March, his ordeal was syndicated news. Modesto Vareschetti, a 32-year-old Italian miner, became a household name.

The fact that the newspaper chose May Gibbs to depict this miraculous rescue was a testament to her standing as a local artist. It acknowledged the versatility of her ability and vindicated her long and lonely dedication at art schools in London. Additionally, it showed faith in her ability to produce a strikingly effective illustration at very short notice.

Within two days of the rescue, May had found a diver's suit to give exotic fidelity to her depiction and had then submitted her commissioned piece. 'A Light in the Darkness', appropriately, borrowed the religious overtones of a succouring angel arriving in a blaze of light and delivering mankind from peril. It depicted Frank Hughes, a miner and former deep-sea diver who achieved the rescue with the help of a team of volunteers. Luckily, or providentially, Vareschetti had found an air pocket on a narrow ledge above the water, and every day Hughes took food, drink, matches, candles, tobacco and messages of comfort and guidance to him.

It is not difficult to see why May's newspaper illustration was reissued as a postcard. The saga electrified all of Australia. Across the other side of the country, the *Sydney Morning Herald* avidly reported the story for readers in the eastern states. The newspaper made the significant claim that this unfolding rescue had focused the eyes of the nation: 'Day after day … the people of the Commonwealth have been watching with growing tension … and the Commonwealth joins in a chorus of congratulations and rejoicing at the success that has crowned so magnificent a series of heroic efforts'.

Seen in this federated context, one which reveals nearly unprecedented national interest, it is not surprising that the story became a proud assertion of national character. No wonder it was seen as extending the united strengths and values extolled in Australia's recent baptism of fire in the Boer War. Readers were reminded that 'Young Australia has shown his mettle on South Africa battlefields' and that 'there is a valour equal to the best that a

The newspaper illustration of the miner's dramatic rescue captured the public's imagination and was reproduced as a postcard.

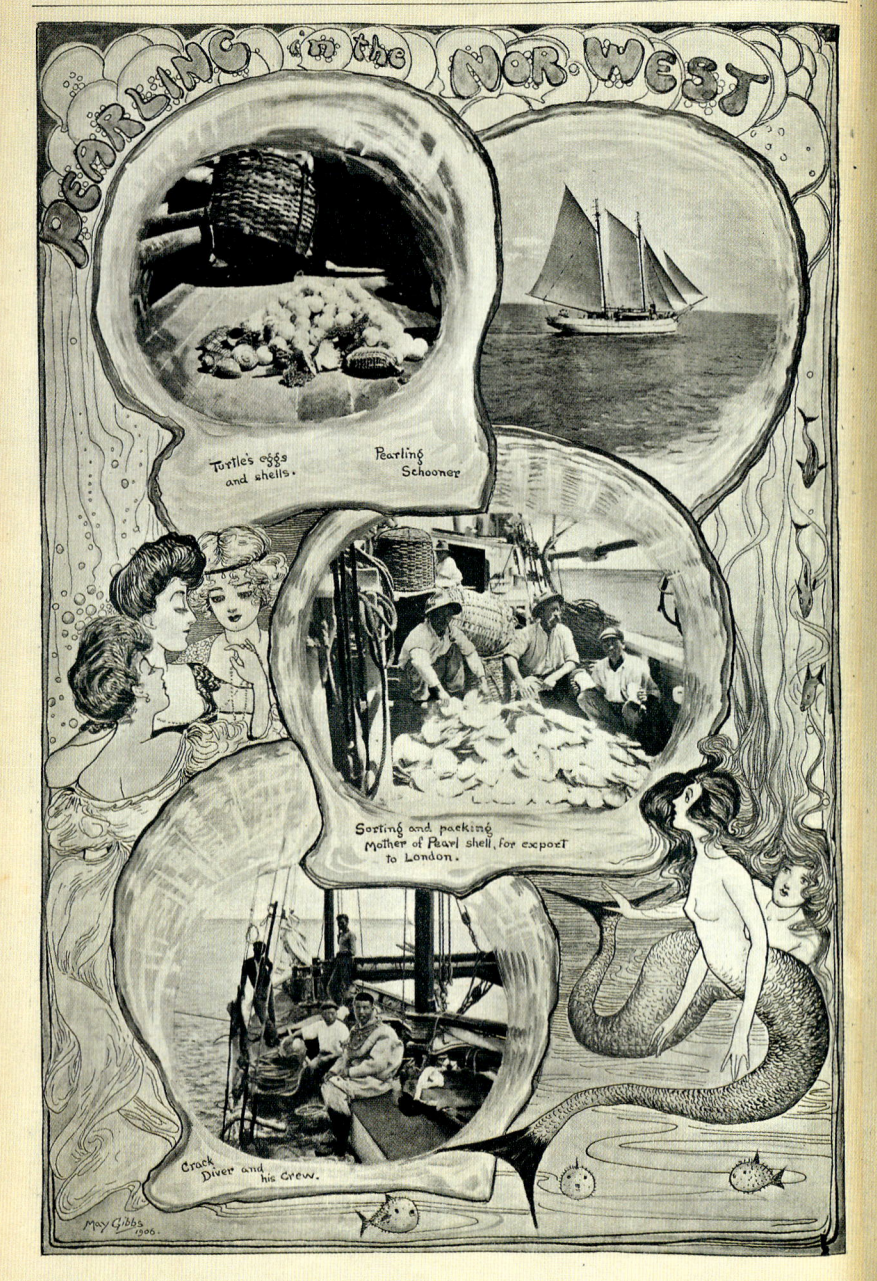

Pearling in the Nor'West

Turtle's eggs and shells.

Pearling Schooner

Sorting and packing Mother of Pearl shell, for export to London.

Crack Diver and his Crew.

May Gibbs, 1906.

soldier can show, and that saving life is better than taking it'. Only seven years later, on the eve of a world war, Australia was to feel these same Commonwealth bonds as never before. May then responded with a whole series of postcard images of the gumnut corps as she answered a call for another, much greater need.

The success which May achieved with this dramatic image for the *Western Mail* was enhanced on 25 December by her depiction of 'Pearling in the Nor West', which was given full-page status in the same newspaper.

Although Western Australia had made its name—and its wealth—from gold, the pearling industry was another colourful and exotic addition to the state's portfolio. Pearling had been part of the colony's economy ever since the 1860s, and by the mid-1880s the newly established township of Broome had become a bustling port for the luggers. Within a generation it would become the centre of the largest pearling industry in the world, with nearly 400 luggers based there and more than 3500 people fishing for pearl shell. By then, fully three-quarters of the world's shell would come from Australian waters.

Although pearling had an obvious allure, the reality of the industry was radically different from any picturesque imagining. The early luggers were sail-powered and could only deploy one diver and his apparatus at a time. Most of these divers were Japanese and Malay men who struggled along in lead-weighted boots, peering through inch-thick faceplates as they scooped oysters into their bags. These divers could make a fortune, but it was very dangerous work. Inferior equipment, a lack of basic safety regulations and an ignorance of the medical dangers of deep-sea diving meant that many lives were lost. Furthermore, only the year after May's illustration was published, two hurricanes devastated Broome—in April and December 1908, the wildest storms in Western Australia's history claimed around 200 lives and practically destroyed the state's pearling fleet.

But perhaps not surprisingly, it was the romance of the industry which May chose to capture in her illustration. She did this by creating an eye-catching layout: four photographic illustrations of pearl shells framed within a decorative cartouche of mermaids, fish and fashionable beauties admiring their pearls.

Over a decade later, in 1921, May was to reaffirm the illustrative potential of underwater exploits, and of pearling in particular. *Little Obelia*, her

FACING PAGE: 'Pearling in the nor west', a montage of fantasy illustration and photographs, published in the *Western Mail, 1907.*

FACING PAGE: *Little Obelia* was published in 1921. In old age May reflected 'I thought how lovely it would be to have a little town under the water.'

third major children's book published in Australia, introduced an undersea variation on her bushland baby stories. She used the book's striking cover to depict Obelia enthroned in an oyster shell and holding a magnificent pearl. It is possible that some of the inspiration for this character came from a reproduction of a seventeenth-century European masterpiece which May treasured. Today, visitors to Nutcote, May's beloved home for the last forty-four years of her life, can see this print hanging above a mantelpiece: Johannes Vermeer's *Woman with a pearl necklace*.

A few months before 'Pearling in the Nor West' appeared in the *Western Mail*, May Gibbs was one of the thousands of hopeful Australasian women who had entered their work in the largest showing of its kind ever held in Australia. The First Australian Exhibition of Women's Work was heralded in Western Australia, as elsewhere in the country, by a preliminary state exhibition, staged in Perth's town hall on 14 August 1907. As expected, May was among its noted exhibitors. However, what was not expected was her choice of work—Australian landscapes rather than wild-flower paintings. Had her second round of exposure to the cosmopolitan art scene confirmed her view that the botanical genre was becoming somewhat *retarditaire*? Whatever the case, her name as a contributor in this preliminary exhibition was singled out for mention by both of Perth's leading newspapers, and May became one of the ten artists selected to represent her state in the exhibition proper in Melbourne in October and November 1907.

Almost all of these women contributed paintings of wild flowers, and the category itself attracted over 300 entries. This was far more than any other fine arts category in the exhibition—in Australia, it seemed, this was a genre that still reigned supreme. May, however, contributed five watercolours to the 'Best Australian Landscape' class. In such a highly competitive field, the only known accolade she received was from the authoritative critic William Moore, who praised one of her entries as 'a clever study by … a talented West Australian'. But although May was not awarded a prize for any of her landscapes, she showed herself to be a true professional—when Western Australia announced that its own sequel exhibition would open a month after Melbourne's closed, May submitted more new work.

The Australian Exhibition of Art and Work of Western Australian Manufacture took its lead from the Melbourne survey but welcomed entries from both sexes. This proud and independent assertion of the state's wealth on

85

FACING PAGE: A cover for the *Western Mail* with English story-book imagery.

combined fronts—both economic and cultural—was held in Perth's Exhibition Buildings from 23 December 1907 until 8 January 1908. Although West Australian wild-flower paintings remained a popular choice among the fine arts exhibits, once again May chose to show her autonomy. She submitted a figure work in watercolour which was awarded a certificate of merit.

But this was only May's penultimate accolade for 1907. She closed the year with a social triumph at Perth's Cup Day on 28 December. This racing carnival had become Perth's most anticipated social event. The *West Australian* enthused that 'of all social events in the year [it] conjures up in the imagination of the annual visitors the pleasantest associations and keenest excitement'. May's exposure to the best and latest fashion that Perth had to offer through her advertising commissions showed its effect. The extensive newspaper coverage of the event singled her out for mention, dressed in 'white muslin, with lace finishings'.

It is easy, and tempting, to see May as the living embodiment of one of those fashion advertisements over which she had so recently laboured. Her choice of white muslin was decidedly à la mode. The fashion pundits observed that white was 'more popular … this year' than ever before.

If May's achievements reached an apogee in 1907, the following year was only slightly less distinguished. On the social front, May once again revelled in Perth's most elite occasions. At the June opening of the state's new art gallery, described by the *West Australian* as the 'most brilliant function held in Perth for very many years', May was among the 400 guests who had assembled to greet the governor, her stylish sense of couture providing copy for the local press. A month later, the annual Society for the Prevention of Cruelty to Animals (SPCA) fancy-dress ball at Government House gave May another occasion on which to shine when her mother organised a set of costumed revellers from South Perth.

On the artistic front, in March 1908 May designed an address to farewell her old headmistress from Bishop's Girls' College—Amy Best was leaving the state after a distinguished educational career. And in August, May was acknowledged for a poster she created for a minstrel show in aid of the charity Our Boys' Institute. May also continued her contributions to the *Western Mail* with six full-page works, including two for its special Christmas number.

SUPPLEMENT TO THE "WESTERN MAIL"
CHRISTMAS NUMBER, DEC. 25, 1907.

The CHILDREN'S CORNER

by "Aunt Mary"

May Gibbs
1907

FACING PAGE: A cover for the *Western Mail*, with distinctly Western Australian flora and fauna imagery.

Among all the work that May produced throughout 1908, one example stands out for its unique status: on 13 June, a short story by May Gibbs entitled 'Parson Dick of Pinginup' takes up almost an entire page in the *Western Mail*. Because it appears never to have been cited until now, a short synopsis of its narrative is necessary to reveal its hitherto-unknown value.

The story opens with an eight-year-old boy, Pat, enticing his pet possum to play with him. Pat shares a bush hut with Parson Dick, who has cared for the boy ever since he was deserted by his drunken father. The strength of affection between the pair is shown by the trust which Pat has been given by the parson. He has written a letter which he entrusts to the boy with the promise that it will be posted if he should die. This farewell letter is addressed to an English actress whose love he had renounced in order to fight his 'fiend'—an addiction to morphine. 'You could not love where you could no longer respect', he had told her. Then, fearing that neither his love for her nor his sacred office were sufficient to overcome this fiend, he had emigrated to Australia. When the parson collapses, little Pat fears the worst and fulfils his promise, completely unaware of the consequences. The parson revives, but he has no regrets about the letter being sent. By releasing the woman he loves, he has allowed her to be free to marry another.

As sentimental and unoriginal as the story might be, it still manages to engage the reader. The black sheep who emigrates to the colonies to fight his demons might be a cliché, but May's story creates enough mystery to retain interest and sufficient affecting pathos to arouse concern. Is it possible that, at this time, May Gibbs was seriously considering a career as a writer or journalist? The answer might lie in the fact that, from 1905 until May's last visit to London in 1909, she found that her standing as a popular female illustrator was not as undisputed as it once had been. A new Australian illustrator had entered the field—Ida Rentoul, who went on to achieve international fame under her married name of Ida Rentoul Outhwaite.

Ida Rentoul's work had increasingly gained exposure and popularity. Throughout the five years in question, she published at least eight significant illustrated works—although she was a decade younger than May, she still managed to eclipse her rival. Even more frustrating was the fact that Ida also encroached upon May's hard-won profile on her home ground: the Melbourne-based illustrator was consistently represented in the *Western Mail*. And while May had started those years as the cover artist for that

Western Mail

Xmas Number

Dec. 25. 06.
No. 10

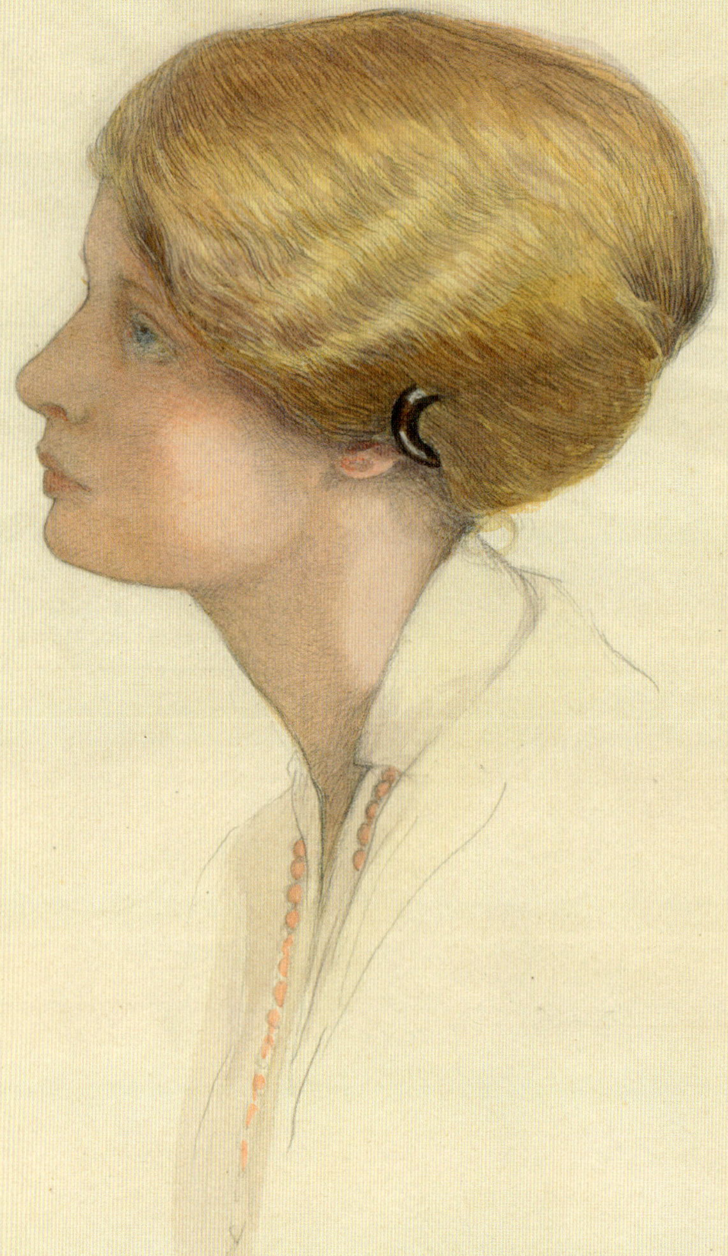

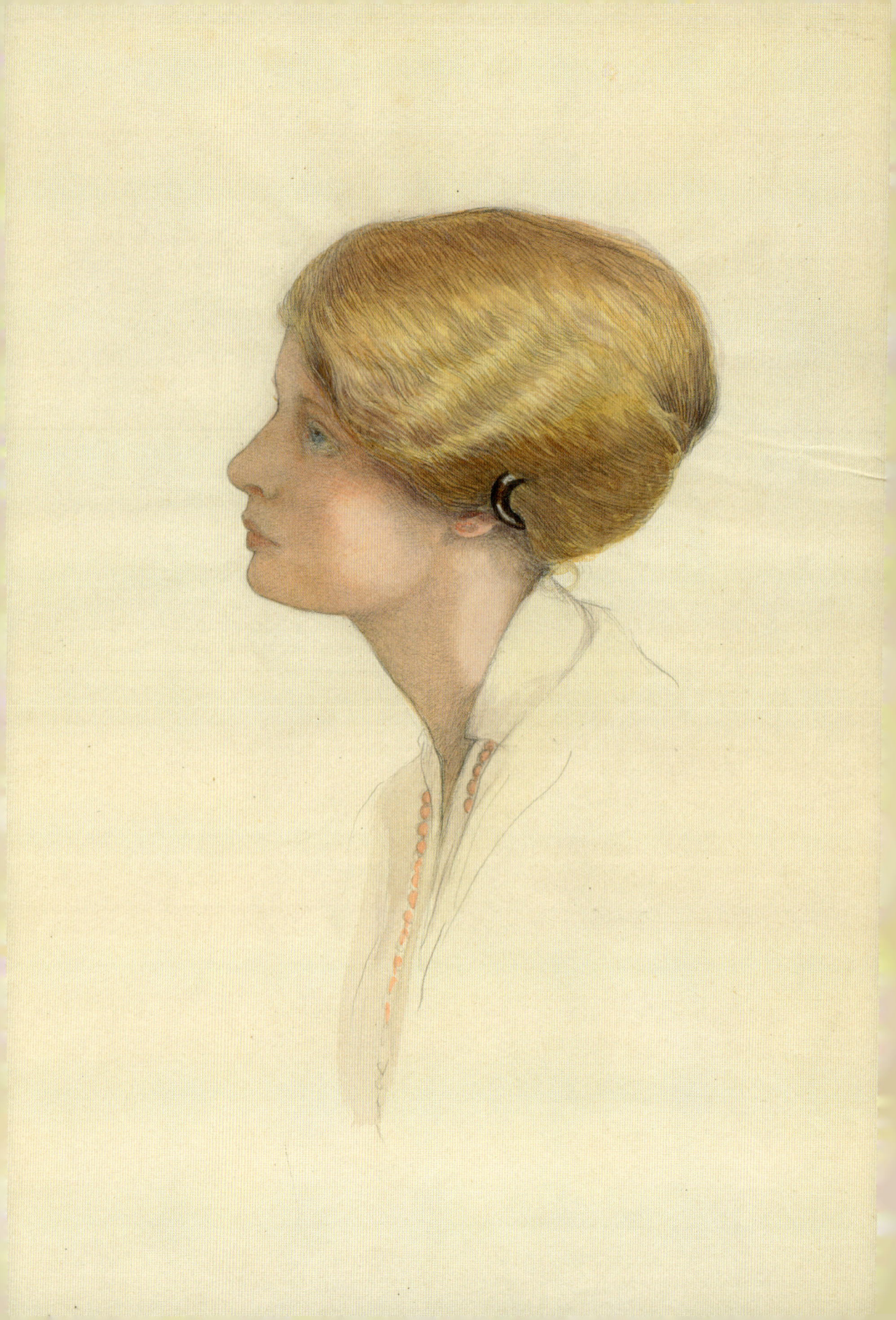

paper's most prestigious issue, the Christmas number, by 1909 Ida had usurped even that honour. Furthermore, to add to the ignominy of all this, Ida had received none of the professional training that May had undertaken!

In May 1909, May was given a significant reminder of the vibrant cultural life that she had left behind in Europe. Her family played host to a celebrated family of musicians whose fame was taking them around the world. The three Cherniavski brothers, ranging in age from fifteen to eighteen years, were making the first of what would be five tours to Australia over the next two decades. Leo, Jan and Mischel were Russian-born musical prodigies who had fled their homeland with their father to escape the persecution of Jews in 1904. Starting in Vienna, they had established their name across Europe before travelling to South Africa in 1908 and then on to Australia, where they were scheduled to appear in Melbourne, Sydney, Perth and Kalgoorlie. While their popularity was no doubt enhanced by such a dramatic personal story as well as by the novel presentation of three handsome performers from the one family, their musical prowess was undeniable. Furthermore, their willingness to perform outside metropolitan centres guaranteed a wildly enthusiastic reception.

May's engaging pictorial mementos of their visit are evidence that her early years were filled with incident, with a wide variety of social and cultural occasions and with an exuberant family life.

Also in Perth's small cultural clique at this time was another Australian. Lionel Logue moved to Perth from Adelaide in 1906 and established himself as a teacher of elocution, voice production and dramatic art. He became a frequent performer in local concerts and charity benefits. Moving in the same milieu it is inconceivable that their paths did not cross. London was to be the making of Logue just as it was for May, only this Australian was to achieve fame as the speech therapist to the future King George VI.

In spite of all the activities and accolades, May must have felt she was merely achieving provincial triumphs for someone whose horizons and ambitions had been broadened so much. To see the adulation which the visiting musicians attracted and then to compare it with her own situation must have been sobering. As the first decade of the century progressed, May like other Australians of her milieu must have chafed at the cultural and geographical confines of her life, as well as the lack of real opportunity to display and enhance her talent.

By 1907 May's skills in illustration and portraiture had reached a highly developed level.

May Gibbs
1910

from life — at St Monica Brook St Holborn London

Imagine my bed a haystack — while I get a sketch of — ? never gone a lovely little girl.

CHAPTER 7

MAY—THE EMANCIPATED WOMAN

In 1909, May Gibbs made her third—and what was to be her last—journey to London. She embarked on 8 November aboard the *Persic* and remained in Europe until early 1913, the longest overseas stay of her life. We can only lament that we cannot enjoy an autobiographical account of these years. What is clear, however, is that this third period of study and experience in London consolidated May's two previous visits.

In the Australia that May had left behind, there had already been signs that the fortunes of women artists and illustrators were changing. No less a local art authority than William Moore had been urging women for several years to consider art as a profession rather than a mere pastime. In late 1907, a series of articles by him on careers for Australasian girls had devoted an informed and encouraging place to the artist's life. Within a few more years, proud reports in the Australian press stimulated such an overseas exodus of Australian women that three lengthy series of articles appeared in Melbourne magazines. Some of these articles devoted themselves to the major career choices available in London: music, writing and, of course, art.

On May's last visit to London she was determined to build her career as an artist and found an agent to represent her work to publishers.

94

Together, they revealed the triumphs of expatriate Australian women, as well as the possible pitfalls they faced, and offered practical career and travel advice.

And so, although it had been lamented only a decade earlier in the *British-Australasian* that Australasians had made 'but a poor show' in the Royal Academy exhibition of 1900, a complete reversal was now being effected. Upon arriving back in London, May found that the city's art scene was particularly energised by expatriate Australians. The exploits of May's fellow artists and their newly elevated status were to be proudly recorded over the course of several years by William Moore. On 17 December 1912, at no less a prestigious venue than the Royal Colonial Institute, and before an audience of luminaries that included the high commissioner for Australia, he delivered an illustrated lecture which was a testimony to the established art coterie of expatriates who had gained official recognition. Moore quoted some impressive figures: in 1911, 'twenty-four Australians were represented at the Royal Academy, fifteen at the old Salon and six at the New'.

An illustration for a children's book, strongly influenced by the English illustrators of the time.

Although May's third trip to London was made when she was thirty-two years old, she was still accompanied by her mother and a cousin. Did she need and welcome this intense chaperoning or was she irritated and embarrassed by its imposition? What is known is that, after the familiar welcome from the Rogers family and the departure of her mother, May asserted her independence. Her choice of new lodgings was a small attic room overlooking the rooftops of London. From there she again traced the well-worn path to British publishers, hoping to interest them in her growing portfolio of work. Eventually she realised that a literary agent might open doors for her, and she placed her work—and her aspirations—with Charles H Wood of Fleet Street. It was a professional move that soon reaped a dividend.

There had been a significant development in London only a few months before May had arrived. On 26 June 1909, the new Victoria & Albert Museum had been opened by King Edward VII. While May was probably familiar with its collections from her previous visits, she now found a much larger collection with greatly improved display. Its new galleries alternated between long rooms and lofty exhibition courts; rows of cases were set against the museum's plain walls, grouping objects of similar appearance. The change from the bold colours of the 1890s meant that these treasures retained a greater presence. Furthermore, specialist departments had begun

For income May was forced to concentrate on creating illustrations that drew on the period costumes of Georgian England.

to consolidate their fields in the decorative arts. As a focus for the education of designers and craftsmen, the museum was a godsend for May and her fellow students.

A few years earlier, another aspiring illustrator, as unknown then as May Gibbs had been at the time, had benefited greatly from the museum's collection of eighteenth-century costume. That illustrator was Beatrix Potter, whose research had culminated in *The Tailor of Gloucester*, first issued in a trade edition in 1903. Now it was May's turn to immerse herself in the same collections. Her agent had secured her three commissions from a leading British publisher, George G Harrap, and the work demanded close and accurate attention to historical detail.

Throughout the 1930s, Harrap was to establish an impressive reputation as a publisher of finely illustrated books by luminaries that included Arthur Rackham. In May's time, however, its productions were much more modest. Nonetheless, her commissions were part of a series and ranged over six centuries of English social and political history. She had to be exact in her preparation of literally hundreds of vignette chapter headings, textual illustrations and full-page plates. The diverse collections of the Victoria & Albert Museum provided May with necessary examples of everything from armour, clothing and furnishings to household artefacts and toys.

There were, however, to be some distractions from what could have been more of a burden than a joy. For example, in the second in this series, *The Struggle with the Crown*, one of the chapter headings called for a depiction of 'Pestilence, Fire and Treason'. This allowed May an imaginative release from strict documentation and she was able to indulge herself in a bizarre fantasy of wraiths and monsters. Then there was the next in the series, *Georgian England*, which may have provided the most welcome work of any volume. Its many chapter headings allowed May to indulge her love of historical costume, most particularly of children's clothes and the paraphernalia of childhood.

The strain which May faced in undertaking these commissions, published between 1912 and 1913, was startlingly apparent. They required detailed historical research and documentary accuracy. *Georgian England* alone required over 100 individual illustrations. Multiplied across three books, this workload was prodigious. It is no wonder that May's family became concerned for her health and wellbeing.

"Some one coming down the lane —
Dolly waited anxiously"

some mother of more children
sick gent
sick gents wife
mother of some children
Am I not mad yet
Had 8 hours of this! & recovered!
May
Temperature 90 in the shade
Oranges bananas biscuits & sticky stuff

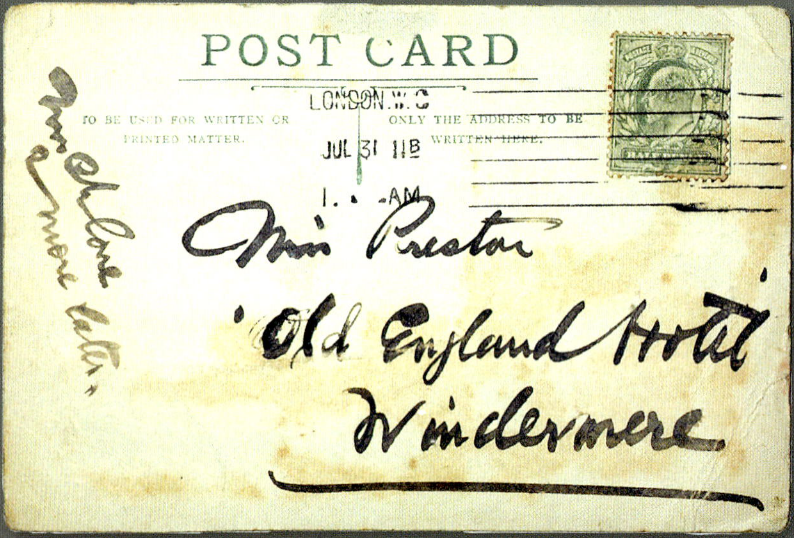
POST CARD
TO BE USED FOR WRITTEN OR PRINTED MATTER.
ONLY THE ADDRESS TO BE WRITTEN HERE.
LONDON.W.C
JUL 31
Mrs Preston
'Old England Hotel'
Windermere
Much love more later.

What cannot be denied, however, is the fact that, as an illustrator, May finally found a metier and a style during this last London exposure. She certainly discovered that one area of historical research needed to fulfil Harrap's commissions was particularly welcome—the demand for a detailed depiction of children's costumes from the past. As a child herself in the 1890s, she had appeared in historical and fancy dress, while as an adult in the 1900s, this interest had evolved into much more elaborate presentations at the annual SPCA costume balls held at Perth's Government House.

May's involvement in these productions had been varied: she had been a regular participant and a recorder of their costumed finery for the pages of the *West Australian*. The work she performed in this latter role had been regarded highly enough for it to secure a full newspaper page in the wake of the 1906 ball. The challenge and the allure for May were obvious from a contemporary description in the *Morning Herald*:

> Costumes of periods long since past appeared for a second ... and famous characters of history and fiction entered into the eye's fleeting glimpse ... till it appeared that the barriers of Time had been swept away and the dead generations had been awakened and hauled up the ladder of centuries to dance a figure with a band of twentieth-century merrymakers.

May had also been an artistic collaborator with her mother in organising some of these annual fancy-dress sets. The creative stimulus involved was recognised in the fulsome descriptions which these occasions warranted in the local press. The 1908 event, for example, was described in the *West Australian* as being 'of quite absorbing interest for many weeks beforehand to those who are getting them up'. The qualities they were seen to demand were those in which May obviously excelled: 'originality and taste and ingenuity' such that 'the stately, the comic, the dainty, the historic, the lovely, the picturesque, all vied one against another for the glory of giving the most pleasing effect'. Only a short time later, in London, May surely found that this cumulative experience was another source of inspiration for her costume illustrations.

In 1913, with the renewed confidence of Harrap's significant commissions to her credit, May finally crossed the threshold of the British publishing world. But while she had been busy creating a world in her imagination, the real world had been changing.

Herbert's postcards to May (above) and May's postcards of life in England (facing page) were usually self-deprecating. May depicted herself holding her hat on her lap saying 'If not mad yet, when —?'

May took her sketchbooks everywhere, finding constant opportunities to sketch characters.

The London to which May Gibbs returned in December 1909 was not the same London she had left in 1905. Increasingly, it had become a city under siege. Although the traditional signs of warfare were not immediately apparent, the streets of London, its public forums and its press were all under fire from strident protest and verbal attack. Since the founding in October 1903 of the Women's Social and Political Union (WSPU) by Mrs Emmeline Pankhurst and her eldest daughter, Christabel, its members had become increasingly militant. These defiant women had even been given a newly coined name—suffragettes.

This word was first used by London's *Daily Mail* in 1906 to denote the new, aggressive style of woman agitating for social reform, including female suffrage. It quickly became loaded with emotion and a variety of meanings. At first, the suffragettes were content to limit the tactics of their campaign to writing letters of protest, heckling Cabinet ministers and public speakers, and holding marches. At this stage, they were using the only sanctioned means available to the gentler sex. However, faced with growing derision and animosity—from both sexes—the suffragette movement began to adopt a new militancy. The movement recruited across all classes and occupations and energised the formation of many allied groups. And at least one of these groups attracted May Gibbs.

The early twentieth-century campaign for women's suffrage united and mobilised women in a manner unprecedented in Western history. It politicised thousands of women of all classes across separate continents, and women's organisations proliferated—some advocated moderate action while others preached a more combative approach. These women united in meetings, parades and demonstrations to attain political equality. For women artists like May Gibbs, this meant a deployment of their particular arsenal of weapons: the design and production of illustrations, cartoons, posters, postcards, banners, pageants and paintings for the cause.

The training and employment of women as artists was, of course, only one strand of the suffragette campaign. Larger issues such as the division of labour in the house and at work, the consequences of increased education and employment opportunities, the place of women in a broadening sphere that embraced family, community, state and Empire, and the definition and regulation of female sexuality were all more central to their concern. And all the while these suffragettes were questioning the meaning of femininity and the position of women in public life.

101

An illustration from one of May's first children's books published in London, *About Us*.

FACING PAGE: May experimented with various characters and styles, including the pen and ink illustration featuring a bunyip-style character.

In this context, it is worthwhile casting our eyes back. Three years before arriving in London for the last time, May Gibbs had contributed a detailed black-and-white illustration to a Perth newspaper. 'Shipping in Fremantle Harbour' was a crowded gallery of shipboard vignettes, obviously inspired by May's own travelling and taken directly from her shipboard sketchbooks. It was set within a full page of text on 25 December 1906: 'Women's Position in the State'. It must be acknowledged that May's drawing did not specifically illustrate this accompanying text; it was more of a decorative centrepiece imposed onto a frank assessment of social life and attitudes of the time. This combined placement, however, could not have failed to affect May, particularly when she read that 'for many years to come women in Western Australia will remain but the lesser man'.

While this 1906 illustration did not concern itself with the position of women in society, within a year, May's perspective began to show. In 1907, she contributed four full-page illustrations to the Christmas number of the *Western Mail*. One of these was a witty satire on modern society entitled 'The One Unwanted Gift', in which a bewildered Father Christmas vainly attempted to interest members of both sexes in his 'gift' of Cupid. In retrospect, it was a gentle forerunner of the more assertive political cartoons she created for the suffragette cause while she was in London.

Although May Gibbs could never have been called a militant suffragette, her very presence in London throughout 1910, pursuing an independent career, granted her some alliance with feminist principles. While the prejudice that women were sullied by contact with the rough-and-tumble of a working life had largely been refuted, there was now a battle to have them accepted into the political life of Britain. And May herself was living proof that this battle could be won. May, like her fellow countrywomen, had already achieved suffrage. By November 1908, Victoria had adopted women's suffrage; it was the last state of Australia to do so. May's presence provided a defining example for English women of what could be achieved.

To many Londoners, the increasingly visible action being taken by women agitating for suffrage was unprecedented, incomprehensible and, sometimes, appalling. Militant suffragettes were pronounced 'unwomanly' for their transgressions into the public sphere and even 'unsexed' for daring to supplant the traditionally masculine role of active protest. It was somewhere in this mix of moderates and militants that May Gibbs would find a role. She transformed her personal ambitions as an artist and a woman into service for a collective mission.

103

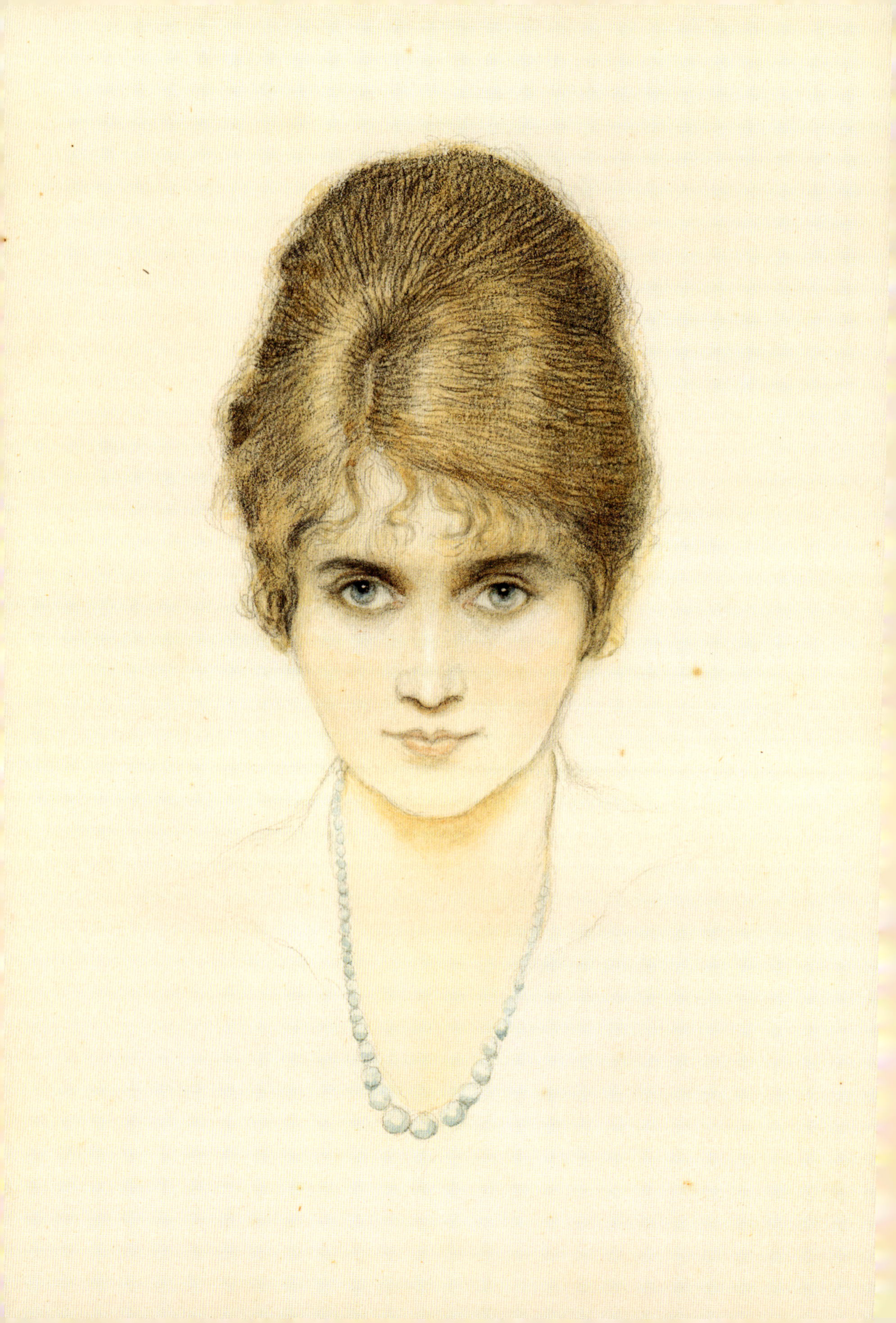

CHAPTER 8

WOMEN ON THE MARCH

Almost everyone who was in London in mid-1910 was witness to an extraordinary event. May Gibbs was certainly there when the suffragettes staged one of their largest and most effective public spectacles. On 23 July, two suffrage processions converged on Hyde Park where forty platforms had been erected for a range of speakers, one specifically for Australian and New Zealand delegates. The processions featured an 'Artists' Contingent' and a 'Colonial and Foreign Contingent'—either of which could have attracted May Gibbs. What is certain is that a 'Miss Gibbs' was recorded only the day before in the *Votes for Women* periodical as a 'banner captain' in one of these processions. It is tempting to think that this namesake could have been May!

At the same time, a battle of sorts was also being staged on another front: London's art world. While we have no diaries to show that May Gibbs actually attended any of its avant-garde exhibitions during these years, it is inconceivable that she could have remained unaware of its highly publicised rebellions. The Bloomsbury Group's modernist showings, including Roger Fry's post-impressionist exhibitions in 1910 and 1912, provoked the public to levels of outrage and mockery similar to that which they bestowed on suffragettes.

May was a confident portrait artist and between 1921 and 1924 all of May's contributions to the annual exhibition of the Society of Women Painters were portraits.

A political cartoon by May Gibbs on the cover of *The Common Cause* depicts the British Home Secretary, a young Winston Churchill (centre), being lectured by the newspaper magnate and proprietor of the *Times*. Both were against women's suffrage.

May herself bridged the worlds of art and protest in early 1911 when she began contributing illustrations and then cover designs to one of the leading suffragette journals—*The Common Cause*. Published weekly from 1909, this journal gave a voice to the National Union of Women's Suffrage Societies (NUWSS), the largest organisation promoting women's suffrage. The NUWSS had a network of regional branches throughout Britain and its executive committee included some of the most distinguished women in the country. Significantly, these women had chosen to follow a moderate path rather than the militant one advocated by Mrs Pankhurst. The very title of their journal spoke of this resolve. It was meant to refute the idea that women's suffrage would cause division and antagonism between women and men.

After being entrusted with producing two vignette black-and-white portraits of English politicians for *The Common Cause* edition of 23 March 1911, May was quickly promoted to a position as its cover artist. Over the next five months, her ability was recognised by the commissioning of six such prominent contributions. The visible value of these covers presumably encouraged the periodical's editors to appreciate the need for ongoing, rather than sporadic, cover presentation. By May 1912 they had instituted a permanent front-page illustration.

May's first cover, which appeared on 13 April 1911, was to be the most powerful of all her commissions. It depicted the opposing sides of the suffragette 'battle' locked in debate. On 7 April, Cicely Hamilton and GK Chesterton publicly debated the motion that 'the demand for the enfranchisement of women is a symptom of progress'. This was a highly anticipated and much publicised confrontation, held before a large and impassioned audience which included George Bernard Shaw, who was very supportive of the suffragettes. At the time, Hamilton was well known as a playwright, actress, journalist and suffrage speaker. Her *Pageant of Great Women*, which had premiered in November 1909, had become a highly popular stage presentation with suffrage groups throughout Britain. Chesterton, who was a noted Edwardian man of letters, epitomised all that was retrograde in liberated thinking.

After this pair delivered their impassioned arguments, it was stated in *The Common Cause* that no mere report of the words spoken could convey the dynamics of the meeting: 'the interest lay so much in the piquant contrast of temperaments, in the voice and gesture and face and figure of the combatants'. It was precisely this contrast, this confrontational stance, which was captured so skilfully in May's cartoon.

The occasion was so significant that May still recalled it in great detail a lifetime later. Maureen Walsh quoted her as saying: 'The small Queen's Hall was filled and I had to stand leaning against the wall, one knee up to hold my book while I sketched'. The two speakers obviously made a great impact upon the artist. She described Cicely Hamilton's manner as 'intensely nervous' with 'a way of flinging down her soul as a gauntlet, that would have put her at the mercy of any debater'. As for Chesterton, May's word portrait was equally succinct: she saw him as 'a happy philosopher revelling in his own philosophy'.

May's debut cover for *The Common Cause* was nothing less than a triumph. With a great economy of line, it juxtaposed Hamilton's thin angularity against Chesterton's black and rotund expanse of dress suit. By rejecting all the fussy ornamentation which was typical of so much illustration at the time, May was able to focus on the stiff and beseeching arms of one and the seated complacency of the other. Much of the drama of the occasion was conveyed in the direct gaze between the pair, and May's sparse pen strokes depicted them locked in verbal battle. So highly publicised was this debate that a variant of the same illustration was published in *The Christian Commonwealth* at the same time.

By this stage of her life, May had had years of experience in capturing such moments of action. It was obvious that her vignettes of tennis matches, which had been published in the *Western Mail* only a few years earlier, had now matured into a style offering both forthright impact and originality. May must have taken a ringside seat to have been able to observe the verbal sparring of this debate in such minute detail.

Fulfilling such commissions for *The Common Cause* meant that May had to attend lectures and rallies, immerse herself in the excitement (and danger) of protest and hear firsthand the polemics that energised the movement. This was an environment which fostered dedicated friendships and alliances, forged in defiance of authority and flouting the accepted modes of feminine behaviour. May soon became part of this solidarity by forming a friendship with a young suffragette, Irene ('Rene') Heames. It was to be a significant alliance with lasting consequences.

The debate between Cicely Hamilton and GK Chesterton 'that the demand for the enfranchisement of women is a symptom of progress' graphically portrayed by May Gibbs on the cover of *The Common Cause*.

FACING PAGE: A comic depiction of May's everyday life in England for the family back home.

In Walsh's biography, May recalled the 1911 debate as a defining moment in her life. She specifically remembered that 'Miss Hamilton introduced herself as thirty years of age and unmarried'. What the speaker actually said was conveyed in a blunt question to her audience and recorded in the magazine *The Vote*: 'Do you suppose that forty or fifty years ago a woman would have dared to stand up on a platform and say without the slightest shame that she was thirty and unmarried?' May could have certainly empathised on both these counts—at the time of the debate she had been a few years older than Hamilton and was also unmarried. The insight from this experience was never forgotten. 'When I looked about the crowd,' she recalled, 'I realised there were a lot of us in the same state'.

Only two years earlier, Hamilton had published a famous polemic against what she saw as the enslaving state of marriage. Many of the same sentiments which energised *Marriage as a Trade* were repeated in the 1911 debate, and one of its major conclusions was something which May's own life at the time heartily endorsed—she was living proof that 'in the recent history of women nothing is more striking than the enormous improvement that has taken place in the social position of the spinster'. Indeed, May would eventually return to Australia well able to endorse one of Hamilton's central points—the assertion that some women could be proud to have fought their own way through the world and that 'the lack of a husband is no longer a reproach'. The same sentiment was central to Hamilton's argument in the debate. Knowing her audience well, she was able to assert with absolute confidence that 'there are women in this room who have felt like myself, that the attraction of men was not the only thing that would bring us happiness in the world'.

While May could not have failed to react positively to Hamilton's appeals to individual strength and self-reliance, she was equally unlikely to have felt any sympathy for Chesterton's chauvinistic and arrogant assertions. Perhaps most of all, she was angered by his claim that women were 'better off not mixing in the excitement of the market-place'. As someone who for years had earned a living in the commercial world of illustration, she had no regard for such pomposity and prejudice.

At this time, London was home to a significant coterie of Australian women who were, like May Gibbs, mainly middle-aged, middle-class and unmarried, and who were involved at all levels of the suffragette

Locked out!

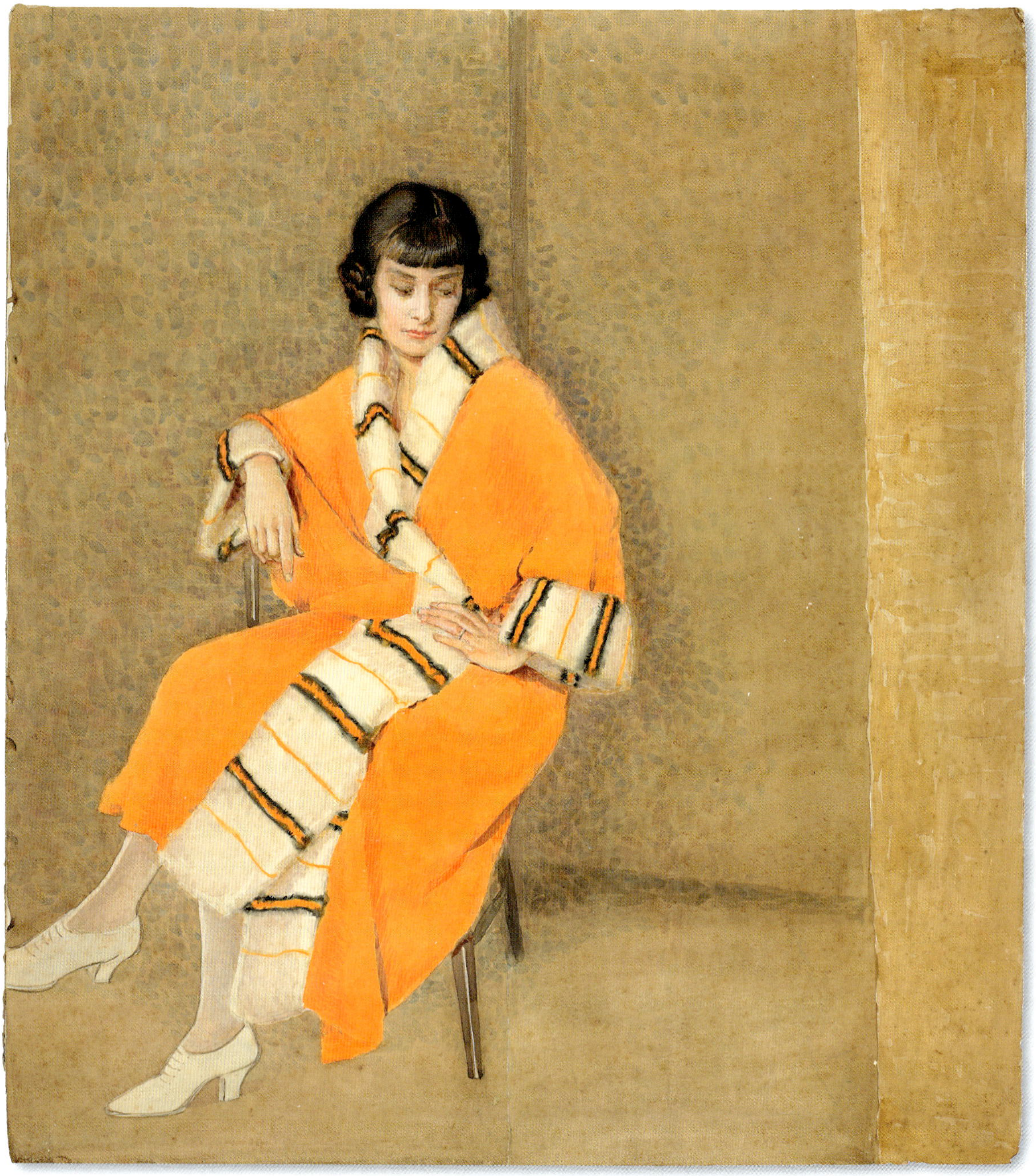

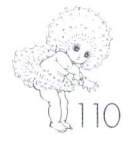

movement—from speakers on the same platform as the Pankhursts to members of the Artists' Suffrage League, which had been set up in January 1907, and the more recently founded Australian and New Zealand Women Voters' Committee. It is frustratingly unknown whether May gave her support to either of the last two groups. Because the suffragette Dora Meeson Coates was the most prominent Australian woman artist in the whole movement, her contribution has tended to overshadow that of at least two others: Ruby Lind (the sister of Norman Lindsay) and May Gibbs.

The Artists' Suffrage League was responsible for much of the visual propaganda for the whole movement and was committed to a belief in the effectiveness of art as a weapon in their armoury. The league not only designed banners and placards for the marches but also commercial items like postcards, illustrated booklets, Christmas cards and calendars. These were sold as far afield as America. Though they were described by Myra Scott as 'unsophisticated, lightly amusing publications', in 1910 alone, the league reported the sale of almost 75,000 items. The postcards designed by Dora Meeson Coates were particularly in demand.

While it is unfortunate that, according to Elizabeth Crawford, 'no membership lists survive', it was highly likely that, while May was in London, her illustrative skills were also recruited by the league. The call for women artists in London to contribute to the united cause was pervasive. Articles regularly appeared in suffragette journals exhorting women from this profession to realise their potential. *The Common Cause* was particularly forthright in its plea. As early as July 1909, it had advocated for what it called an 'agitation by symbol'. It recommended using 'signs and emblems and pictures … processions, and many other visible and audible displays'. By February of the following year, it was proclaiming the important place that art and artists could take in the movement: 'Never in the annals of our country have pictures played so large a part in politics … and enormous sums of money have been spent … in this pictorial warfare'.

The year in which May Gibbs entered this 'pictorial warfare' with her six cover illustrations for this journal happened to be a milestone year for suffragettes. The Women's Coronation Procession that was held in London on 17 June 1911 was the largest and most spectacular women's march of the period, strategically timed to coincide with events which would guarantee worldwide attention: the coronation of King George V and the

May met Irene 'Rene' Heames, an active member of the non-militant National Union of Suffrage Societies, at a rooming house in London. The two attended meetings together and May began to contribute illustrations to *The Common Cause* and *The Christian Commonwealth*.

The Women's Coronation Procession through London attracted huge crowds. It was an event not to be missed and included a contingent of women from Australia and New Zealand.

Imperial Conference of the Empire's leaders. Australia was well represented: London was alive with Commonwealth and state parliamentary delegates as well as visitors.

Carried at the head of the Australian and New Zealand contingent in the procession was a banner designed by Dora Meeson Coates. But even more pertinent to May's milieu was the fact that students from London's art schools, ranging from the Slade and the Royal Academy to less prestigious sources, were recruited to help design and stage the procession's floats and historical costumes. Perhaps as many as 60,000 women marched that day.

The whole event almost upstaged the two official coronation processions held only five and six days later. The pageantry was, in fact, so successful that it may have blinded many onlookers to the serious questions it raised—questions as to the very value of the royal hierarchy and of entrenched political power itself. There was, however, no doubt about the women's solidarity. For the first (and only) time, militant and more moderate societies joined forces. This ecumenical gathering was given even greater presence by combining national, imperial and international supporters into a cohesive procession. The resulting sense of cooperation, as well as the rivalry between the groups, resulted in strenuous efforts to present the greatest number of participants with the greatest possible decorative effect. It was achieved with a procession which stretched for an astonishing eleven kilometres!

Considering May Gibbs' long history of involvement in creating historical costumes for Government House parties back in Perth, it is hard not to see her contributing to the Australian contingent's Pageant of Empire or to the Pageant of Queens. It is equally possible that she marched with one or other of the artists' groups represented: the Artists' Suffrage League or the Suffrage Atelier. It is inconceivable that May and her new ally, Rene Heames, did not contribute to the staging of this procession and participate in its progress, or that they could have been content merely to witness things from the sidelines.

May's recruitment as an artist by the suffragette cause allows us to compare her with the most dedicated of all the suffragette artists, Sylvia Pankhurst. May was born only five years before this second-eldest daughter of Mrs Pankhurst and there were significant similarities, initially at least, in the lives and careers of the two young women. Both were raised in an aesthetically aware environment, and from childhood both were determined to become artists. In their school years, both girls were praised for their drawings—

VOTES FOR WOMEN

Women's Coronation

PROCESSION

(Five miles long).

Saturday, June 17th,
START 5.30 P.M.

Route via:—TRAFALGAR SQUARE,
PALL MALL, PICCADILLY,
KNIGHTSBRIDGE.

**70 BANDS!
1,000 BANNERS!**

THE PROCESSION will march to Kensington, where great meetings in the ROYAL ALBERT HALL and in the EMPRESS ROOMS will be held by the Women's Social and Political Union, at 8.30 p.m., in support of the Woman Suffrage Bill.

Speakers:
Mrs. PANKHURST, Mrs. PETHICK LAWRENCE, Miss VIDA GOLDSTEIN, Miss CHRISTABEL PANKHURST, and others.

Tickets for the Meeting in the EMPRESS ROOMS for Numbered and Reserved Seats, price 2s. 6d. and 1s., can be obtained from The Ticket Secretary, W.S.P.U., 4, Clements Inn, W.C.

For all further plans and particulars read the weekly newspaper VOTES FOR WOMEN. (Price One Penny.) It can be obtained at all newsagents and bookstalls.

Printed by ST. CLEMENTS PRESS, LIMITED, Portugal Street, Kingsway, London, W.C.

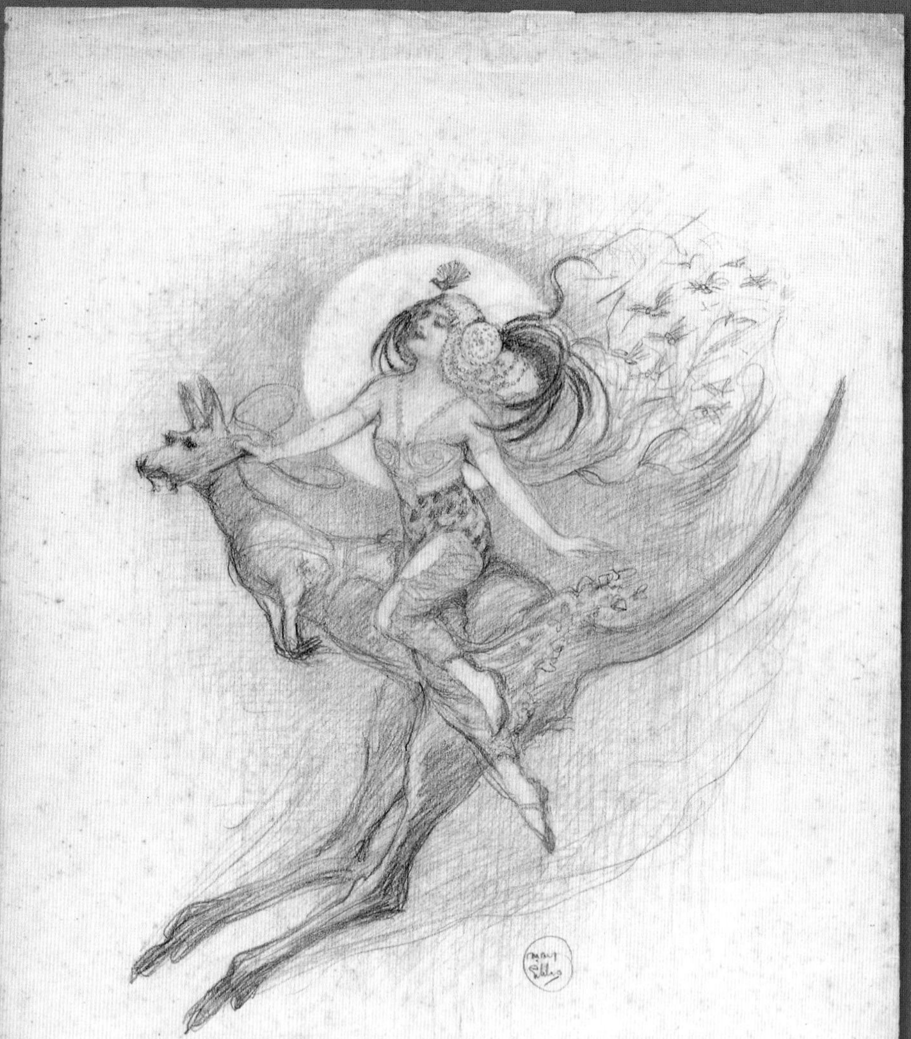

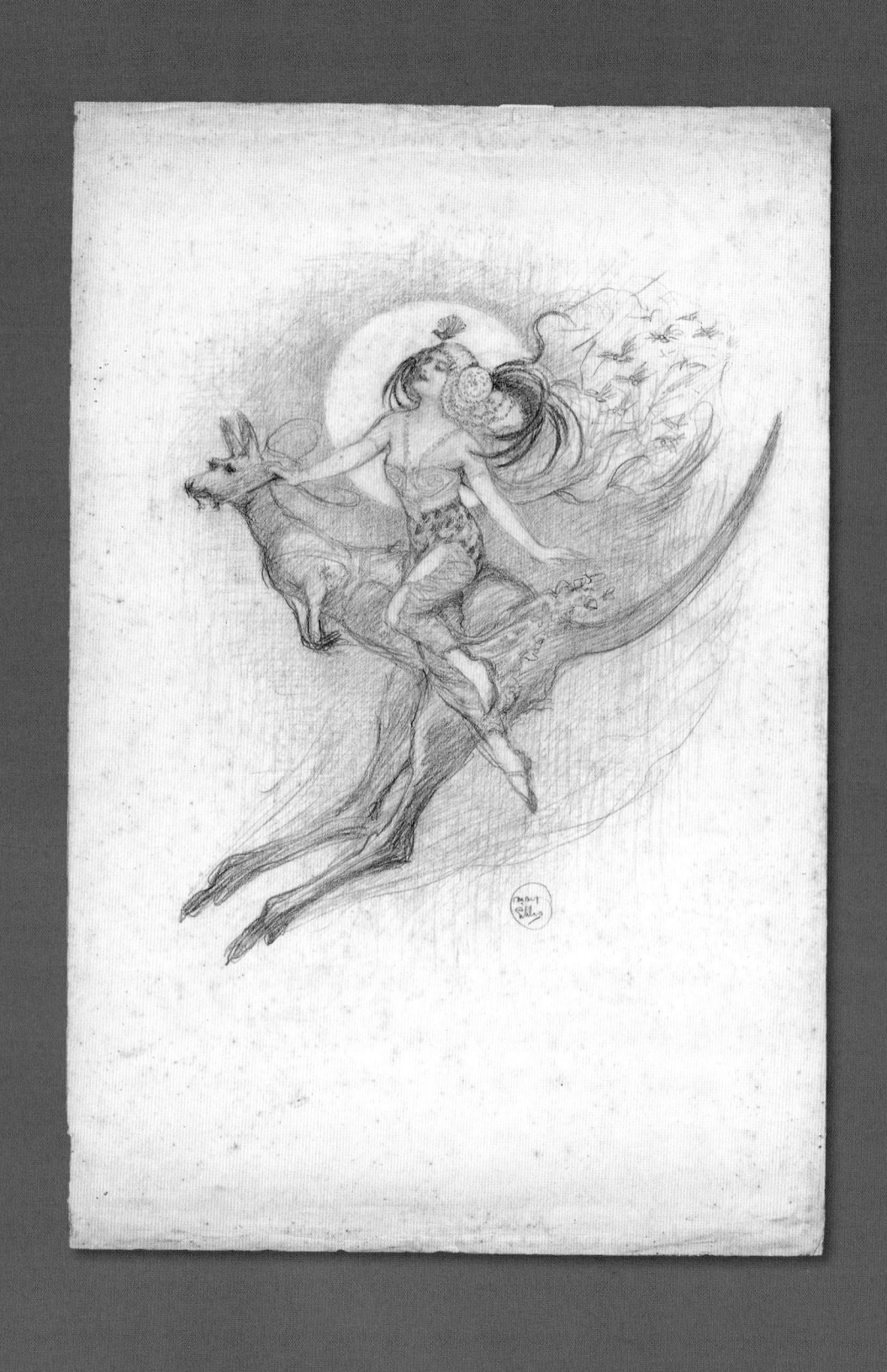

May's design for an address to Queen Victoria in 1896 was matched by Sylvia's for the Prince of Wales when he visited the Manchester School of Art, where she was enrolled at the turn of the century. As young adults, and probably in the same year, both attended evening classes at the Chelsea Polytechnic. And finally, both won awards and recognition during their student years.

However, as she rallied to the suffragette cause, Sylvia began to neglect her art studies. Inevitably, she was drawn into her mother's activities for the WSPU. In 1906 Sylvia founded the London branch of the union and began to design major decorative schemes for suffragette events in her pre-Raphaelite style. That year also marked her first experience of prison life and force-feeding, horrors which caused her to question the ultimate cost of her commitment. In an autobiographical essay, Sylvia is said to have described 'the idea of giving up the artist's life, surrendering the study of colour and form, laying aside the beloved pigments and brushes, to wear out one's life on the platform' as 'a prospect too tragically grey and barren to endure'. It is sad that, even with this awareness, by 1910 Sylvia Pankhurst's artistic ambition had been completely replaced by dedicated political efforts. One has to ask if her highly prominent example was a timely warning which May Gibbs herself heeded.

Besides Sylvia Pankhurst, there was another prominent suffragette with whom May Gibbs could well have identified. This was Marion Wallace Dunlop, a militant suffragette who is remembered today as the movement's first hunger-striker. In mid-1909, when she was imprisoned and then released after almost four days without food, her example encouraged other women to adopt this extreme form of protest. Within months, the government was forced to introduce force-feeding into its prisons to counter this growing trend. Thereafter, Dunlop was prominent in organising the artistic decorations for the major London processions of 1910 and 1911. Even more pertinent in any context with May Gibbs is the fact that Dunlop was a children's book illustrator working for the suffragette cause, and that her most celebrated book, published in 1899, depicted 'flower babies'.

In 1912, May turned her attention back to mainstream publishing when she managed to secure her most significant commission yet. Entitled *About Us*, it marked May's debut as a combined author and illustrator. The first version of this episodic little tale had actually been offered to Perth publishers a

An unpublished illustration of a 'modern' woman riding a kangaroo by May Gibbs.

Mimie rides a kangaroo for May's unpublished children's book, *Mimie and Wag: Their Adventures in Australia*. *Mamie* [previously Mimie] *and Wag* eventually appeared in an English setting.

FACING PAGE: *About Us* was released by publishers in London and New York in 1912.

few years beforehand as *Mimie and Wag: Their Adventures in Australia*. But, unfortunately, the children's book publishing scene in Perth at the time was virtually nonexistent. May had brought some of these nursery-rhyme illustrations with her to London in 1909, hoping they would interest a British publisher. Presumably on the advice of her agent, Charles H Wood, she soon accepted that the Australian characters and settings in her nursery-rhyme projects did not appeal to British taste. But with typical fortitude and determination, she refused to be overwhelmed by rejection. Her solution was a clever amalgam of characters from two unpublished works which she introduced into a quintessential London setting—it was the very view over the rooftops from the room that May had taken for her third sojourn in the city.

May reprised the characters of Mimie and Wag, and placed them on the rooftops of Victorian and Edwardian London—a fantastic realm inhabited by chimney pot people. She invented a whole new world which existed alongside the everyday one but was unknown to those who lived out their lives down below. It was a formula which she would turn to even greater account once she was back in Australia, where she created the treetop world of the gumnut babies—as the modern critic Juliet O'Conor has asserted, the characters from Chimney Pot Land foreshadow May's bushland babies.

By transferring the setting to England, May had ultimately attracted the interest of publishers in both London and New York. Clearly, it was a project close to May's heart. Indeed, the story's protagonist, Mamie, was autobiographical—this was the name by which May was always known to her family. Nevertheless, it has to be admitted that the whole concept was very derivative and the jejune story ended disappointingly. It was as if May could find no original resolution to her tale and so relied on the old formula of a protagonist waking from a dream. Even so, the book had one redeeming feature—its artwork, particularly the imaginative chimney pot people. They were May's only original touch and their elements of caricature and grotesquerie owed much to her sustained observation of personality and type. More of this fantasy and stronger narrative skills could have lifted the book to much greater heights.

Even with these small triumphs to her credit, however, as the new year of 1913 began, May resolved to return to Australia. The combined effect of overwork, severe London winters and the looming threat of war was enough

117

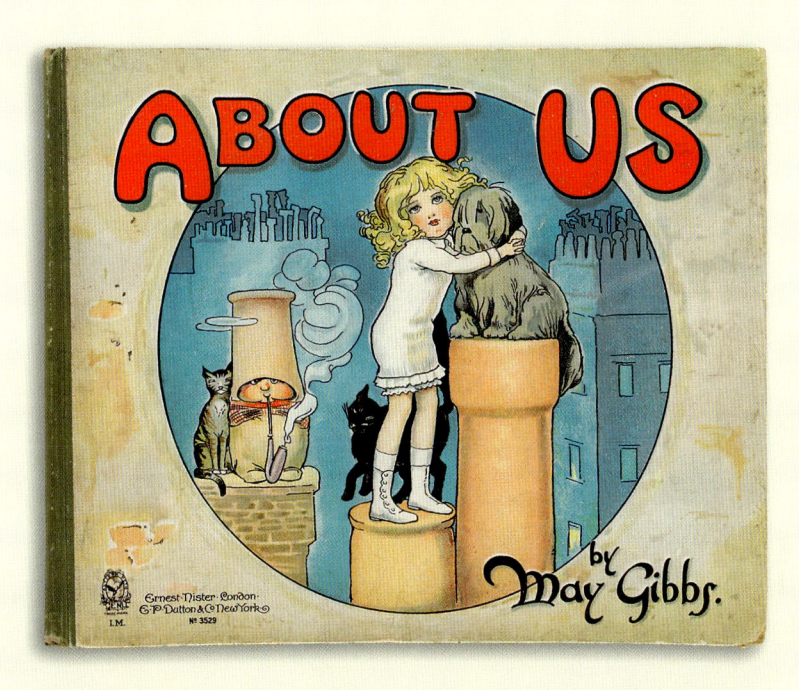

May's wattle flowers would appear in many guises in her later books and cartoons.

for May to make this heart-wrenching decision. Shortly before she departed, she experienced a highly poignant reminder of Australia—on 27 January, London celebrated Wattle Day for the first time. This anniversary, later called Australia Day, had been inaugurated only the year before in Australia. Overseas, the Australasian Section of the Royal Colonial Institute in London quickly followed this lead. So, too, did the great department store Selfridges, which filled its Oxford Street store with wattle blossom in a show of solidarity with Australasian banks and offices throughout the city.

Everywhere, it seemed, people wore buttonholes proudly displaying sprigs of Australia's national flower, which had been specially imported for the occasion. The unmistakable perfume and sight of these flowers, let alone the memories which they evoked, surely affected the thousands of Australians then in London. Only three years later, May would create her Wattle Blossom Babies, first on postcards, in 1916, and then in a series of five booklets, beginning in 1918.

By the time May Gibbs had completed her third and last period of London training and was finally beginning to make her name as an illustrator, the Australian exodus of aspiring women artists was being seen in a less rosy light than previously. In contrast to William Moore's earlier enthusiasm, a new round of advice in *Everylady's Journal* offered some sensible cautions. 'It has to be remembered', the journal advised, 'that the [London] market is overcrowded, and the pay poor'. It concluded with a sobering statement: 'Unless a girl has had considerable experience and success in Australia first … she will be foolish to come to London with any idea of making a living at black-and-white work'. But neither this nor Norman Lindsay's later diatribe against modern art would dampen their enthusiasm: 'If travel could make an artist,' he scornfully observed in 1921, then 'any bagman could paint'.

May had been twenty-three years old when she had first embarked for London. She was thirty-six years old when she took her final voyage home. With three periods of prolonged and intense art training and cultural exposure behind her, she was now more than ready to make a new beginning back in Australia. Not only was she confident enough, and determined enough, to seek an independent career away from her family, it was also providential that, as a highly trained illustrator, she was returning to an Australia which was beginning to see her professional career choice as a valid role for a woman.

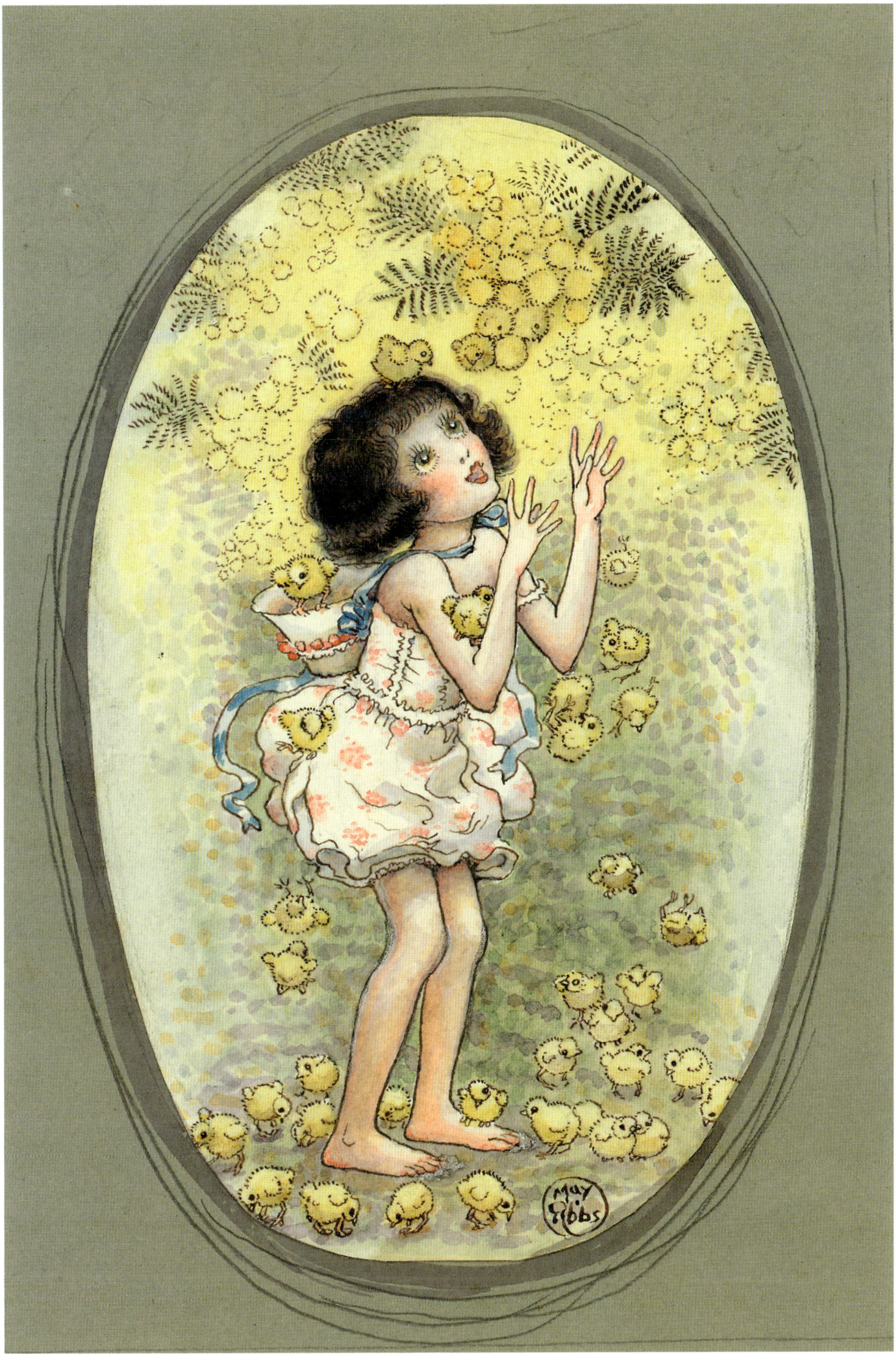
May Gibbs

Her now formidable academic record and a portfolio of published and unpublished work boosted her chances in the less competitive Australian market. Furthermore, she arrived with fortuitous timing—on the eve of World War I, there was a demand and appreciation for nationalistic Australian images like never before.

These advantages aside, a professional book illustrator, let alone a woman artist with some obvious affinity with children's book illustration like May Gibbs, still faced serious challenges in Australia. Unlike their British counterparts, Australian children's book illustrators did not have a choice of classic texts to inspire and tempt them. In May's generation, the British luminaries in the field could reinterpret works from *The Arabian Nights* and Shakespeare to *Alice's Adventures in Wonderland* and *Peter Pan*. No Australian publisher could or would compete with this domination.

The genesis of children's book illustration in Australia really dated from only twenty years before May's gumnut booklets began to appear. In 1897, when no local illustrator could rely solely on commissions for books, it was the academically trained George W Lambert whom Angus & Robertson chose to illustrate Jessie Whitfeld's *Spirit of the Bushfire*. The novelty of its production was cause for proud comment in the Australian press: 'No such elaborate illustration has hitherto been attempted in Australia before', claimed the *Bulletin*. The claim was quite justified—Lambert's thirty-two full-page black-and-white plates were without precedent in Australian book production. Nevertheless, it has to be admitted that the artist's first (and last) excursion into the fantasy realm was less than successful. His pedestrian illustrations featured fairies who resembled classically draped drawing-class models, solidly earthbound rather than ethereal creations.

Within two years, the first Australian to produce a coherent output of children's book illustrations appeared. When David Henry Souter illustrated Robert Irvine's *Bubbles, His Book* for William Brooks in 1899, the publisher could proclaim its justifiable pride in what was a unique local production. In December that year, the book was described in the *Sydney Morning Herald* as 'perhaps the most ambitious effort of an Australian [publishing] house by Australian men for Australian children'. Souter's contribution, in contrast to Lambert's, was both decorative and whimsical and guaranteed to enchant a young audience.

And so when May arrived back in Australia, it was to find, providentially, that the first generation of Australian book illustrators to make the genre their major pastime was emerging. Already, Australian publishers were competing with their British counterparts for a share of the local book market, particularly the children's sphere. The beginning of this shared market is clearly shown in the publishing history of that classic work by Ethel Pedley, *Dot and the Kangaroo*. Although the 1899 first edition was printed in England, a competing Australian edition appeared in 1906. In 1913, when May Gibbs chose to return from London, not only did the first anthology of Australian poetry for children appear at this time, but local support enabled Ida Rentoul Outhwaite to publish no less than her sixth major, illustrated work.

May Gibbs was set to make her own name in this evolving marketplace. It would be back home in Australia that she would at last find her unique illustrative style—one that built on the past decade of academic training yet drew its inspiration from her adopted country. The fact that she became one of the rare birds of passage to achieve commissions, fame and fortune has been well documented. What has not been significantly detailed before are the preceding years—the years of hard work, training, dedication and daring which made all this possible.

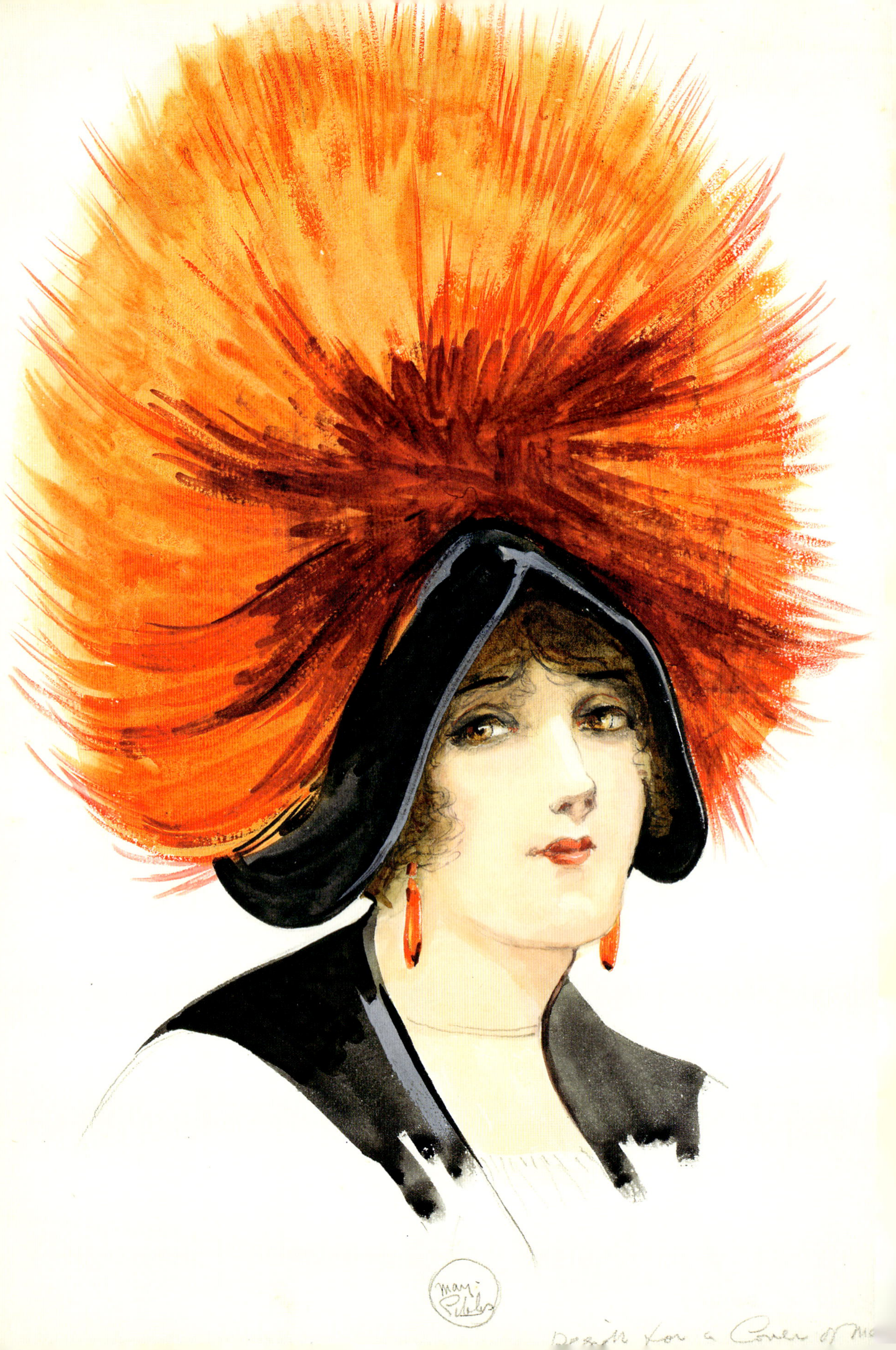
Design for a Cover of

CHAPTER 9

'CUT AWAY FROM HOME'

Returning to Australia after three years of exposure to suffragist principles and practices, May seemed destined to remain a spinster. For the moment, she appeared to subscribe to the feminist view of marriage—that it was imposed by a patriarchal society intent on keeping women subservient; that marriage was an institution which mitigated against women gaining independence by working for a living and achieving professional status.

It is not unreasonable to suppose that May Gibbs returned to Australia with the words of Cicely Hamilton's argument still ringing in her ears: 'Before your duty to your children, or your duty to your husband comes your duty to yourself'. It was likely this perceived duty to oneself which gave May the resolution and the courage to seek her full potential. At this stage of her life, she had reached a turning point: she had realised that the issue of independence was an issue of identity. To stay in Perth with her family would be to consign herself to a backwater existence where she would waste her potential on a variety of unsatisfying and minor cultural projects.

May had learnt more than artistic technique during her latest London sojourn. After all, one of her first defining decisions after returning to

May returned to Australia more determined than ever to make an independent living from her art.

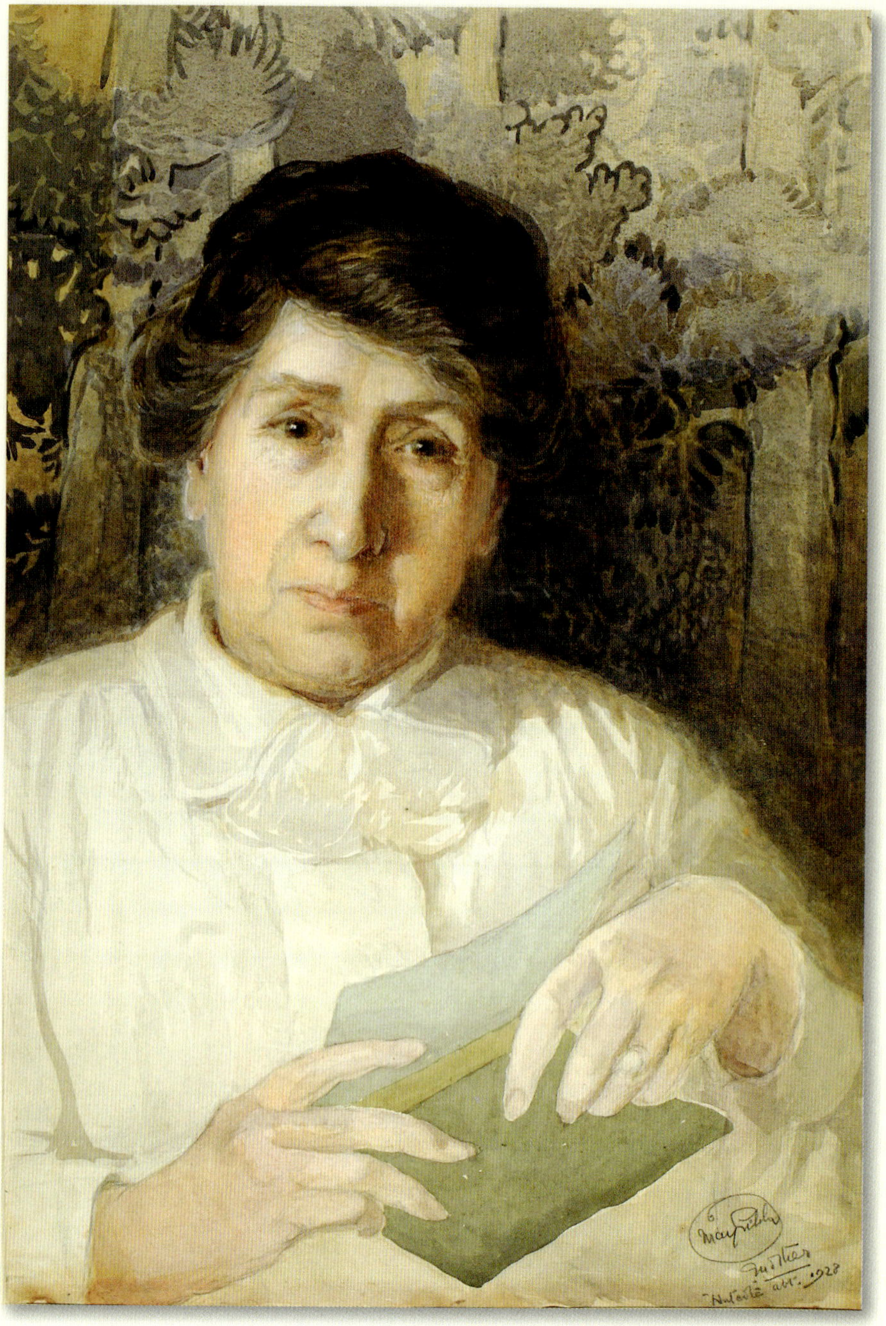

Western Australia was to exhibit defiance, self-assertion and an overthrow of authority—all attributes which she had seen her suffragette sisters display. May Gibbs did this by arriving in Australia with her friend Rene Heames. Unfortunately, May's mother could not comprehend the ties that bound these two women together. She was totally opposed to what she saw as an intrusion and an unwelcome influence. Is it possible that she reacted so antagonistically to Rene because of the bad press which the suffragettes were getting? However, if the battle for suffrage had long been won in Australia, it was now May's turn to achieve a victory here on a more personal front. She and Rene were to leave for Sydney, where they would share boarding rooms in Neutral Bay.

The depth of May's estrangement from her mother and the conflicting emotions which it aroused can possibly be gauged from an unpublished short story of May's, first quoted in Maureen Walsh's biography. This story, presumably written in 1913 just after the break, has been seen as autobiographical in its analysis of family discord. The central character in May's story revealed her difficult relationship with her mother.

'When I broke away mother was terrible', May wrote, presumably putting all of her own anguish into this fictionalised version of events. 'I'll never forget how she sat as if she were turned to stone when I kissed her goodbye—she didn't say a word, it nearly broke me.' The justification and reasoning of the story's heroine surely voiced May's own determination: 'I've no doubt we're all meant to be married but if you can't the next best thing is to cut away from home and make some sort of place in the world for yourself.'

Presumably, Cecie Gibbs saw May's short stay in Perth and her abrupt departure, after her daughter had been away for more than three years, as a sign of militant behaviour—a legacy from her London associates. A more objective opinion might have easily interpreted it as less bellicose and, once again, as something more in line with Cicely Hamilton's moderate example, which she had detailed in her book *Life Errant*: 'My personal revolt was feminist rather than suffragist; what I rebelled at chiefly was the dependence implied in the idea of "destined" marriage, "destined" motherhood—the identification of success with marriage, of failure with spinsterhood'. Certainly, what May achieved was an open admission of her desire for power and control over her own life.

Early in 1913 on their return to Australia, Rene Heames helped May to pursue her career in Sydney, where they handcrafted a range of calenders and cards as they had for the suffragette movement in London, but this time using May's Australian themes.

FACING PAGE: A portrait by May of her mother, Cecie, completed when her parents were visiting Sydney in 1923.

FACING PAGE: May Gibbs' cartoon 'The Modern Maid' appeared as a full-page cartoon in the *Western Mail* in October 1913.

It is valid to interpret May's experience with the suffragettes as a direct impetus and inspiration to the artistic career which unfolded in Australia. The areas of artistic endeavour which the suffragettes promoted would be the same ones May would turn to her advantage: designing cover art, calendars and postcards would make her into a household name across the whole of Australia.

May was only one of many Australian expatriates who fled London throughout 1913 as the threat of a European war loomed larger and larger on the international horizon. Even so, it must have been a heart-wrenching experience to leave behind the cultured and independent life she had been leading. Almost a decade earlier, in October 1905, a long editorial in the *West Australian* had extolled the pioneering work of such expatriate artists: 'it is the wanderers', it prophesised, 'who have done most to help forward the day when this country will, artistically speaking, be able to stand on its own feet'. Although May must have been forlorn, even despairing, at the prospect of leaving London, did she dare to hope that her own contribution to Australia's artistic independence was about to begin? Certainly, in her own way, May Gibbs was poised to fulfil the *West Australian*'s optimistic forecast. She was determined to repudiate the traditional roles granted to her sex from the sidelines of the art world: as artist's model, mistress or muse.

Significantly, the Australia in which May arrived in 1913 was radically different from the one she had left in 1909. There was proof of this in two highly significant events in the opening months of that year. Together, they proclaimed that this was not the staid and economically precarious country May had first left in 1900. Even with talk of a war in the offing, there was a newfound optimism in her homeland. Although none of Australia's cosmopolitan advances could match the attractions that May had left behind in London, these two events augured well for the nation's future: they were the commencement of construction of the east–west transcontinental railway in Kalgoorlie and, soon afterwards, the laying of a foundation stone for a national capital in Canberra.

The year 1913 was one of geographical and emotional upheaval as May Gibbs strove to relocate and re-establish her life and her career. But although she was a stranger to Sydney, she was no stranger to hard work. At thirty-six years of age, and with years of professional art training and publishing experience behind her, she was ready to make her mark.

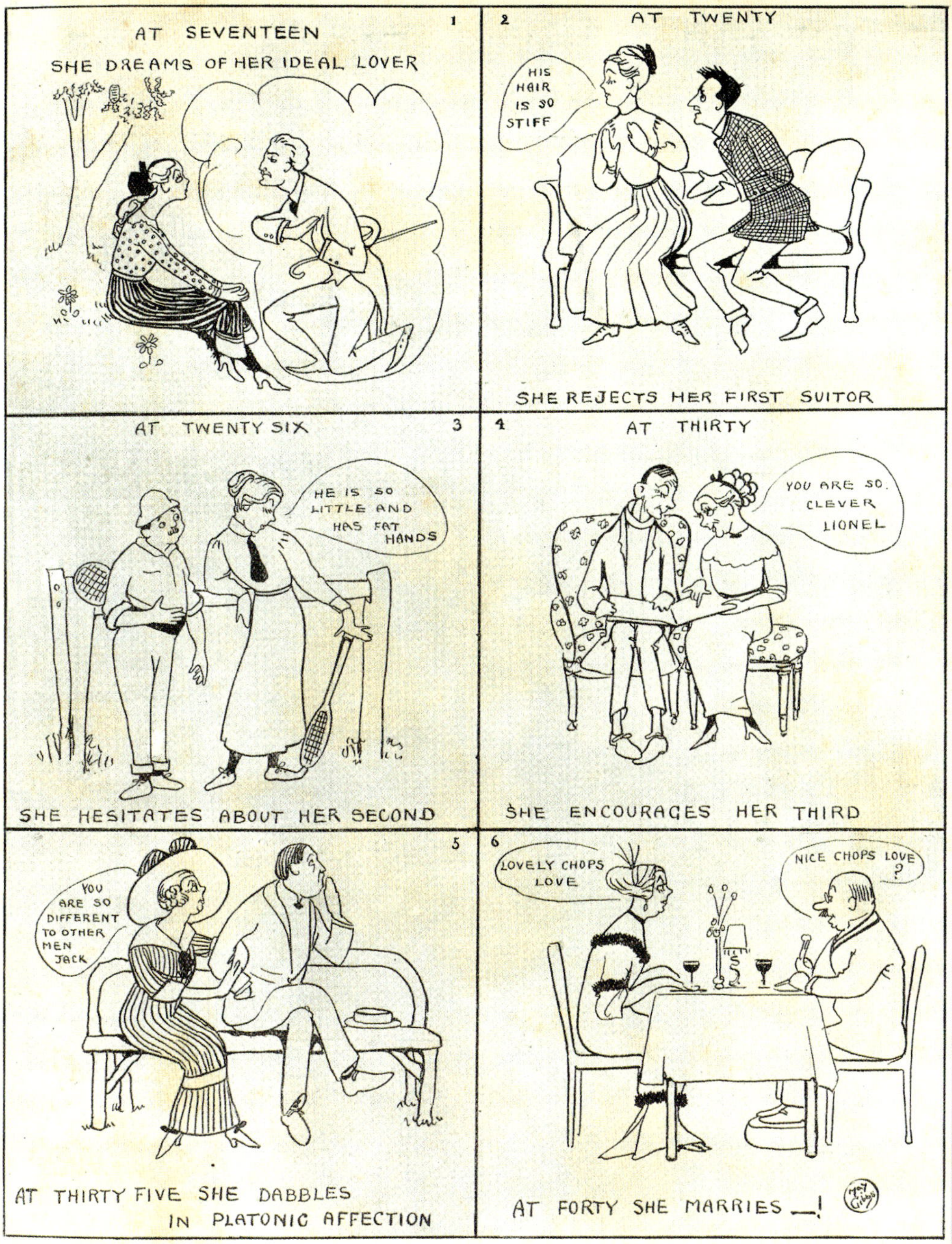

THE MODERN MAID.

FACING PAGE: An idea for the cover of *The Lone Hand,* one of the most sought-after commissions for cover artists.

Before she moved over to the east coast, however, May first tried to re-establish her lucrative contact with the *Western Mail* in Perth. In April 1913 she contributed one full page and one half-page of sporting vignettes to the newspaper. She also began a new, adult series of comic cartoon blocks which continued until 5 December. As a sustained and completely new format for the illustrator, this series showed a distinct advance in May's pictorial skill and comical characterisations.

As a pioneering woman cartoonist in Australia, she was at the forefront of a whole generation of female followers. By the time of World War I, and certainly in the interwar years, notable women would be working as professional cartoonists.

These women included the McCrae and Paterson sisters, who established a casual but regular profile in *Aussie,* the *Bulletin* and other magazines of the 1920s and 1930s. We might even conclude that Percy Leason, the Australian master of the comic narrative block, took his lead from May and refined the same format. His comic vignettes linked by a running narrative or situational comedy were highly popular throughout the 1920s. May occasionally continued this successful format until mid-1916, when work on her gumnut-baby booklets completely consumed her time.

The most consistent source of inspiration in these adult cartoons was the comic or satiric potential which May found in fashion or costume. Typical of this series was an offering questioning 'Fashions appropriate to the season'. Here, her delight in the bizarre was conveyed using a masterful economy of line. What has never been appreciated before is that it was this sustained body of cartoon work for an adult audience, reliant on short, amusing episodes, that would eventually stand May in good stead in producing over forty years of gumnut cartoon strips for children.

May's significant decision to move to Sydney was as much a desire to distance herself from Perth and establish a stimulating career as it was an assertion of her right to an independent lifestyle. And there were other major considerations. Sydney offered more opportunities for an aspiring illustrator than any other city. The offices of the *Bulletin,* of the monthly magazine *The Lone Hand* and of the publisher and bookseller Angus & Robertson were all centred there. This impressive triad lured many aspirants to their offices. Like May, they came in search of commissions, fame and fortune.

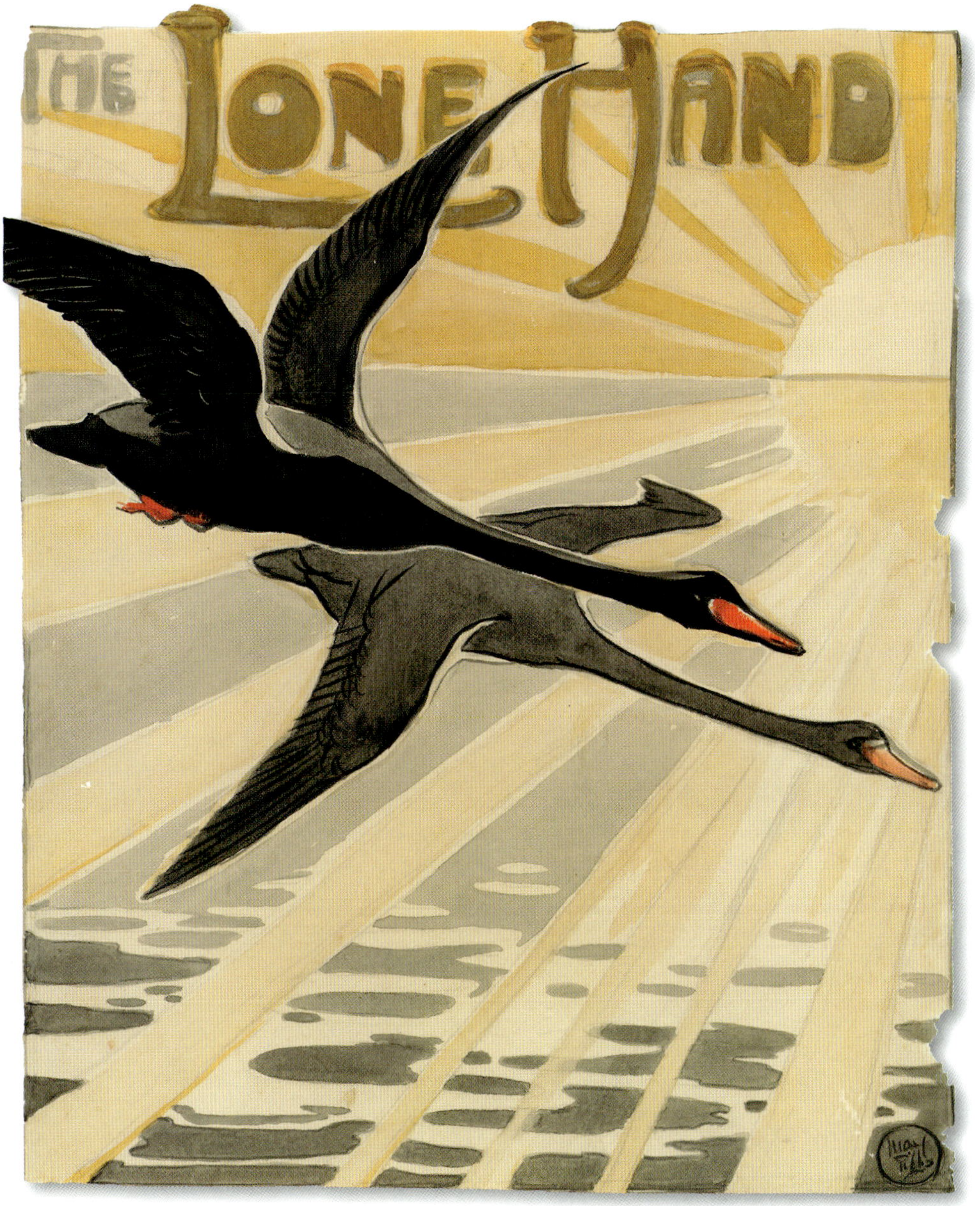
THE LONE HAND

Bib and Bub sat in a Gumtree, thinking.
Suddenly—they heard a strange noise.
Climbing down, they saw something disappear and ran after it.
"It went in this hole" said Bub" What can it be?" said Bib.
Then down they fell.
Mr Kookaburra, awakened by screams, flew over "Ah!" he said.
And hiding, made a noise like a mouse.
Up came Mrs Snake.
He pounced upon her, chopped her up, and—
Out sprang dear little Bib and Bub.
May Gibbs

24 NEW Bib & Bub Stories
One hundred & forty four Pictures to Colour
WE painted these to show the way we do it
Bib
Bub
May Gibbs

Just after May left Perth, her mother's worst fears were confirmed: a militant English suffragette delivered the ultimate sacrifice to the cause. On one of the most celebrated racing days in the English calendar, Derby Day (4 June), Emily Davison threw herself under King Edward's horse. This extreme protest was an immense shock and Davison was given a martyr's funeral. The suffragettes organised an infinitely more sombre occasion than their coronation procession of 1911, with ten brass bands and 6000 marching women solemnly following Davison's hearse. Some of them carried purple silk banners emblazoned with Joan of Arc's final words: 'Fight on, and God will give the Victory'.

Once in Sydney, May created a new profile: between June and December she contributed two colour covers and various black-and-white vignette illustrations to the *Sydney Mail*. She began with a number of enchanting illustrations depicting children and their pastimes. Although these were modest, they clearly showed where May's forte lay—in depicting the world of childhood without any undue and cloying sentiment.

For May, 1913 was to end with a significant accolade. This was a commission to illustrate work by one of the most popular writers of children's books in Australia—Ethel Turner. Her eight-part weekly serial for the *Sydney Mail* was enhanced by May's skill in depicting childhood. A close look at the vignette heading which announced the serial's title on 10 December reveals something utterly new—the public debut of the gumnut babies. Hidden among the detail of this intricate cartouche was a small family of bush babies peeping shyly out of their gumnuts.

Only a week earlier, May had taken out a Commonwealth copyright registration. Among the wealth of commissioned work which she undertook—cartoon blocks, magazine covers, sporting cartoons and illustrations for a children's serial—nothing was more personal or more original than this one single item of ephemera, which became one of Australia's iconic designs: her gumleaf bookmark. Although the modest debut of the babies would be used to announce Ethel Turner's serial, it was in these bookmarks that they achieved their shy autonomy.

Three years later, in an article for the *Theatre Magazine*, May told of the birth of these gumnut babies. This concept, of a gumnut baby peeping over the top of a leaf-shaped bookmark, had reputedly come to May 'in the middle of the night'—presumably, some time in November 1913. Its genesis

May's cartoon strips 'Bib and Bub' and 'Tiggy Touchwood' were so successful they ran in newspapers for over forty years.

The Sydney Mail

PRICE THREEPENCE

was a simple need: May 'wanted a good Australian book-mark'. As she cast her mind about for local inspiration, she thought of a gumleaf 'as a pretty thing' but wondered 'if she could only make it interesting [on] both sides'. Her solution arrived in a moment of utter inspiration: 'I awoke, and in fancy saw peeping over a long gum-leaf a little bush sprite, with a gum-nut on its head'. It was from this deceptively simple yet utterly charming idea that May Gibbs' entire Australian bushland fantasy was to be born.

At first, May and Rene produced these bookmarks as handpainted items which were sold for the then-considerable sum of five shillings each. However, the immediate and popular demand for a greater supply meant that production by hand had to give way to commercially printed multiples and these were soon issued at sixpence each. As slight as these pieces were, they were eventually enough to encourage the first substantial article on May and her evolving career in the Australian press.

The Sydney newspaper the *Sun* obviously considered the bookmark a significant item of Australiana and reproduced both sides of May's design. It used them as a device to frame her portrait and added a lengthy and highly enthusiastic appreciation:

> Haven't you seen them, peeping with great wonder-wide blue eyes under the green gumnut-cap, tiny button of a mouth, and wee pink fingers clinging to the gumleaf edge, or the equally fascinating back view of miniature round, pink body and small, curled toes …?

And if this accolade was not uplifting enough, the year closed with some welcome rapprochement between May and her parents. On 29 October, May's parents travelled across to Sydney for a family wedding. Three of May's cousins also made the trip to serve as bridesmaids at the marriage of Roy King and Mabel Preston. May's contribution to the occasion was to create an illustrated menu for the wedding party which depicted a traditional Cupid figure in one corner. These naked cherubs had been intruding into May's designs and her thinking for some time now. Surely they were the unacknowledged precursors of her gumnut babies.

The gumnut babies bookmark first sold as handpainted copies. In a later interview May said, 'When World War I started my job folded … fortunately someone asked me to make them a bookmark and I designed one with a gum leaf and two funny little animals peeping over the top'.

FACING PAGE: An idea sketched in watercolour for a cover of the *Sydney Mail*. Eight of May's covers were published by the *Sydney Mail* before the outbreak of war.

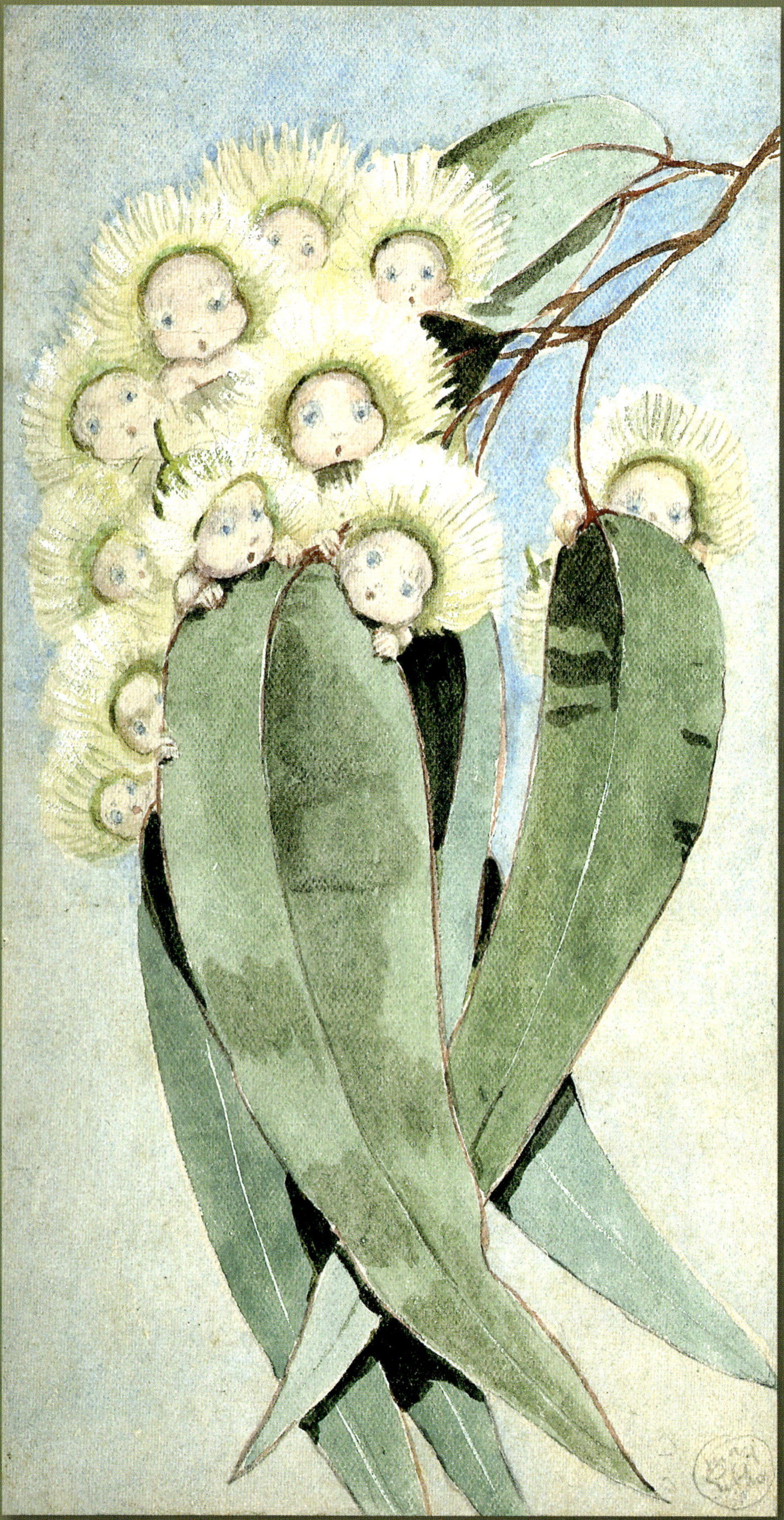

CHAPTER 10

'GUM-NUT BROWNIES'

Within a few weeks, the unassuming debut of May Gibbs' gumnut baby design in Ethel Turner's serial was completely transformed into a centrestage appearance: the first issue of *The Lone Hand* for 1914 welcomed in the new year with no less a gathering than thirteen gumnut babies on its cover. Surely it is tempting to ask if there was some prescience here on May Gibbs' part, some intimation of the coming war? Had May intended the babies, gazing round-eyed and innocent out of their secure home in the trees, to be seen as hidden and protected by their camouflage of khaki leaves?

Certainly, May's fluctuating emotions, raised by the ever-growing threat of war, should have been offset by seeing this work reproduced as a colour cover for the most prestigious literary magazine in Australia. Significantly, the January issue of *The Lone Hand* introduced what we now know as gumnut babies by another name—on their debut they were 'Gum-Nut Brownies'. It seemed as if May was still wavering between British folklore and a purely Australian derivation for her fantasy. Perhaps, also, she was prompted by a children's story which Molly Barrington had contributed to the *Sydney Mail* only the month before. In that tale, the 'Brownies of the Bush' had

The gumnut babies were to become May's most famous and popular characters.

A cartoon by DH Souter in *The Lone Hand* depicts a woman artist attempting to sell her sketches to the editor – the caption: 'A really nice girl brought a sketch which must have taken her days to produce'.

FACING PAGE: A portrait by May Gibbs likely to have been completed at her studio in Bridge Street, Sydney in 1916.

been introduced as 'very fond of children, but too shy and timid to come very close to them, or to allow themselves to be seen'. This timidity was to become the defining characteristic of May Gibbs' miniature world when the first bush-baby booklet was finally published nearly three years later.

The year 1914 was one of new opportunities and even greater successes for May, whose output continued to grow. The range of audiences for which she provided illustrations, from adults to children, and her willingness to accept all manner of commissions, from vignettes to colour covers, placed her firmly in the competitive world of the freelance illustrator who sought work wherever it could be found. This professional challenge was amusingly captured in a cartoon by David Henry Souter in *The Lone Hand*. Although May was only one of a number of women making successful inroads into a previously male-dominated commercial art world, she was at the forefront of such female efforts, and she was certainly set to become the most successful woman cover artist of the decade. Thereafter, the arrival of *The Home* magazine in 1920 created a whole generation of Australian women cover artists who followed in her footsteps.

Despite these successes, however, the year was not without its setbacks. Although Sydney was a world away from the suffragette battle still being waged in England, May could not remain immune to cabled news of its latest protests. One of the suffragettes' newly instigated tactics for grasping public attention must have seemed particularly abhorrent to her. This was the campaign which inaugurated a season of attacks on artistic masterpieces in national collections in Britain. It began on 10 March 1914 when a suffragette slashed a Velasquez nude of Venus in the National Gallery, inspiring similar acts across the country. The resulting shock and outrage was such that, for a time, women were denied access to some galleries. It seems impossible to imagine that May would have endorsed this radical strategy, one that struck at the very heart of all that she treasured most.

What shocked May more? The dreadful death of a suffragette martyr trampled under the hooves of King Edward's horse on Derby Day the year before, or this slashing of Old Master paintings? Back in Australia, where the battle for suffrage had already been won, there was little outlet for the strong political passions which had been aroused in London. May's illustrative work would have to suffice. Was it any wonder, then, that these years spent establishing a new life in Sydney were extraordinarily busy and productive?

Sketch Portrait (Harry J. Western Artist)

May's illustration used on the cover of Gem of the Flat.

Between late 1913 and January 1916, May contributed eleven colour covers to Sydney magazines. Earlier, in Perth, she had created magazine and newspaper cover work—mainly in black and white—as well as covers for art-exhibition catalogues. But it was in these Sydney commissions that May showed the full maturing of her technique into creative and eye-catching work. Over fifty years later, when she was ninety-one years old, the memory of these covers was still potent enough for May to single them out for mention. In 1968, when she went on record for the National Library of Australia, she said: 'I used to do anything that came into my mind that made an effective cover … a fancy idea … a face with it'.

Four of these cover designs were portrait works. Even at this stage, on the very eve of creating her wild-flower baby imagery, we see that May was still producing work which demonstrated her wide-ranging art training and ability. One early article highlighted this versatility, something which is all too easily forgotten today. 'She excels in other branches of her art', the Sydney *Sun* enthused in March 1917, before going on to identify 'sketch portrait work, at which she is kept constantly busy with private commissions'. Even the overwhelming success of the first two gumnut booklets at Christmas 1916 did not, initially, convince May that she should abandon her avowed speciality for 'portraiture, cartoons, and caricatures', an assertion she had made in an article for the *Theatre Magazine*.

Indeed, for almost another decade, examples of these 'private commissions' still appeared. Between 1921 and 1924 there were four rare occasions when May contributed to group exhibitions in Sydney: in the annual exhibitions of the Society of Women Painters, she showed portrait works. Presumably, it was the pressure of producing books and ongoing comic strips thereafter which eventually curtailed this portrait work. It was only one of the artistic avenues which May might have followed further if the gumnut imagery had not committed her to a lifetime of work for children's books. The *Sydney Mail*, for example, was so taken with her work for their (adult) covers that they originally commissioned twenty-five examples. Only the advent of the war, which introduced a passion and a demand for overtly militaristic cover art, sabotaged these plans.

May's first commission in Sydney for publication in a less ephemeral format than its magazines was offered by Angus & Robertson, the biggest publishers of children's books in Australia immediately before and after

Federation. At the beginning of 1914 it commissioned her to illustrate *Gem of the Flat* with a colour cover which would also double as the frontispiece. But May's work for the girls' novel by Constance Mackness was disappointingly bland. Presumably, May had accepted the offer because it was a commission from a major Australian publisher. However, in March, a few months before publication, she admitted to the project's managing editor that she had found the narrative 'very dull'. Clearly, she knew she was destined for better things and was confident enough to assert her opinion—she declared the story to be 'rotten'.

After May's first commission from Angus & Robertson had proved to be utterly uninspiring, she must have been delighted to almost immediately receive a second chance to prove herself. She was contracted to illustrate *Scribbling Sue and Other Stories* by Amy Mack, another children's book destined for that year's Christmas market. After the disappointing text of *Gem of the Flat*, this new book engaged May, not least for the opportunity to present grotesque characters. The bizarre bushland 'brownies' who had clambered around the illustrated title to Ethel Turner's serial could now achieve their autonomy.

Scribbling Sue was part of Amy Mack's prodigious output of highly popular Australian children's books, and for May to have her name on its titlepage was an endorsement of her own growing reputation. Before this, one full-page illustration which doubled as a cover had satisfied the publisher; now May was engaged to provide five full-page plates in colour. *Scribbling Sue* played a seminal role in developing May's pictorial vocabulary. Obviously, this book was infinitely more to her taste than *Gem of the Flat* ever could have been—not the least for its grotesque, original characters, both on land and on sea. It was this element which inspired May's first major children's book commission in Australia.

Amy Mack's title story concerned a little girl who started writing her name indiscriminately on walls, doors and fences, and then proceeded to tree trunks. This concept of 'scribbly-gum writing', the creation of a whole text waiting to be discovered in the bush, was something which appealed so strongly to May that it became central to the evolving world of the bush babies. The story continued with the introduction of a little man dressed in the 'red tips of the gum saplings', and with 'a strange little wooden cap' on his head, who berated Sue for her constant scribbling and her defacing of the environment.

May's illustration of a little man dressed in red gum leaf tips for the cover of *Scribbling Sue and Other Stories*.

THE SYDNEY Mail

PRICE THREEPENCE

Wednesday,] [April 29, 1914.

Principal Feature:
The Shakespearean Fete.

GILBEY'S DRY GIN.
TUCKER AND CO., SOLE AGENTS, SYDNEY.

What was significant was that, in the process of depicting this fantastic embodiment of the bush, May introduced her own bushland denizens. She brought them out of the treetops and put them into active roles in the bush. She realised that they could be protagonists in a narrative rather than merely static creations on bookmarks, postcards and magazine covers.

Because children's books received little critical mention in reviewing columns during this era, it is rare to find anything more than a cursory listing of the works in which May was making her earliest appearances. And disappointingly, these rare comments were usually limited to a simple plot summary, without any mention of illustrations. The one exception to this was the commentary voiced in the periodical *Western Women*. It, alone, gave value to May's contribution to *Scribbling Sue*, noting that her illustrations were 'always a most attractive addition to a book or magazine', and that 'her humorous touches are like glints of sunshine'. Admittedly, these are opinions by an understandably proud home-state publication.

Also significant in 1914 was a clearly autobiographical cartoon which May produced for the Sydney press. On 21 January, the *Sydney Mail* published her 'Post-Impressionist's Impression of a Week-end on the Blue Mountains'. The first of the six panels depicted the artist at an easel, her floor littered with discarded drawings, a towel to cool her aching head hanging nearby. The hardworking and harassed illustrator was obviously May herself, with her recognisably unkempt hair and unflattering profile. In the succeeding panels, she was lured away for a weekend of sightseeing in the mountains, with an end piece depicting the exhausted artist back home, recuperating from her 'holiday'. The appearance of May's own clearly identifiable portrait and pastimes in these blocks was an indication that her move to Sydney had provided her with new inspiration and independence.

What is of greatest import, however, is that this very excursion to the mountains could have provided the direct inspiration for the first gumnut baby. An article by Jean Chapman quoted May's significant belief: 'it's hard to say … if the bush babies found me or I found the little creatures'. She was, however, certain of one thing: that they were inspired by 'memories of West Australia's flowers and trips to Blackheath' in the Blue Mountains.

May Gibbs used her own weekend in the Blue Mountains in a cartoon that appeared in the *Sydney Mail*.

FACING PAGE: Both the gumnut babies and the kookaburra, that decorated the *Sydney Mail* cover in 1914, were to become major characters for May Gibbs.

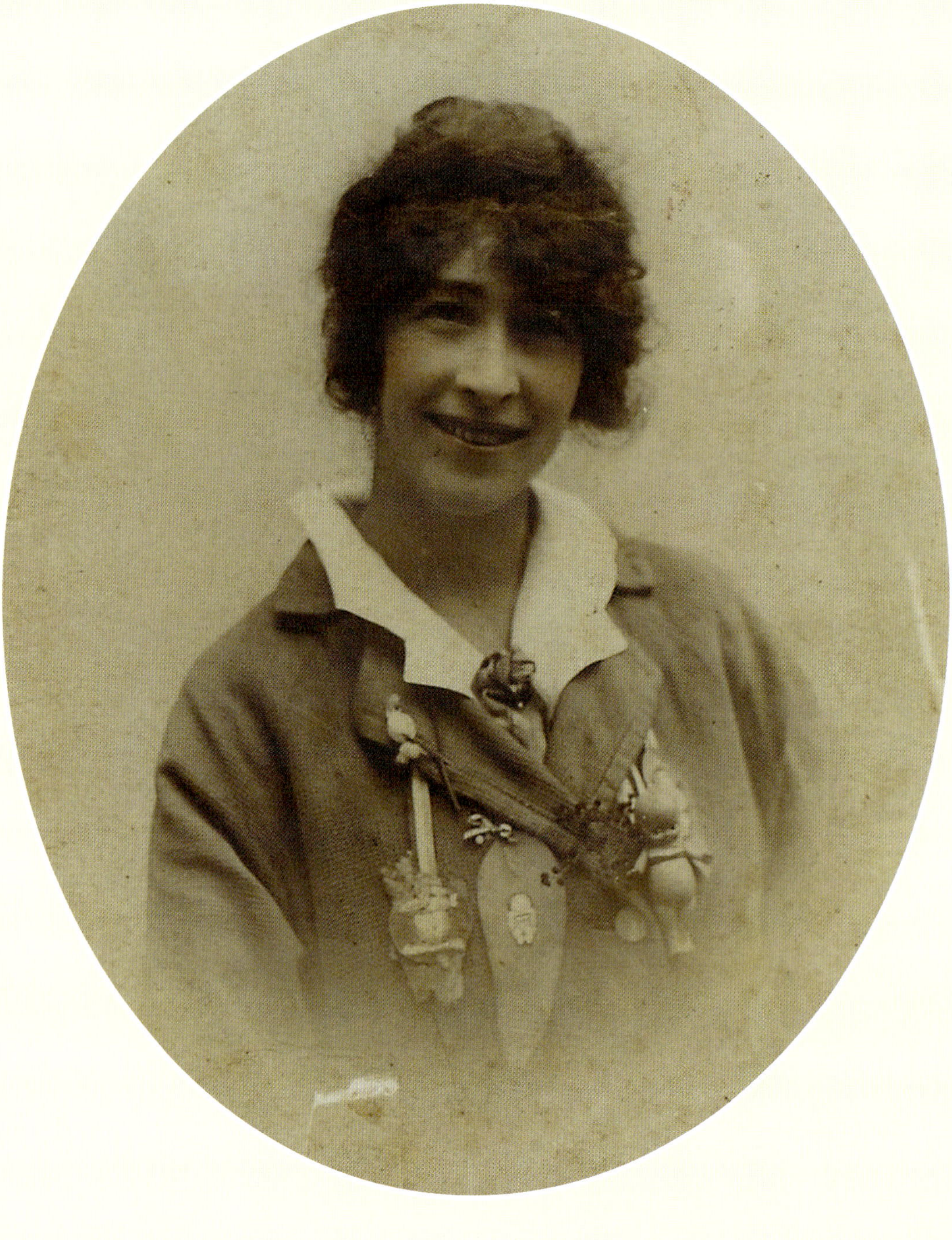

CHAPTER 11

THE GUMNUT CORPS GO TO WAR

As 1914 unfolded, Australian events and developments seemed, increasingly, to be dwarfed by the international news that forecasted an imminent war in Europe. One welcome respite which May enjoyed from this apprehension was Australia's victory in the men's singles tennis final at Wimbledon. The family's interest in tennis had been spurred by Ivan Gibbs' progression into major league tournaments in Western Australia. Clearly, the entire Gibbs family would have been proud when the Australian Norman Brookes defeated his German opponent in England in an epic match on 1 July.

Only a month later, however, news of another battle against German opponents swept any thought of sport from the headlines. And this battle would be infinitely more protracted than a five-set tennis match. On 3 August 1914, Prime Minister Joseph Cook pledged that, in the event of a war, Australia would place its vessels under the control of the British admiralty, and he offered to raise an expeditionary force of 20,000 men. The next day, Britain declared war on Germany and, on 5 August, Australia fired the

A portrait of May Gibbs with some of her gumnut creations.

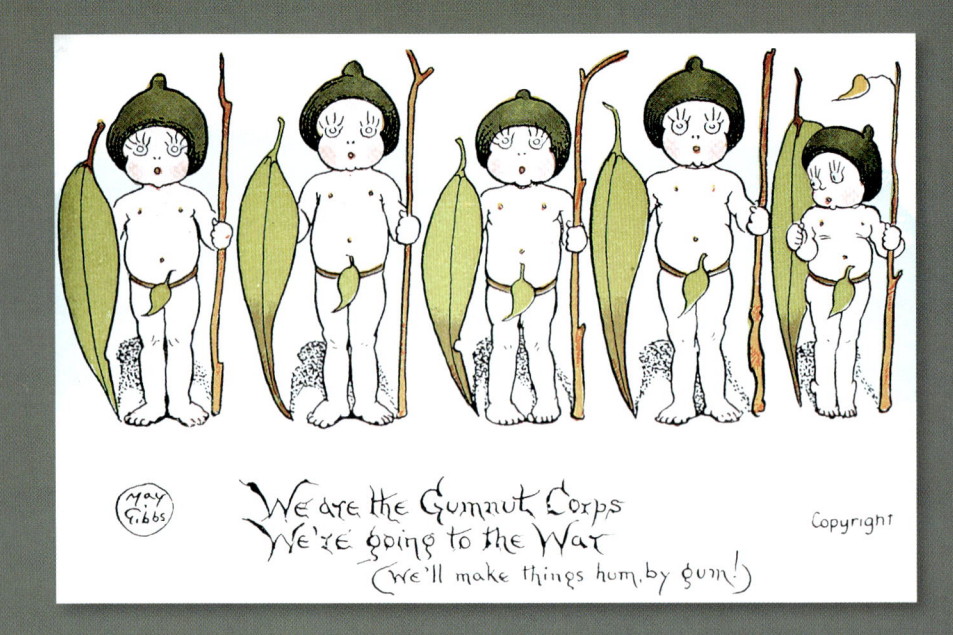

We are the Gumnut Corps
We're going to the War
(We'll make things hum, by gum!)

The Girls I left behind me

first Allied shot in the conflict as it prevented a German steamer from leaving Melbourne.

If these news items were not enough to heighten fears, the stark reality of war struck May on a more personal level. On 5 August, a German ship was sunk while attempting to lay mines in the Thames estuary. The enemy ship carried the name *Konigin Luise*. Although it was a different vessel sailing under the same name as the ship that had taken May to London in 1900, this news was still a chilling reminder. A week later, Australia started recruiting troops and within only ten days the fittest 20,000 of them had been enlisted.

Although this was a European conflagration which had been anticipated for some years, its arrival was deeply unsettling. May's immediate, and sensible, reaction was to find a release in her artwork. The result, an autobiographical cartoon, was published on 20 August in the *Bulletin*. (Although it was a significant accolade to be published in this paper, this triumph was never to be repeated for May.) With a war looming on the horizon, May had depicted herself and Rene sitting side by side, reading the latest newspaper reports. Rene voiced the 'terrible thought' that gave the cartoon its title when she said to May: 'If the enemy came they might seize us girls to be their wives'.

These two (nearly) middle-aged spinsters were voicing a genuine and tangible fear. Although it was a fear that was cleverly undercut by May's self-deprecating humour, there can be no doubt that the uncertainty and vulnerability which the spinsters expressed was also felt by the nation as a whole. These fears were greatly allayed in November that year by the spectacular achievement of HMAS *Sydney* in sinking the German warship the SMS *Emden*. It was to be only another month before the first Anzacs arrived in Egypt.

On the home front, May Gibbs was one of many thousands of women eager to make their own contribution to the war effort. Soon after the declaration of war, the regional branches of the Red Cross united into a national body which empowered women as nurses—the only active role that Australian women, unlike their British counterparts, were given in the war. But May was desperate to find a meaningful and satisfying outlet for her particular abilities. And in finding a place for her patriotic contribution, May had at least one distinct advantage—her experience as a cover artist

TERRIBLE THOUGHT.
SCHOOL SPINSTER *(to Art spinster)*: "*If the enemy came they might seize us girls to be their wives.*"

May's first and only cartoon to appear in the *Bulletin*—May and Rene worrying about the possibility of war in 1914.

FACING PAGE: Postcards created by May that reflected a uniquely Australian sensibility for the troops.

Postcards were a way for May to contribute to the war effort. They were included in the Red Cross parcels sent to the troops.

for women's suffrage. This experience was re-energised when she began a series of Australian postcards. Like her covers, these were works of propaganda for a war effort, albeit one waged on a different battle front. In 1968, in the year before she died, May recorded her memories of this turning point in her long life, telling the National Library of Australia:

> When the war came, I did the Gumnut cards, because I wanted to do something for people to send to the soldiers … [I] promised the printer that I would pay him as soon as I had the money in, and he was nice enough to print them for me before I gave him a penny.

May created over thirty of these postcards during the war years. At first, they were not overtly inspired by the conflict but were simply images of May's earliest flower babies. For example, the first of these, 'Flannel flower babies', was registered for copyright in January 1914, followed by 'Christmas bell babies' in September. Thereafter, it is thought that the first of May's distinctive wartime cards appeared in two related series. Both of these were black-and-white images of kookaburras or kangaroos printed on different coloured backgrounds, and they carried distinctively Australian sentiments. They included two matronly kookaburras sitting side by side on a gum branch, knitting. Like the spinsters in the *Bulletin* cartoon, they, too, confessed their fears: 'Your old Aunts are very anxious about you'.

Another was even more touching: Mr and Mrs Koala and their baby eagerly read news from the front and, grateful for this, reminded the Anzacs that such a 'letter brings joy to the Old Home'. In a time of censorship and paper shortages, it was nonetheless an effective message that the assault on the emotions of those left at home could still be lightened. Another example, perhaps the most sophisticated image of all, was a motherly kangaroo with a joey in her pouch, tending a camp fire: 'We'll keep the billy boiling, dear, till you come marching home'. At the time, these cards were unique: there were no others that matched their charm, their unforced Australian sentiment and humour, or their originality.

By the end of 1914, May had begun to make a name for herself with a steady output of whimsical items of ephemera: calendars, pictures and postcards, all of which were noted in the daily press with more than passing affection and appreciation. May entered into the country's national life simply by creating little pictures, fancy cards, bookmarks and magazine covers of native flowers. Composite sheets of her illustrations were printed

May Gibbs
Your old Aunts are very anxious about you
copyright

May Gibbs
We'll keep the Billy boiling, dear, till you come marching home.
COPYRIGH

CALENDAR

for her to cut up and paste onto calendars and cards. All these items were crafted by May and Rene Heames in May's Bridge Street studio, in inner-city Sydney, and then distributed through such local outlets as the Roycroft Library. It became a wartime cottage industry.

In mid-December, the *Sydney Morning Herald* enthusiastically reported on this handicraft's 'loving and fanciful treatment, with its quaint turn of humour … [catching] the fancy of … admirers'. It noted the distinctive contribution which May had made to the Christmas season: 'That she uses altogether Australian flower and leaf forms in her artistic work is one of the chief charms which Miss May Gibbs manages to infuse in all she does.' In recognition of how significant her ephemeral output had become, it continued: 'Her little pictures and fancy cards are now well known, and this artist deserves congratulation, because nothing seems to tempt her away from her chosen path of naïve simplicity.' May Gibbs, it concluded, 'with a way of her own … has certainly made her mark'. And which native blossoms did the newspaper single out for specific mention? They were the very ones which, within a few months, had morphed into individual booklets featuring flannel flower and Christmas bell babies.

What is believed to be the first example of a May Gibbs calendar has a date pad for 1914 and is a laboriously handcrafted item decorated with a Dolly Varden figure. This was obviously inspired by May's acknowledged love of the books of Charles Dickens, in this case *Barnaby Rudge*. In the 1890s, May and her mother had designed costumes based on Dickens' characters for groups of guests of the Government House balls in Perth, and this calendar maintained that interest.

It has to be admitted that this utterly conventional and sentimental design showed none of May's usual flair and originality. Actual pieces of lace were used to embellish the figure, which attracted the admiring gaze of Cupid. However, in her calendars for the very next year, May forsook such trite images and introduced gumnut characters instead. When Sydney's Society of Arts & Crafts held a Christmas sale of gifts in December 1914, May offered her new series of designs to some acclaim. 'Among the collection of novel and useful articles suitable for the season', said the *Sydney Morning Herald*, were 'some charming calendars by Miss May Gibbs, who has made a special study of fairy lore, as suited to Australian child-life'. Within two years, May's cottage industry was turning out a welter of items for the

At first May and Rene created handmade items such as bookmarks, booklets, cards and calendars, then as demand increased May could afford to have them printed.

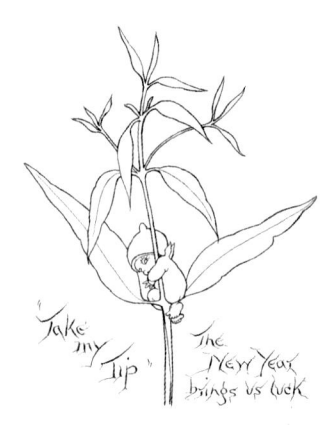

FACING PAGE: The war created a demand for nationalistic iconography.

showcase event of the society—its annual exhibition. In October 1916, the specific contribution of May's 'calendars, cards and bookmarks' was again cause for comment by the daily press.

These efforts sparked a regular series of calendars, which, astonishingly, continued to appear until the 1950s. The intervening years offered a great choice of designs, usually at least two per year—indeed, the examples for 1945 existed in no fewer than twenty-one different formats featuring bushland characters! Perhaps the largest and most striking of all May's calendar designs was the one she issued for 1919. She printed a large backing board with a circular device and gumleaf pattern to echo the smaller circle in the bottom corner which enclosed her trademark signature. Cut to shape and laid down within this large circle were no fewer than a dozen wide-eyed gum-blossom babies. They peeped out at the world through this circular window and offered the viewer a 'sweet greeting'. Their message was inscribed in scribbly-gum writing on the front of the calendar beneath, and the whole was finished with a tie at the top. It is a welcome and unlikely survivor from almost a full century ago.

Some time around 1920, a teenage Pixie O'Harris, who went on to carve her own niche as a children's book illustrator, visited May in her studio. Her later recollections included a memory of these calendars: 'Where ever one walked in the city streets, one saw for sale delightful small calandahs [sic] and other novelties'.

May's inspired creations were so utterly Australian that they ultimately conquered the heart of the nation. At last, she could channel all her passion and experience and newly won independence into creating her own world. The way she signed her works became the final vindication of that independence: she had created a firmly drawn circle that enclosed her name. It was a complete, self-sufficient and assertive stamp of authority.

'Ow's things?

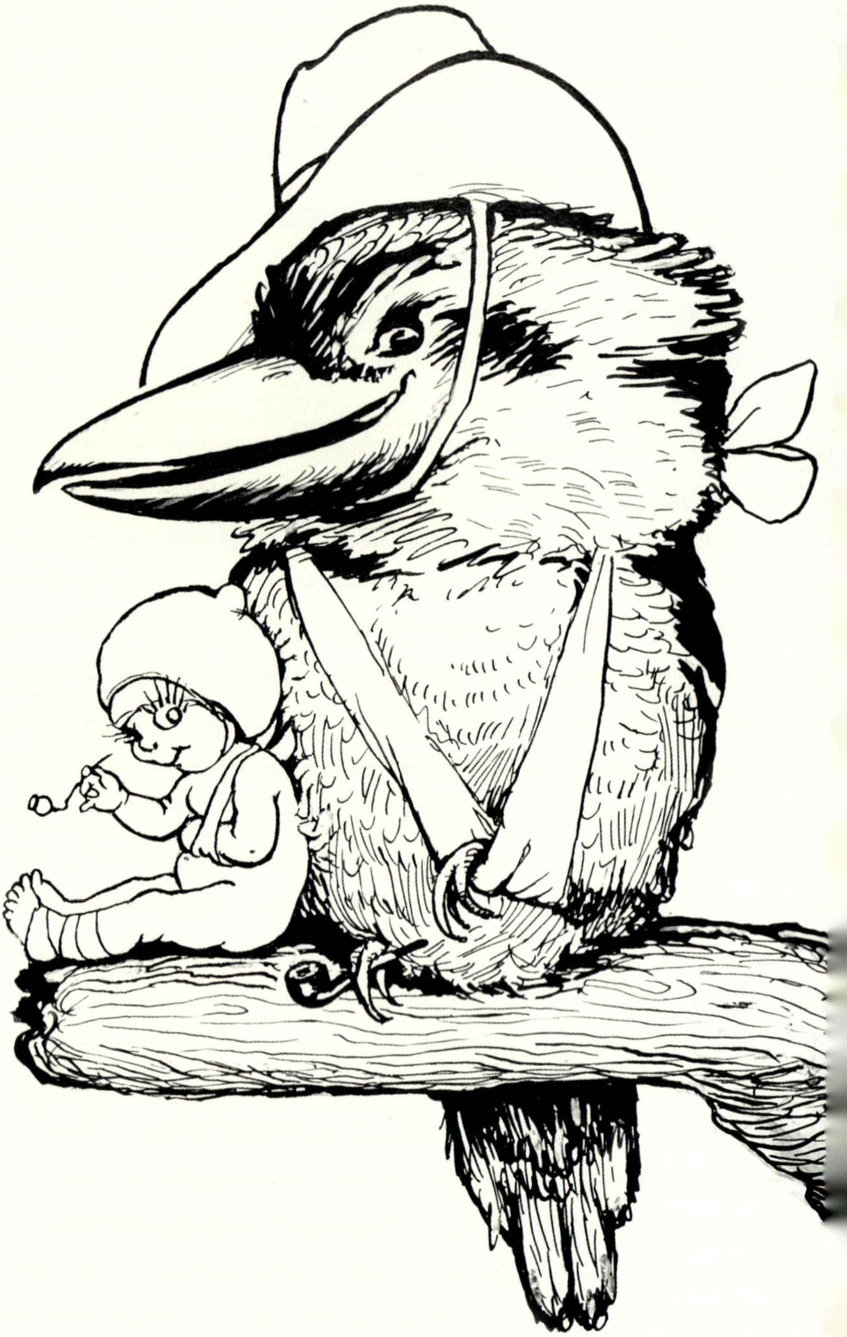

CHAPTER 12

'SISTER SUSIES SEWING SHIRTS FOR SOLDIERS'

Like so many other Australians of her time, perhaps May had also desperately clung to the popular opinion that the troops would be home by Christmas 1914. Yet even as this fond hope faded, May and her family must have been greatly relieved that she, at least, was back home. The question now was what May's options were—besides creating more gumnut cards—as an Australian woman wanting to contribute further to the continuing war effort.

It was, of course, a much less difficult question for a male to answer. Consider the example of fellow Australian artist Arthur Streeton, a highly respected painter who was a regular exhibitor at the Royal Academy. Streeton was a frequent traveller between Australia and England, but he was now temporarily stranded in Australia. The German ship on which he had been booked for his next voyage to England had been seized in Sydney by the Australian government at the outbreak of war. But Streeton remained determined to make his trip, and he finally disembarked in England early in 1915. The geographic path he took, the reverse of May's, was as much a turning point in his artistic career as was her decision to return home. By

This kookaburra illustration carried the tag line 'Are we downhearted?'.

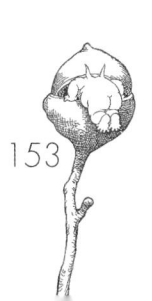

May's World War I postcards were so popular she created a whole series.

1918, he had become one of ten expatriate Australians appointed as their country's official war artists.

An Australian woman artist did not have this choice. For such women on the home front, the role of nurse was the closest they could come to active duty. But not all Australian women were suited to becoming nurses, and it was unfortunate that there were no other validated occupations for them. Their largest representative organisation, the Australian Women's National League, as well as others like the Australian Women's Service Corps, offered their strength to the government. These women were willing to enter a range of occupations, from drivers to factory workers, taking over traditional working men's roles to release them for enlistment. But the government was steadfast in its refusal to accept these offers, and Australian women had to devote themselves to what were considered more appropriate duties. Sewing rabbit-skin vests and shirts, and knitting socks, mittens and mufflers, all for the Australian Comforts Fund, became nationwide occupations.

By April 1915, the patriotic fervour of the first months of the war was dreadfully shattered. Already, the conflict was proving to be more protracted than most had predicted, and the carnage and loss at Gallipoli delivered a further, terrible shock to all Australians. Although the national resolve was strengthened the following month when Lieutenant-Corporal Albert Jacka won Australia's first Victoria Cross of the war, the country's emotions had become very mixed by that December—although successful, the evacuation of the Gallipoli peninsula in that month was an infinitely sad leave-taking. Throughout this time, Australian women searched for a meaningful role and a way to make a tangible contribution to their country's war effort.

The most significant opportunity for such a contribution came on Australia Day, 30 July 1915. (It was not until 1935 that all Australian states celebrated Australia Day on 26 January.) Patriotic signs and symbols were everywhere in sight, with many people wearing buttonholes of wattle. But it was in the very vanguard of that day's official procession through Sydney's streets that the most moving sight was evident. It was there that the crowds were given the unmistakable evidence of Anzac sacrifice—and for many, the reality of the war finally hit home. It had been three months since the Gallipoli landing, and wounded soldiers had begun arriving home. Leading the procession, in the governor's carriages, in cars and in military ambulances, were wounded Anzacs. It was a sight that caused an outpouring of pride and emotion.

155

Throughout that day, collectors tirelessly encouraged the crowd to donate money for the wounded—as the *Daily Telegraph* put it, to 'show the world that the generosity of Australia's people at home is not unworthy of being bracketed with the gallantry of her soldiers at the front'. The result was unprecedented. On that day, over £400,000 was raised across New South Wales. The *Sydney Morning Herald* reported that, as the procession of wounded Anzacs moved along, they were assailed with 'a shower of coins … until the floor of their motor car [was] covered with silver and copper'. The bombardment was even compared to 'that day in April' in Gallipoli, 'when they were under shrapnel fire'. But the generosity of the crowd was not limited to this shower of donations.

Sydney, in particular Martin Place, was crowded with stalls and street vendors, all trying to tempt the immense congregation to purchase items for the war effort. 'Wherever one looked', the *Daily Telegraph* reported, there were 'stalls heavily laden with goods which patriotic donors had sent in', sold by vendors getting 'fabulous prices for trifles'. Many of these goods had been handmade by thousands of women volunteers. Their efforts were rightly described in the same newspaper as a 'great charity mobilisation'.

The *Daily Telegraph* of 30 and 31 July described how 'the intersection of all streets [have] their special stall attractions', and said their offerings ranged 'from the most grotesque golliwogs to fine bas-relief plaster casts'. Among these stalls, Sydney's lady mayoress and the members of her sewing guild had their own stand. Sewing shirts and knitting socks for soldiers were highly practical ways for Australian women to contribute to the war effort, and these contributions were sorely needed. Once the Anzacs had arrived in Egypt, they were only able to purchase cheap cotton socks of the poorest quality, which wore out within days of strenuous marching. A touching appeal to the lady mayoress from an Australian woman in Egypt who had observed this problem was widely quoted throughout 1915. It urged 'Sister Susies' to greater efforts by encouraging 'the Australia[n] people to give … two pairs of socks and one warm shirt every three months to the troops'.

Any Australians who heard it would undoubtedly have been familiar with the term 'Sister Susie', which referred to these industrious seamstresses. Its derivation from one of the most popular songs of World War I made it a catchphrase across the nation and, indeed, across the world. It was, in fact, one of the very few songs which came close to rivalling the popularity of

'It's a Long Way to Tipperary'. As a British patter song, no doubt much of its appeal was due to its tongue-twisting lyrics which were first made famous in a London revue in late 1914. Thereafter, it swept the world, being performed in revues and in pantomimes, as a solo song, and even delivered as an amusing recitation; in America, Al Jolsen's recording of it in 1915 was a guarantee of instant success.

The song's amusing premise was simple enough. Soldiers would rather spurn Sister Susie's good-natured relief efforts than wear her itchy and far-too-feminine shirts:

> Some soldiers send epistles, say they'd rather sleep in thistles
> Than the saucy, soft, short shirts for soldiers sister Susie sews …
> When we say her stitching will set all the soldiers itching,
> She says our soldiers fight best with their backs against the wall.

In Australia, the song was first sung in the theatrical company JC Williamson's pantomime *Cinderella*, which opened in Melbourne on 19 December 1914. May Gibbs herself might certainly have heard it performed in Sydney, where the show opened on 20 March 1915. JC Williamson built on the publicity potential of the pantomime's most popular tune by running a competition to add a new alliterative chorus to their sibilant soldier song.

May Gibbs made her own contribution to the 'Sister Susie' push in the early months of 1915. Among the first tentative steps she took in formulating her wild-flower baby imagery, before it appeared fully fledged in the five booklets she released between 1916 and 1920, there was one that has eluded researchers until now. This ephemeral item introduced not one or two gumnut babies, but a whole family. Or perhaps it was a virtual gumnut 'army', for there were no fewer than fourteen of them! The title of this image, printed in scribbly-gum lettering, read: 'Sister Susies Sewing Shirts for Soldiers'. It was a caption for a sewing circle of gumnut babies, all of them sitting along a tree branch and engrossed in their work. Some sewed blue-striped shirts while some knitted socks. Their thread/wool came from two industrious spiders, and all these efforts were being overlooked by a bespectacled, matronly kookaburra. Next to her, in final acknowledgement that this was a patriotic sewing circle, was a Red Cross satchel.

Clearly, May was presenting another role for her patriotic little Australians. This image derived from the same inspiration that marched the gumnut corps

The popular postcard 'Sister Susies Sewing Shirts for Soldiers'.

OVER PAGE: The original pen and ink illustration.

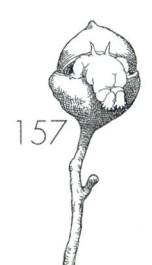

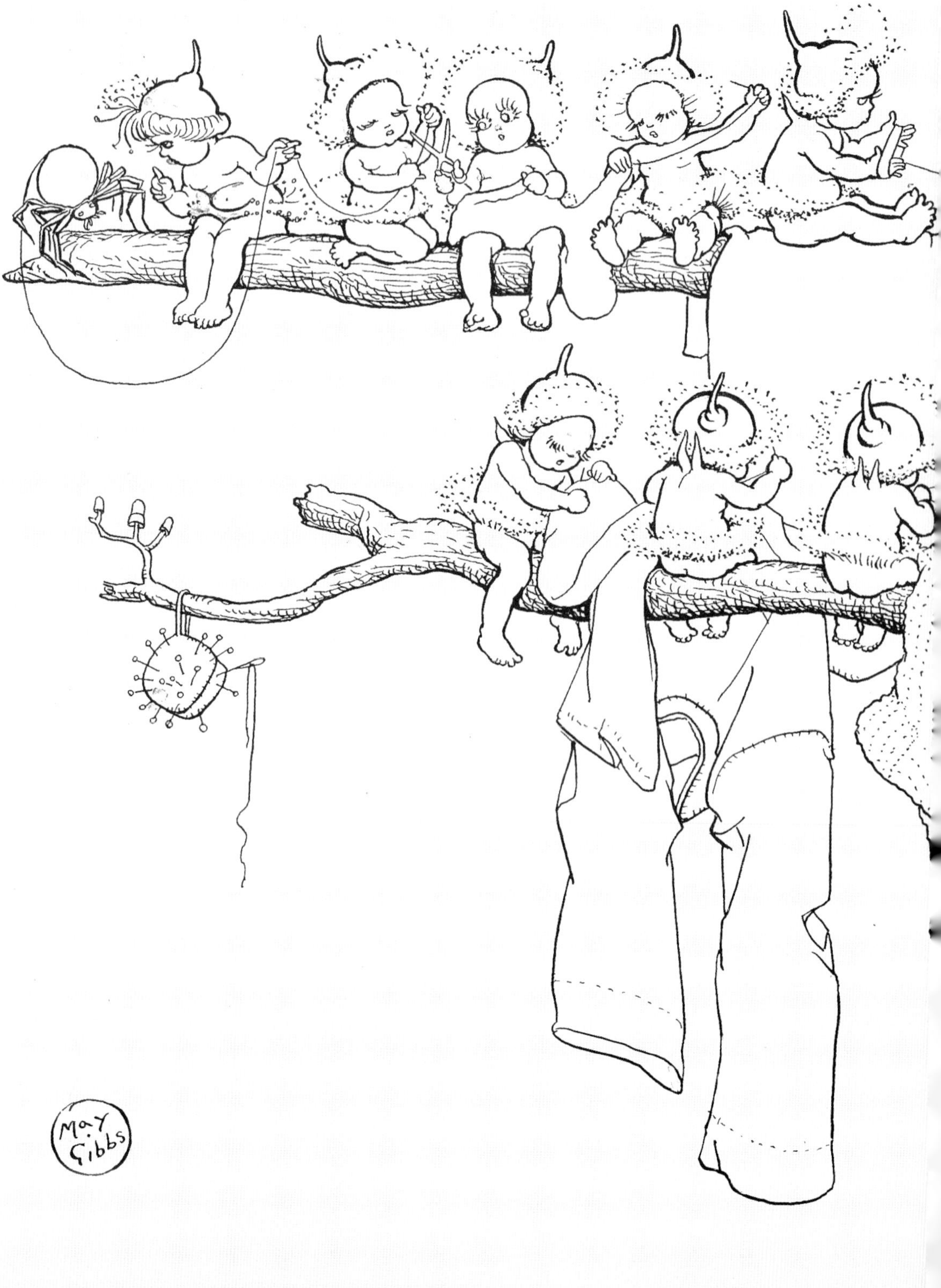

May
Gibbs

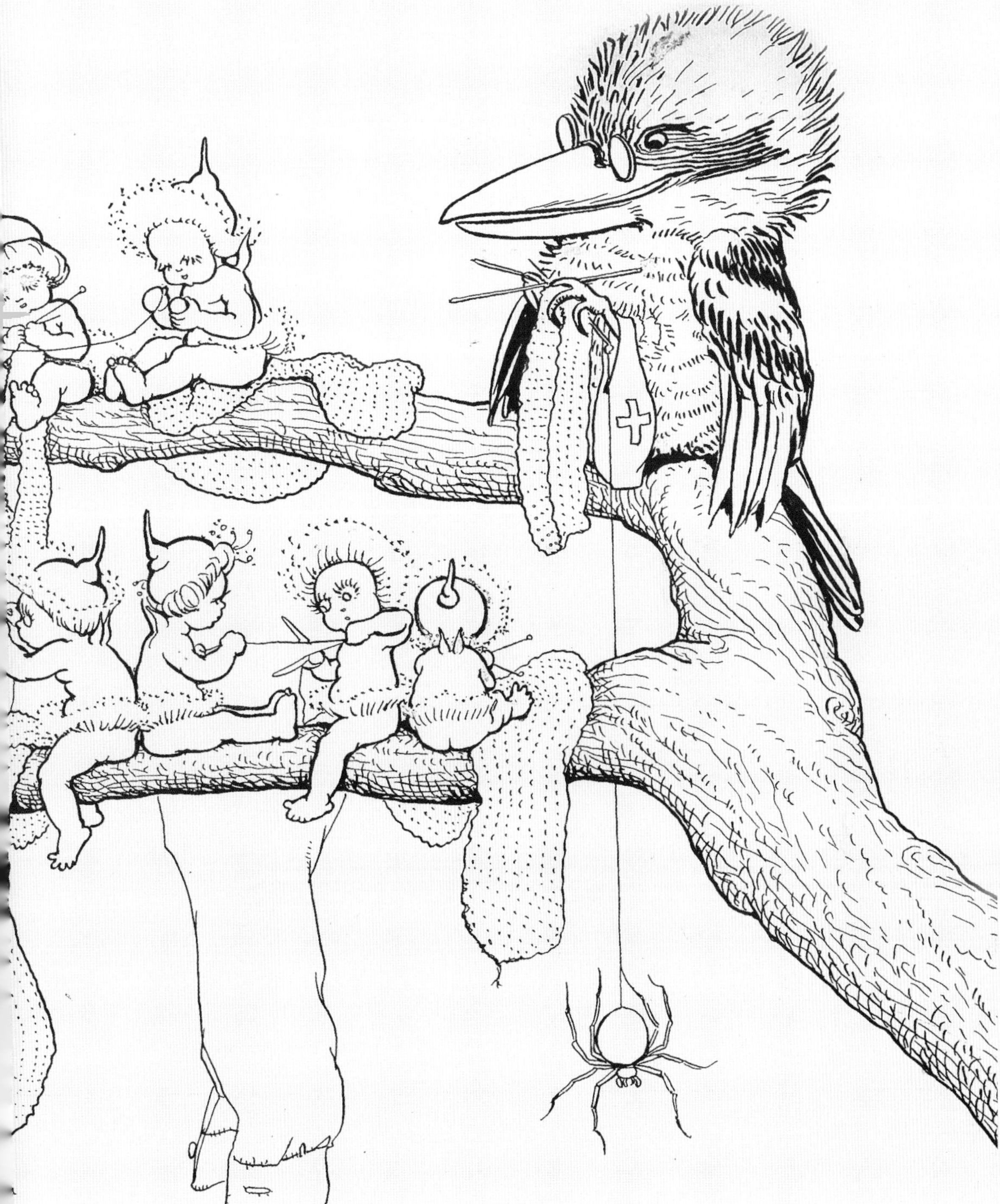

Gumnut Babies

off to war on a postcard. They left with a determination to 'make things hum, by gum!'.

In September 1915, an extensive article on May's work in the Sydney newspaper the *Sun* disclosed that these 'fourteen demure little Gum Nuts', which all appeared on a postcard, had a genuine existence—they had been inspired by a real-life knitting group. The image was described as representing '14 girls who meet together and sew for their soldier friend away fighting, and Madame Kookaburra represents their kindly directress'. May's pride in the success of this postcard, which became possibly the most disseminated of all her designs, was understandable. 'No work has ever before given her such genuine pleasure,' it was reported, 'for she worked with the knowledge that they were going out to the gallant lads, and were something essentially typical of their native land'.

The same article revealed that the Red Cross had sent this postcard out to diggers across the world: 'Every parcel that is despatched contains a card of the Sister Susie Gum Nuts'. The image was soon reprinted in an enlarged, hand-coloured version and was very possibly sold to raise funds for the Red Cross. It was produced with a concern for its flimsy nature. The fact that it was strengthened with a backing board and mount meant that it was obviously designed to be an item of pictorial propaganda which would be kept and treasured rather than discarded. It is thought that May's hand-coloured print was sold at one of the many stalls which were erected across Sydney on Australia Day 1915, presumably at the one which traded as a 'Sister Susie' shop.

The evolution of May's imaginative world continued in a book published in October 1915—Edith Graham's *A Little Bush Poppy*. One of its nine full-page plates was a significant peepshow into the miniature world that May was creating. In this dream fantasy sequence, May took illustrative liberties. She could not resist introducing her own characters: a line of gumnut babies, a gum-blossom baby and other, various wild-flower fairies. It was an imaginative addition to the work: in the words of May's first biographer, it involved an eight-year-old boy 'looking on in wonderment at the meeting of the fairies of the old world with the bush sprites of the southern continent'.

Then, in mid-1916, only months before the first wild-flower baby booklet was issued, May created a sequel to her 'Sister Susie' image. It was another ephemeral delight—again, a separately issued, hand-coloured patriotic

The first of May's series of highly successful books was *Gumnut Babies*. Published in December 1916 it sold out immediately.

FACING PAGE: May's popular wild-flower babies began to appear on covers and cards. In September 1914 the second of three covers commissioned by *The Lone Hand* was published.

OVER PAGE: An unfinished sketch for an illustration that was to feature dozens of little babies.

image. Its pairing of a kookaburra in a slouch hat with a gumnut baby presented them as iconic Australian soldiers bearing the marks of war: both wore slings. Like its predecessor, this image was also inspired by a popular World War I song. And it, too, was given a title in gumnut lettering, an appropriately boastful message which was rendered with great gusto by the Aussie troops: 'Are we downhearted?' May's imagery clearly answered that question with a resounding and uplifting denial.

Just when May first heard this British song is unknown. Certainly, it had become so popular with the Anzacs that more than one report of the Gallipoli landing in April 1915 had made mention of it. Adelaide's *Advertiser* reproduced this 'letter from the front': 'During that first awful day as the wounded were being taken back to hospital ships they passed troops landing, and the wounded men shouted out as they passed the boats, "Are We Downhearted?" and the answering yell was "No"'. Later that year, May might have attended a musical revue staged in Sydney's Little Theatre which had taken its title from the song. Her musical upbringing and her experience performing on stage throughout her childhood would have made both this song and 'Sister Susie' into instant sources of inspiration as she searched to make her own contribution to the war effort.

This image was slightly reworked into a full-page colour plate for a fundraising anthology, *The Westralia Gift Book*, in aid of YMCA military efforts. This was a compilation by writers and artists from Western Australia which was issued at least as early as August 1916. The quick recognition afforded May Gibbs by Australia's publishing world after her return from London, as well as her graphic contribution to wartime sentiment, were attested to by the inclusion of her work in yet another major gift book only weeks later—the *Australian Soldiers' Gift Book*, presumably issued at the beginning of December. Once again, May was accorded a place in fine company with other leading Australian book illustrators of the day, such as Norman and Lionel Lindsay. Her full-page plate 'What's That?' featured a massive draughthorse turning its head to question the diminutive gumnut baby perched on its back.

'Sister Susie' and 'Are we downhearted?' are two major items by May Gibbs that deserve rescuing from obscurity. These separately issued creations showed May working at the height of her illustrative skill and inspiration. Furthermore, along with her magazine covers, they showed

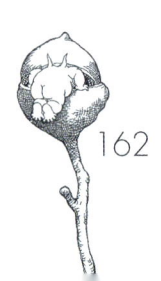

THE LONE HAND

FLANNEL FLOWERS.

September 1914

THE DEFENCE OF AUSTRALIA BY COLONEL FOSTER

6D

SAVE

the

The title page of the *Gumnut Babies* book in May's scribbly writing.

FACING PAGE: *Wattle Babies* was another of May's wild-flower babies books.

how she refined the characters who were about to assert their autonomy in five individual booklets. All of them would be introduced by what became something of a signature with May—her scribbly-gum writing.

By the end of 1916, May Gibbs' name was firmly entrenched in the Australian consciousness. On 26 October, the *Bulletin* commented that the gumnut babies 'who blink at you in countless Christmas calendars' had made May Gibbs 'one of the best-known of our younger women artists'. Indeed, throughout the war years, May's output of pictorial propaganda, which lightened the hearts of a whole nation, was fondly acknowledged. In March 1917, the Sydney newspaper the *Sun* said: 'In thousands every week now, the whimsical cards and other art productions from Miss Gibbs's prolific brush and pen are being sent to our boys in the trenches, and each breathes a message redolent of home as no more serious mementos could.'

May's achievements were even noted in a fine-art context with an accolade from a critic, William Moore, who became Australia's leading art historian of his time. And what would have flattered May even more was that this notice was given in the most prestigious art periodical of the day, the London *Studio*. Writing in September 1916 in that journal, Moore proudly included May's work in his serious consideration of Australia's achievements in national art. 'May Gibbs', he declared, 'has struck a new line in depicting the Bush as a land of fairy folk of her own imagining'. Because May was still some months away from publishing her first gumnut booklet, it is clear that the critic's praise could only have been based on the ephemera and magazine covers he had seen. This was an extraordinary accolade and, remarkably, one that remained unnoticed for almost a century.

By the beginning of 1917, quite astonishing sales figures for May's work were being quoted. Her growing family of bushland babies was reported to have sold over 50,000 copies in each of its varied formats. The popularity of all these items was impossible to ignore, and there was no doubt about the positive reception which the hard-driven Anzacs gave to this pictorial bombardment. 'Pack up your troubles in your old kit bag and smile, smile, smile' was one of the most popular and enduring slogans from World War I and, like the song, May Gibbs' humorous cards and drawings certainly lifted Australian spirits. Inspired by a resurgent sense of her own Australian identity, May's messages to a war-torn Australia could not have been better timed.

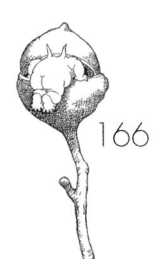

May Gibbs

H. S. Gibbs —
Nov. 1923

CHAPTER 13

'HUMANS PLEASE BE KIND TO ALL BUSH CREATURES'

Throughout the first decade of the twentieth century, an observable change in the attitude of the Australian public towards its fauna and flora became increasingly apparent. A new awareness of conservation developed alongside a burgeoning nationalism. Before this time, the study of natural history and the pursuit of hunting had been closely aligned. They were not only seen as compatible, but even as respectable. However, the growth of bushwalking clubs and of observation with camera and glasses promoted a gentler appreciation of the Australian bush and its animals. A further substantial impetus was the introduction of nature study into the elementary-school curriculum.

This growing chorus of concern had been rallied by a memorable and lonely cry for conservation in 1899. Significantly, this had been the voice of Australia's first classic children's book writer. When she introduced *Dot and the Kangaroo* to the world, Ethel Pedley did so with a heartfelt dedication: 'To the children of Australia, in the hope of enlisting their sympathies for the many beautiful, amiable, and frolicsome creatures of their fair land;

May and JO Kelly built a new home on a steep waterfront bush block overlooking Neutral Bay. They called the house 'Nutcote'.

May was a committed conservationist, known for releasing song birds from cages.

whose extinction, through ruthless destruction, is surely being accomplished'. Her message would resound into the new century, and May Gibbs was eventually to become its new champion.

From Sydney's Neutral Bay, May and Rene took welcome excursions to nearby Manly. This popular seaside suburb had hosted annual flower shows since the 1890s. These, however, had been discontinued when increasing conservation awareness decried their wholesale destruction of wild flowers and their habitats. 'In those days,' the *Sydney Morning Herald* reported in 1911, 'people did not realise the importance of preserving the native flowers. There was no supervision of the gathering, the pickers ruthlessly pulled the plants up, roots and all'. May Gibbs' first major children's book, *Tales of Snugglepot and Cuddlepie*, published in 1918, deplored these wanton acts. It opened with a plea that echoed Ethel Pedley's words of two decades earlier: 'Humans Please be kind to all Bush Creatures,' it begged, 'and don't pull flowers up by the roots'.

After Federation, Australia's indigenous flora and fauna were increasingly represented in the decorative arts, in advertising and on postage stamps. In 1909, this regard was instrumental in prompting the formation in Sydney of the Wildlife Preservation Society of Australia. This was the first such group devoted solely to conservation. Together with other like minded societies, it encouraged the *Birds and Animals Protection Act* of 1918, as well as legislation that prohibited the taking of wild flowers and plants from all public land. Not surprisingly, May became a member of the Wildlife Preservation Society in the 1920s and remained actively involved for over two decades. It was appropriate that May Gibbs was at the forefront of all of this change—its fundamental effect would be nothing less than the town literally acting to save the bush.

Significantly, this initiative was popularised by a well-known writer of children's works at the time—Amy Mack, the same writer who provided May with her first major commission in Sydney. This established author had been contributing short children's stories to the *Sydney Mail*, the *Sydney Morning Herald* and *The Lone Hand* for a decade, and she also had several volumes of essays and collected stories to her credit. The strong conservation theme that permeated almost all of her writing was something which May immediately embraced. In *Bush Days*, Mack wrote: 'Sydney has grown so wide that on every side the bush had had to give way before

WE ARE THE ORIGINAL Gumnuts
BEWARE of all IMITATION
HELP OUR ANIMALS
DOWN with Humans they set TRAPS
CATS are so Cruel
May Gibbs

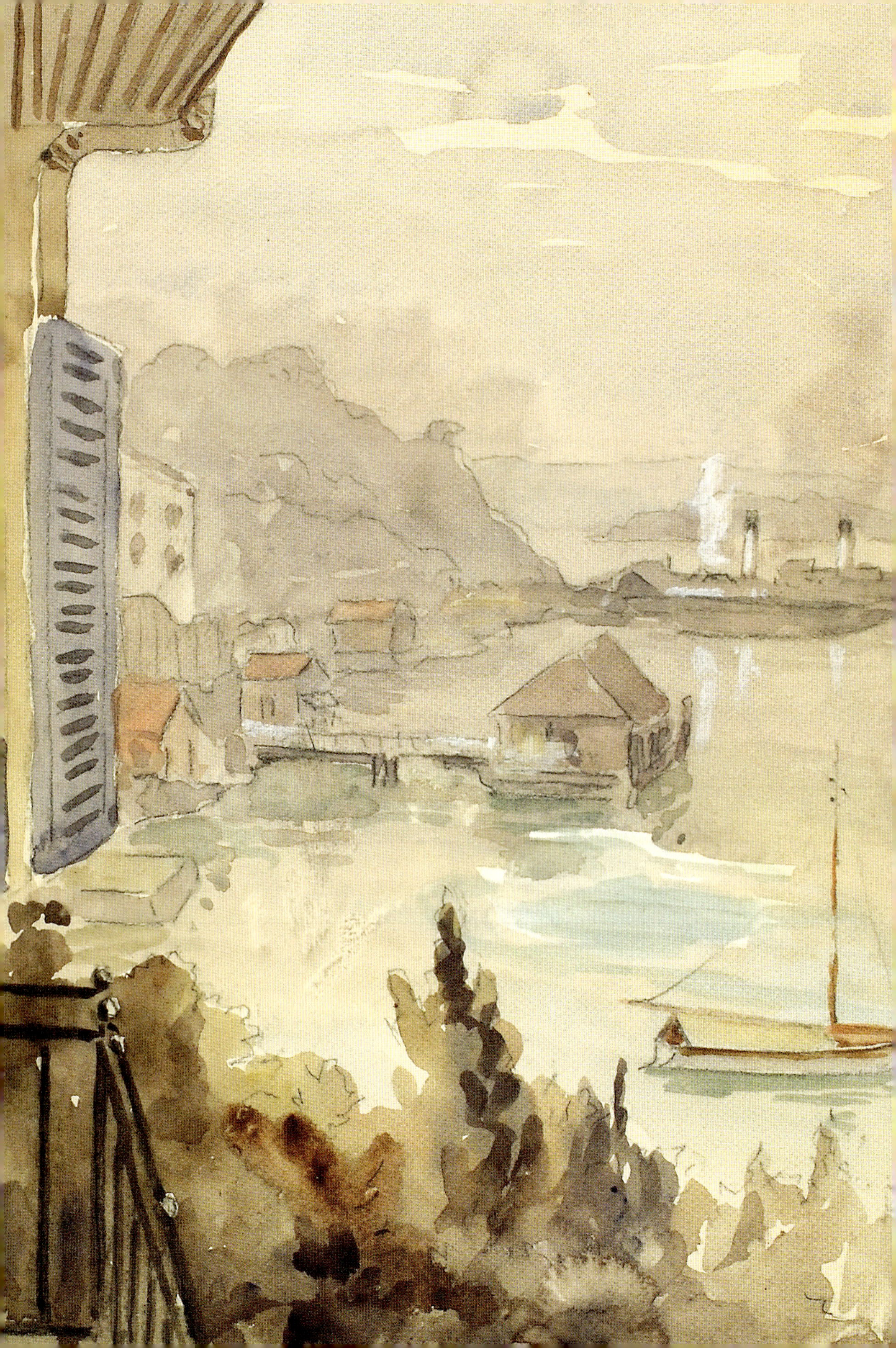

bricks and mortar, trams and trains … till it seems as if, in a very little while, there will be no bush left at all.'

May deplored the encroachment of urban life on the bush as well. In the *Sun* in September 1915, in the most detailed interview she gave before the first of the bush-baby booklets appeared, she clearly echoed Mack's sentiments: 'Miss Gibbs's great regret … is the fast disappearance of the bush in close proximity to Sydney … gradually she has to seek further and further away for her flower models.'

Although Western Australia's wild-flower exhibitions were without serious rival in the east in the 1890s, two similar, highly publicised exhibitions were held in the Sydney Town Hall in 1912 and 1914. Unlike their West Australian counterparts, however, these eastern exhibitions attracted Australia-wide contributions of acclaimed arts and crafts entries. Even though May arrived in the city too late to attend the first Sydney Wild Flower Show, she would have enjoyed one of its features—an award for the best-dressed child in costume as a native flower. As we know, fancy-dress balls had been a popular feature of May's childhood and early adult years, particularly the annual balls staged at Perth's Government House in aid of the SPCA. (In fact, May was to become a member of the Sydney branch of the society immediately upon her arrival, and soon thereafter was given an honorary life membership.)

By September 1914, when the second Sydney Wild Flower Show was held, May was an acclaimed new arrival in town. Although there was no evidence that May actually attended this second show, what made this highly likely was the significant addition of West Australian wild flowers to the event. Fully one-third of the noncompetitive exhibits were of West Australian origin. When these were extolled in the *Sydney Morning Herald* for revealing how 'the plants of our country have entered in no small way into our national life', May surely saw the heaven-sent opportunity for an aspiring illustrator. Perhaps it was this enthusiastic newspaper account of the event which inspired her to create her own signature series of ephemera only months later.

The continuing popularity of fancy dress and costume at the start of the twentieth century was previously unrecognised as a sustained source of May's artistic inspiration. Its most potent result was undoubtedly her series of costumed bush babies. Yet there was more. While May was introducing

FACING PAGE: A watercolour of Neutral Bay from May's home by Herbert Gibbs.

FACING PAGE: An illustration for the unpublished book, *Mimie and Wag: Their Adventures in Australia*.

the bush babies on postcards, she was also designing a series of actual costumes for children. Wild-flower fairies were very much on May's mind at the time—in the same month that these fairies appeared as diminutive illustrations in *A Little Bush Poppy*, they also emerged for another, even more visible, if short-lived, sighting by the Sydney public.

A concert in aid of the Comforts Fund was held in the Sydney Town Hall on 9 October 1915, and all of the costumes in its patriotic parade were designed by May. They comprised the adults' allegorical costumes, which represented each state, as well as all of the children's flower-fairy costumes. The significance of this patriotic event on the home front was clear from its audience, the very upper echelons of society. Among those who enjoyed May's work for this event were the governor-general and various Allied consuls. The *Sydney Morning Herald* reported that, while the colossal organ thundered forth 'a whole series of war-like ballads', the town hall stage filled with a troupe of girls, preceded by soldiers bearing the national flag. This troupe, dressed in allegorical costumes 'picturesquely designed' by May Gibbs, then proceeded around the hall in a patriotic parade.

May represented each state by its trademark product: Victorian wheat, New South Wales wool, South Australian wine, West Australian gold, Tasmanian fruit and Queensland cattle. But her most charming, and original, conception was in her presentation of children embodying Australian wild flowers: wattle, flannel flowers, waratahs and Christmas bells. The inspiration and industry behind this spectacular presentation was not lost—within three months, May had signed a contract for the first of her gumnut booklets. This significant living embodiment of her wild-flower fairies was conceived and presented over a full year before their appearance in *Gum-Nut Babies* and *Gum-Blossom Babies*. This connection has never been cited before; in it we see the worlds of real life and of fantasy intermingle.

May Gibbs went on to do nothing less than create a new and engaging national pictorial vocabulary. The most perceptive contemporary acclaim quite rightly saw it as relevant to all Australians, as something to be treasured by adults and children alike. In the words of an unknown critic, words which the artist valued so much that she proudly clipped them and pasted them into her scrapbook, what she achieved was unique: 'May Gibbs has made a genuine and an original contribution to our Australian folklore'.

175

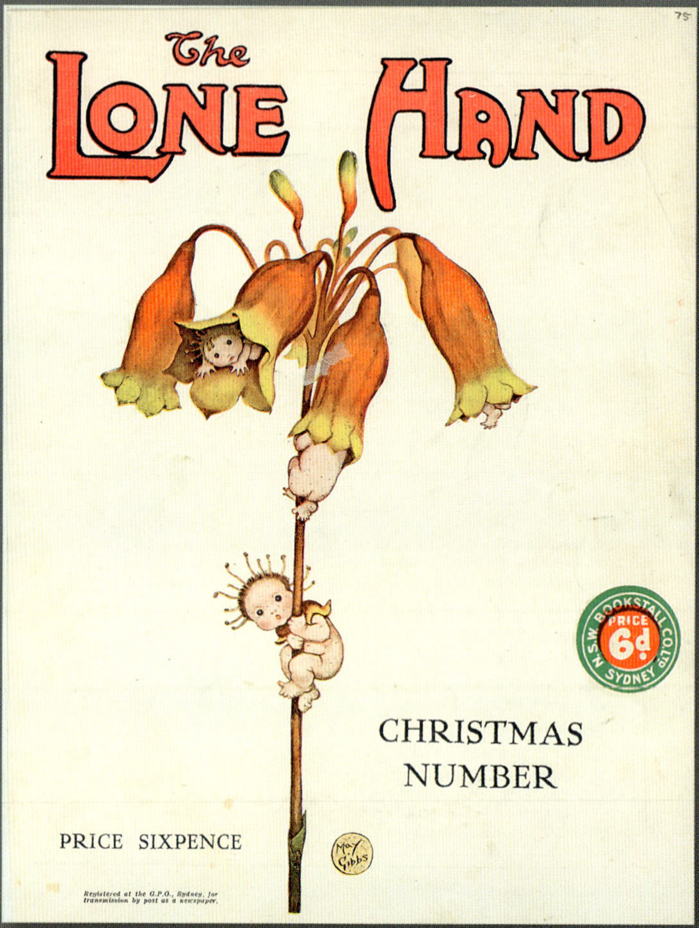
The
LONE HAND
N.S.W. BOOKSTALL CO. LTD.
PRICE
6d
SYDNEY
CHRISTMAS
NUMBER
PRICE SIXPENCE
May Gibbs
Registered at the G.P.O., Sydney, for
transmission by post as a newspaper.

May achieved this by finally completing the task she had set herself in a newspaper interview in the *Sun* in September 1915, which reported that she 'longs to illustrate a book of fairy tales culled from flights of fancy in the Australian bush'. May Gibbs had finally 'come to the conclusion that to realise her dream she must write the book herself'. Throughout 1916, May would work on *Gumnut Babies* and *Gum Blossom Babies*, the first of her five wild-flower baby booklets. With inspired determination, she would write the book herself; she would realise her dream.

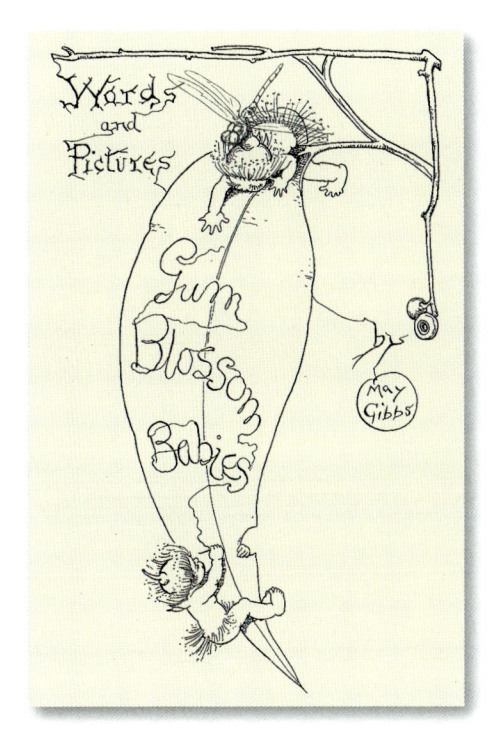

FACING PAGE: May's last cover (of three) for the Christmas edition of *The Lone Hand* was issued in January 1916. The design had already been used on one of her postcards.

Gum Blossom Babies, also published in 1916, was an immediate success and sold out just as quickly as *Gumnut Babies*.

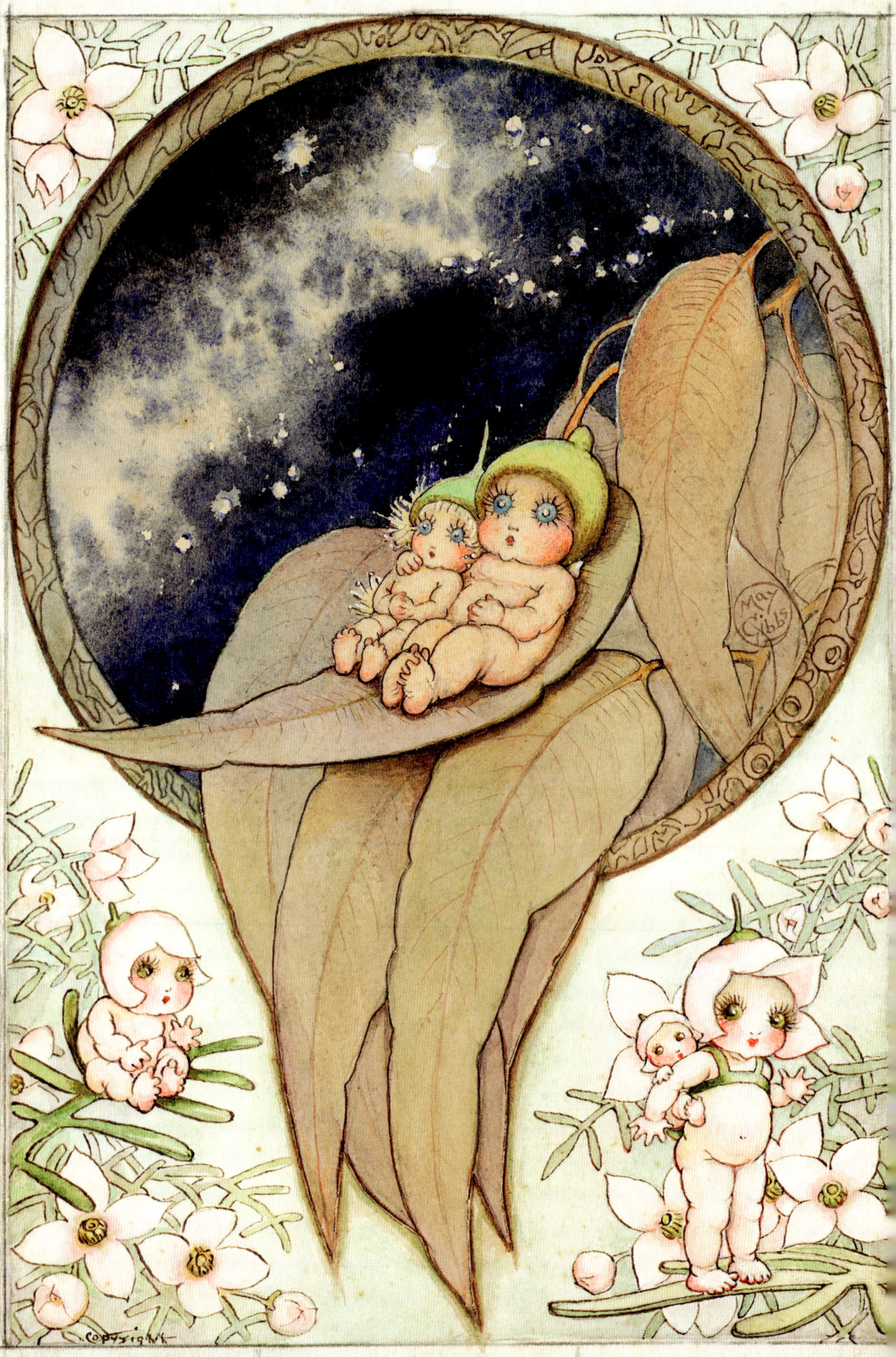
May Gibbs
Copyright

CHAPTER 14

CONQUERING A NATION

As 1916 began, Australia realised that the war was not going to be as short-lived as many people had predicted. The sight of wounded soldiers from Gallipoli had stirred the crowds on Australia Day in 1915, but there were soon to be other, more permanent reminders of the conflict across the Australian landscape. The Sydney suburb of Balmain unveiled a war memorial on 23 April, just in time for the first commemoration of Anzac Day, and the seaside suburb of Manly followed suit on 14 October. Both monuments had enough space on their granite to record additional names—future losses.

Meanwhile, the publication of May's illustrations on magazine covers and in a range of ephemera had successfully introduced an ever-expanding family of bush babies to a welcoming Australia. Between December 1913 and October 1916, she took out Commonwealth copyright registrations on six of these designs: her gumleaf bookmark, flannel flower babies, Christmas bell babies, bottle brush babies, wattle babies and, finally, native rose babies. The imaginative stamina that would have been required to produce these registrations in such a relatively short space of time was clear evidence of May working at the very pinnacle of her inspiration.

The number and scope of the illustrations of wild-flower babies grew and expanded from 1913 when May took out her first copyright registration.

The illustrations of the little bush sprites had found their target, the hearts of Australians.

This inspiration was given an appreciative impetus when May signed perhaps the most significant publishing contract of her career. On 11 January 1916, she completed a memorandum of agreement with Angus & Robertson to deliver to them two 'booklets' entitled *Gum-Nut Babies* and *Gum-Blossom Babies*—May's desire to create a text to accompany her illustrations was finally being realised. Not surprisingly, however, the impressive workload of the early war years, combined with this new responsibility, took its toll. Almost immediately after signing with her publisher, May, exhausted, suddenly returned to Perth. Encouragingly, on 3 March she wrote to Angus & Robertson to reassure them: 'I'm only now recovered sufficiently to go ahead with the Booklets'.

By December 1916, May Gibbs was poised to introduce the first of her five wild-flower baby booklets to the world. Within two years of the launch, she would achieve nothing less than a complete turnaround in the world of Australian publishing. The printing of her series of booklets, starting with *Gum-Nut Babies* and *Gum-Blossom Babies*, was so successful that only one other Australian writer of the time achieved comparable exposure. Together with CJ Dennis, May Gibbs was the publishing sensation of the war years. As with Dennis' work, the publication of May's booklets was a brave assertion of nationalistic pride and the first successful challenge to the imported book trade that had dominated Australia so completely for so long. By the end of 1920, the first two wild-flower baby booklets had sold an extraordinary 65,000 copies in reprints alone!

Among the countless reviews and notices which May's booklets received, one particular notice from March 1919 succinctly placed May's achievement in a national context. This lengthy praise in Rockhampton's *Daily Record* proclaimed that, in May Gibbs, 'Australia has at last produced a writer of indigenous fairy tales'. It then substantiated its claim:

> We have had the ... Old World fairy tale struggling for a foothold ever since the days of the first settlement. But this form of literature was and is an exotic, and it has refused to take root and come to fruition in Australian soil and under Australian conditions. To an Australian-born there is something foreign and hard of comprehension in the elf, the sprite, the brownie, the leprechaun, the banshee, and others of that ilk ... Our Natural is bizarre enough for most of us, and hard enough to fathom, and there is no need to go or look beyond it for image-forming power or suggestion ... Our fairies need to be of hardier mould. They need to be drought resistant ...

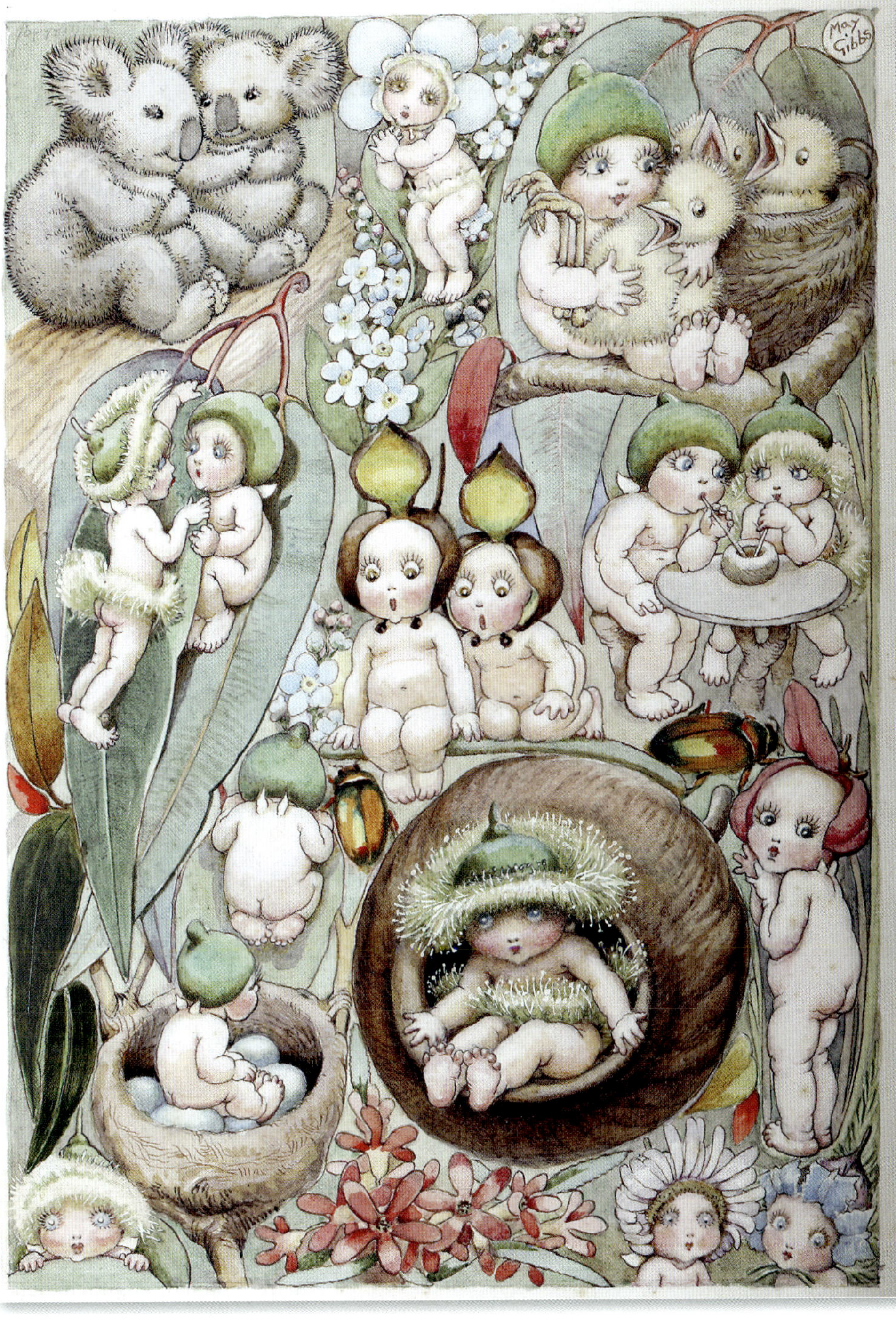
May Gibbs

and time has now delivered the goods in the person of May Gibbs. [She] not only knows her bushland and most of its idiosyncrasies, but she knows the temperament and the form that the fairies must possess if they are to be qualified to live and breathe and have their imaginary existence in that bushland.

This conquest, which highlighted the new regard and unprecedented demand for Australian publications during World War I, was validated on an unexpected front. In April 1918, the Art Gallery of New South Wales hosted a phenomenal loan exhibition of over 550 Australian works. In the words of *Art in Australia*, they were presented as 'an epitome of the work of our painters, pen-draughtsmen and etchers during the last twenty-five years'. Included in this 'epitome' were original book illustrations by the four most significant Australians working in this genre. These works were lent by Angus & Robertson and were a tribute to the local talent they were fostering—the first generation of Australians to create ongoing profiles as book illustrators. May Gibbs held a place there in fine company with Norman Lindsay, Hal Gye and Percy Leason.

In exhibiting these original book illustrations, the gallery became a pioneering Australian institution, giving its imprimatur to local illustrators. The inclusion of an illustration from *Gum-Nut Babies* was a celebration of how completely May Gibbs' creations had conquered the hearts of a nation. Thereafter, the unprecedented numbers in which the five gumnut-baby booklets were printed and reprinted, and the heartfelt welcome they received in a period of national soul-searching and war-torn sentiment, set the gumnut babies on a march to victory.

Perhaps May's own fond 'explanation' of the birth of these gumnut babies—an image of a bush sprite peering over a gum leaf, which came to her in the middle of the night—has made researchers shy off any further debate. However, if the inspiration for the babies did come to May in a dream, they did not arrive without any artistic and cultural forebears. While no-one would dispute the immense and original contribution which the babies made to the pictorial vocabulary of Australia, they still have a genealogy which placed them within an international context.

Alongside the general inspiration of late-Victorian illustrations of flower fantasies by Walter Crane and his contemporaries, there was an even more immediate source of derivation and comparison. From 1909 until well into

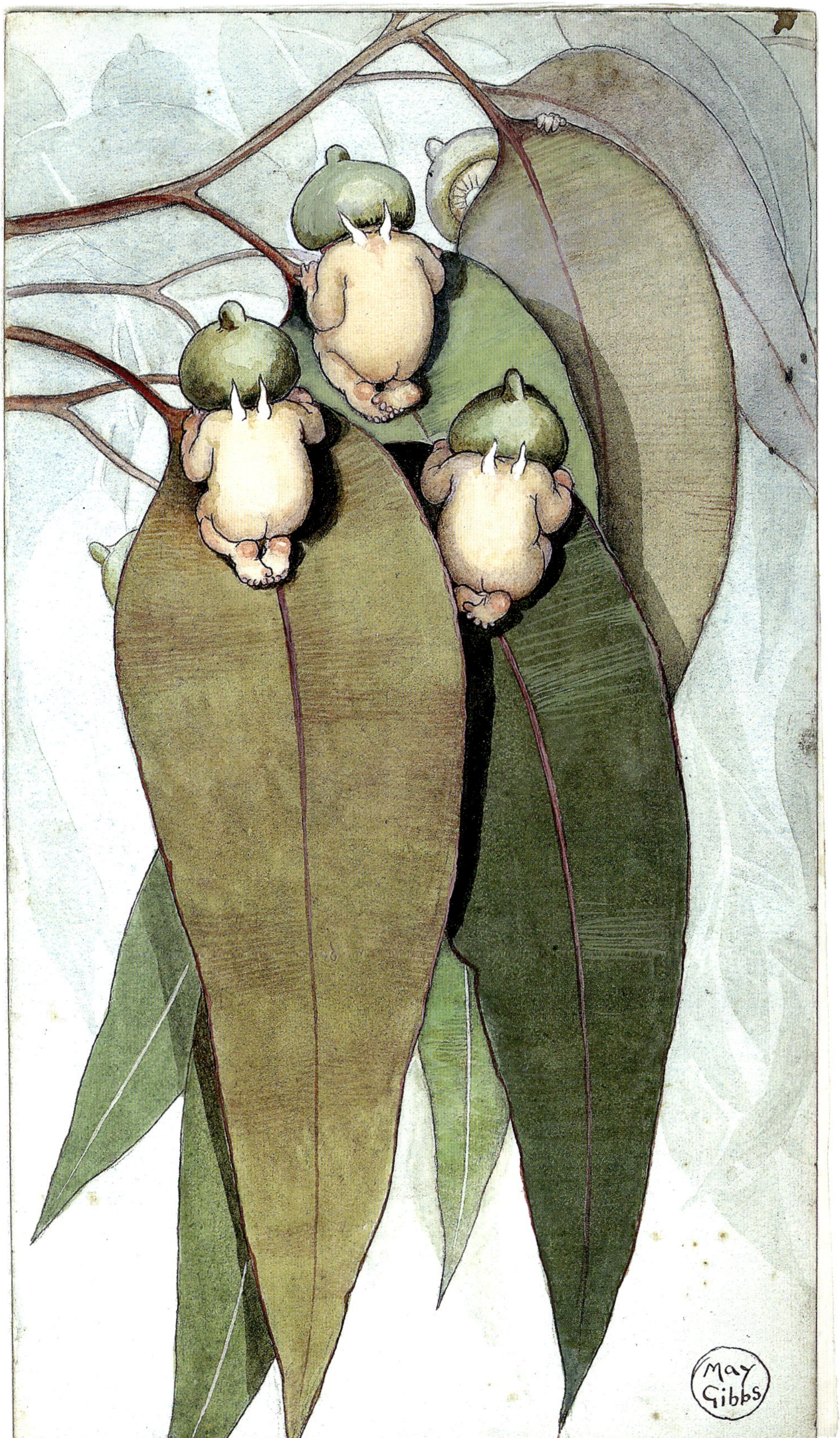
May Gibbs

FACING PAGE: Kewpies, cherubs and cupids were clearly forerunners of the gumnut babies.

the 1930s, the popularity of the Kewpie in magazines, books, postcards, advertising and toys made it an icon of popular culture. In the process, the Kewpie's creator, the American Rose O'Neill, became the most highly paid female cartoonist and illustrator of the early twentieth century.

Parallels between the lives and illustrations of May Gibbs and Rose O'Neill are immediately obvious. Both remained childless, and yet they each created an enduring realm of delight for children worldwide. Their characters continue to entertain us with their perpetual amazement at their own exploits and discoveries, providing an endless source of gently satirical and comic pleasure. Like Gibbs, O'Neill was also recruited into the pictorial war for women's suffrage, and both artists faced demands from an insatiable public to endlessly create comic strips. Until Mickey Mouse usurped its pre-eminence, the Kewpie was the most widely known cartoon character in America; in the Australian consciousness, the gumnuts must be credited with achieving a comparable status.

Like Gibbs, O'Neill attributed the inspiration for her creation to a fanciful source. According to Shelley Armitage, 'she described the Kewpies appearing to her in a dream, tumbling and playing about her drawing board'. As her fame spread, O'Neill became known as 'The Mother of the Kewpies', in the same way that May Gibbs became known as 'The Mother of the Gum Nuts'. And significantly, from their very first appearance, the gumnuts were hailed as an Australian version of the Kewpie.

When the celebrated Australian novelist Miles Franklin first saw the gumnut booklets in London, not only did she write to the publisher to congratulate it on their charm, but she also enthused to friends back in Australia. Writing to Rose Scott in Sydney on 28 December 1919, she described the gumnuts as 'American kewpies but put into Australian settings'. Australian newspapers had already pointed out this comparison. The *Bulletin* had noted that May's gumnuts and gum-blossom babies deserved their wide popularity because 'they are as distinctive as the Kewpie'.

But it was one final, shared attribute that enlivened the lineage of both Kewpies and gumnut babies. Both sprouted tiny wings. The Kewpies did this in homage to the acknowledged derivation of their name—as O'Neill stated, Kewpie was 'baby talk for Cupid'. The gumnuts' link to this forebear is a revealing family history.

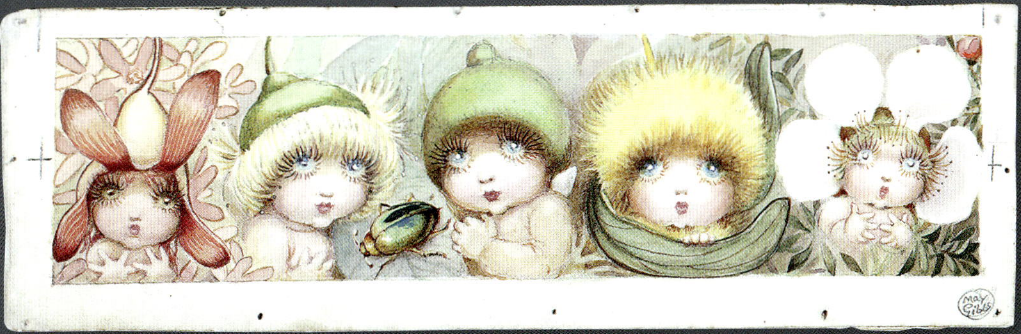
MAY Gibbs

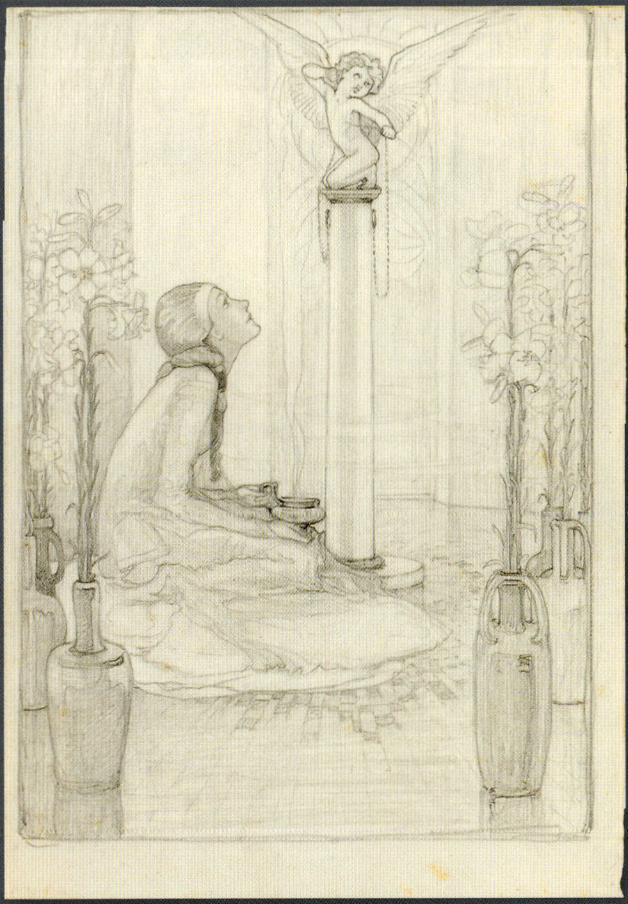

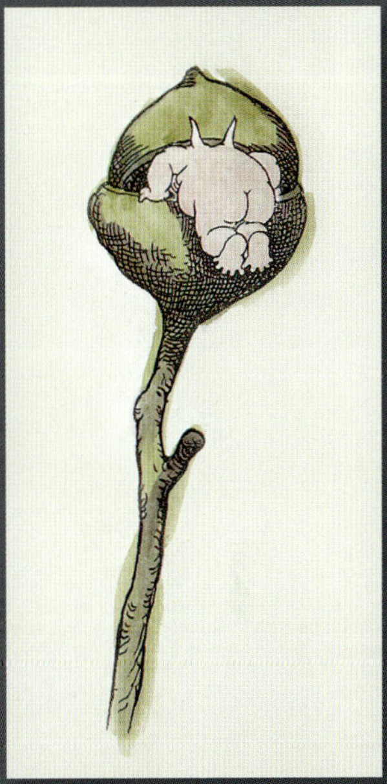

FACING PAGE: Cherubs were among the characters in this Christmas cover illustration for the *Western Mail* in 1907.

As early as 1902, May created a Cupid masthead to announce her series of fashion advertisements for the Bon Marche store in Perth. In it, Cupid took a centrestage position to introduce May's 'Fashion Fancies'. Cupid's introduction, among the more prosaic illustrations of hats and dresses, was May's way of adding a touch of imagination and fantasy to her otherwise workaday commissions. Then, in 1906, May again introduced Cupid (or at least a cherub) into her cast of characters. The cover for that year's Christmas number of the *Western Mail* featured a naked baby doffing his 'New Year' hat.

The same concept appeared in the newspaper's next Christmas annual. This time, three cherubs were recruited to announce the arrival of the new year. There was also a full-page cartoon, 'The one unwanted gift', which presented May's comic appraisal of Cupid as the sole gift left unclaimed beneath the modern Christmas tree. On either side of a bewildered Father Christmas, the sexes had lined up, segregating themselves. The men had chosen the gifts traditionally reserved for women and vice versa. So while the handkerchiefs, sweets, cookery books, fancy work and even toys were enjoyed by somewhat effete men, the philosophical tomes, cigars and sporting equipment attracted the liberated women and girls—in the far corner of the illustration, somewhat daringly for the time, one woman was even depicted smoking a cigarette!

By 1909, the very year in which the Kewpies made their highly acclaimed debut in American magazines, May had returned to Cupid imagery. Perhaps this was synchronicity. Perhaps May saw copies of the American magazines. Or, because May's position as a previously unrivalled female illustrator was becoming increasingly challenged by Ida Rentoul Outhwaite, perhaps she cast about for additions to her repertoire that differentiated her from the young woman from Melbourne. Whatever the case, for the next few years, Cupid was a major pictorial character in May's repertoire—a character, it should be pointed out, that was designed to appeal to adults rather than to children. It is possible that May took inspiration in more than one way from Cupid's example. In 1908 she had taken on the role of short-story writer for an adult audience, and by the following year she had created an entire album of verses and illustrations, again for adults, based on the exploits of Cupid.

With the Season's Greetings to Our Readers.

NURSERY RHYMES FROM THE BUSH

WRITTEN & ILLUSTRATED BY MAY GIBBS.

Mr Centipede & His Boots

Oh Mr Centipede! where do you buy your boots?
I grow 'em in the garden mum, will you have some roots?

It was probably also in 1909 that May reaffirmed her independent outlook by working on a new children's book. She completed eighteen watercolour and ink drawings with the briefest of captions and bound them together. The fact that this project was assembled as a finished dummy, complete with an illustrated and titled cover, means that it was highly likely to have been offered for publication. Entitled *Nursery Rhymes from the Bush*, it was an Antipodean retelling of the classic rhyme 'Hey Diddle Diddle'. While it was inspired by the local colour of Western Australia, its illustrative style was clearly a homage to the great British children's book illustrator Randolph Caldecott. He himself had produced a celebrated version of the rhyme in his 1882 picture book series.

The originality of the setting of the new version was matched by May's characteristic self-deprecatory depiction of herself. This was the hefty 'Miss A. Spoon', who was portrayed dragging an axe along behind her; she had chopped up a log which was now hoisted atop a shoulder. This image celebrated qualities which May certainly displayed: that of a self-made woman taking on the world, undaunted by social convention. May's heroine returned to her bush home, aptly named Spinster Villa. Predictably, perhaps, the spinster then met a rough and bearded bushie called 'Mr A. Dish', who eventually ran away with her spoon! But before this happened, the woman used her civilising touch to transform her rough suitor. Although unseen, Cupid had worked his magic from the sidelines! It was a clear contrast to May's illustrated verse of 1908, in which the female protagonist had rejected her suitor out of hand.

Then, in July 1909, May created a suite of twelve full-page pencil illustrations to accompany some verses, added a cover and entitled the whole *Cupid*. The following year she confirmed her interest in that same theme by progressing to highly finished watercolour illustrations. These works included an accomplished and effective circular drawing of a man accompanied by Cupid, and a larger, highly finished work (perhaps for exhibition) of a man and a woman in a garden, also escorted by Cupid.

Although there are no known works featuring Cupid from her three periods in London, May reconfirmed her interest in this image on her final return to Australia. In October 1913, she designed a menu for a family wedding in Sydney which was decorated with Cupid figures. That design was reused for the first of her calendars in 1914. In October 1915, when the first edition

FACING PAGE: The cover of *Nursery Rhymes from the Bush*. The illustrative style was reminiscent of British illustrator, Randolph Caldecott.

FACING PAGE: May often depicted herself as an old maid, as she does here in this unpublished illustration (May is fourth from the right).

of CJ Dennis' *The Sentimental Bloke* was published, Hal Gye's depiction of its protagonists as cherubs provided proof that this imagery had wide Australian appeal; a comparison of Gye's work with May's is as overdue as it is significant.

Uncovering this growing use of Cupid in May's work only leads us to wonder if there is not a relevance in its continued depiction. Is it too fanciful to see her increasingly pessimistic use of Cupid as a conviction that his arrows would never pierce her heart?

It has already been suggested that May returned to Australia with powerful words spoken by prominent suffragette Cicely Hamilton in 1911 still ringing in her ears—'Before your duty to your children, or your duty to your husband comes your duty to yourself'. There seems to have been some intimation in one of May's earlier, full-page cartoons that she would respond to this call. In 1908, 'An old rhyme in a new place' amusingly depicted a modern maid rejecting a suitor with unexpected self-assurance. This full-page, illustrated verse, with its satirising of modern courtship, was a clear indication of May's independent thinking and an honest appraisal of her own (unlikely) matrimonial prospects.

And surely it was significant that May repeatedly referred to herself as an 'old maid' in her letters and notes, and caricatured herself mercilessly, re-creating her unflattering Gibbs family nose, plain features and dumpy figure. Perhaps when this keen eye was turned on herself, it was never blinded to her personal lack of physical appeal. May's clear-sighted sentiments are scattered throughout her papers in the collection of the Mitchell Library, including one that clearly applied to her own position: 'Old Maid come off your dusty shelf … You still may tie the marriage knot … To marry when you're very very old's the fashion now'.

At the same time, it is relevant to consider the influence of one particular marriage, an extremely successful union that was constantly before May's notice. Her parents gave their daughter more than an artistic example to follow. They gave her the example of their own marriage, which set a standard for marital companionship, amiability and compatibility. Late in life, while being recorded by Hazel de Berg for the National Library of Australia in 1968, May recalled that her parents 'were so happy together' that she 'never remember[ed] them falling out', because they 'were such pals'. But their daughter exhibited a determined vision which, even in her childhood,

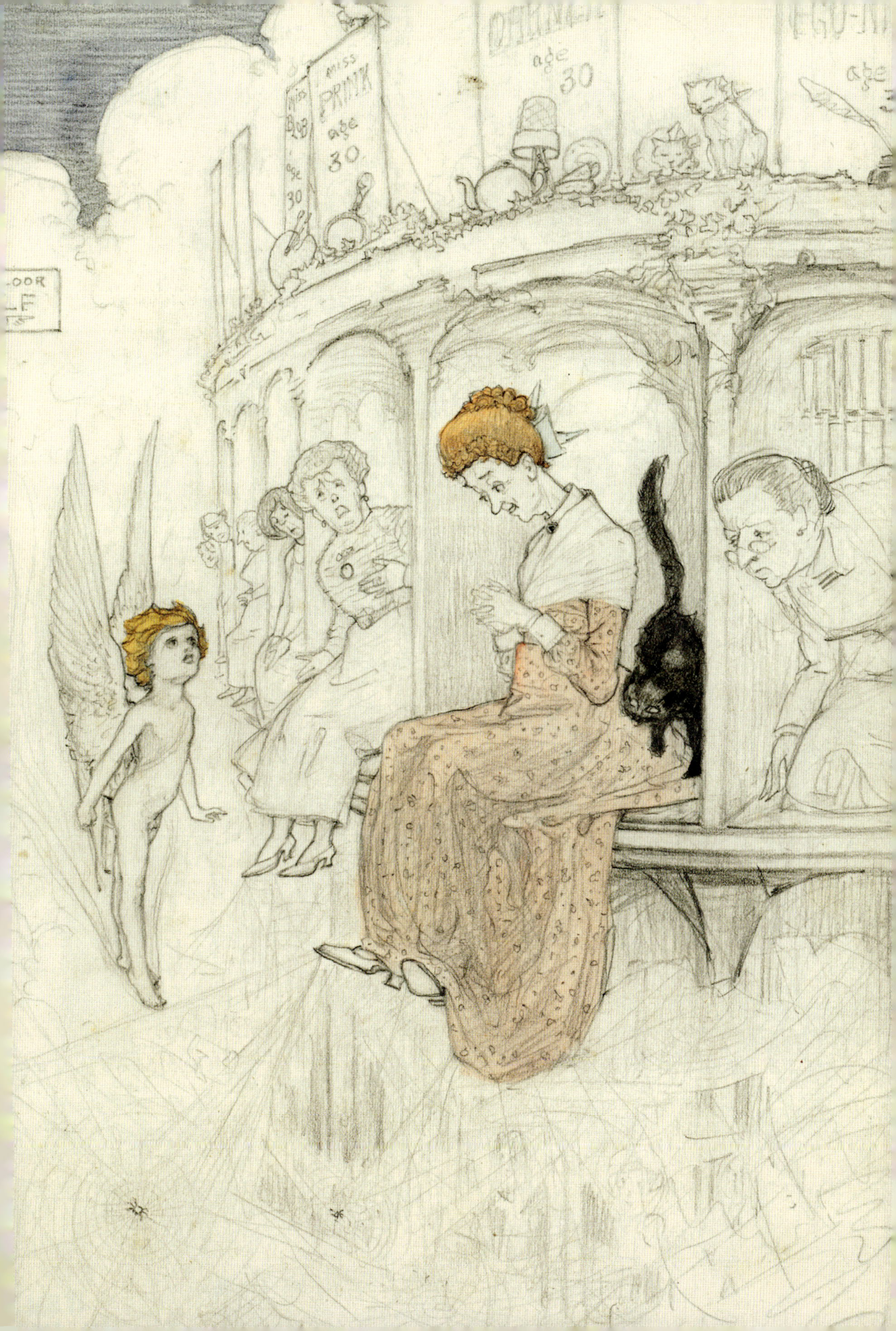
MISS PRINK age 30
age 30
age 30

FACING PAGE: A portrait of JO Kelly, the charming Irishman May married in 1919.

was focused on an independent artistic career. This was coupled with May's appraising artist's eye, which allowed an objective evaluation of her own looks. All of this permitted her to accept, and even use for comic purpose, the notion that she was destined to be an old maid, one who would be left on the shelf herself.

Despite May's feminist sympathies and even, seemingly, a belief that she was destined to remain a spinster, May's life was to change when she met JO Kelly in Perth in April 1918. Irishman James Ossoli (JO) Kelly, a mining agent, was first introduced to May by her father in a letter that suggested him as a potential husband. His impeccable dress sense and intelligent, cultured conversation had clearly impressed Herbert. No doubt after all the years his daughter had remained unmarried, Herbert expected his suggestion to fall on deaf ears. But when May visited Perth in 1918 and they met, JO took an immediate interest in May and a short courtship followed. Exactly a year later, Cupid had pierced her heart and, perhaps to everyone's surprise, including her own, on 17 April 1919 they were wed in a small civil service in Perth. JO returned to Sydney with May and in a rather unusual arrangement they shared a flat with Rene and another of May's close friends, Rachel. With May's successful publishing career dominating their lives, JO happily took over the running of May's business affairs. The perceived duty to oneself, espoused by Cicely Hamilton particularly and by the suffragettes generally, had given May the resolution and the courage to seek independence. It was this outlook that was the making of May Gibbs, the iconic Australian illustrator.

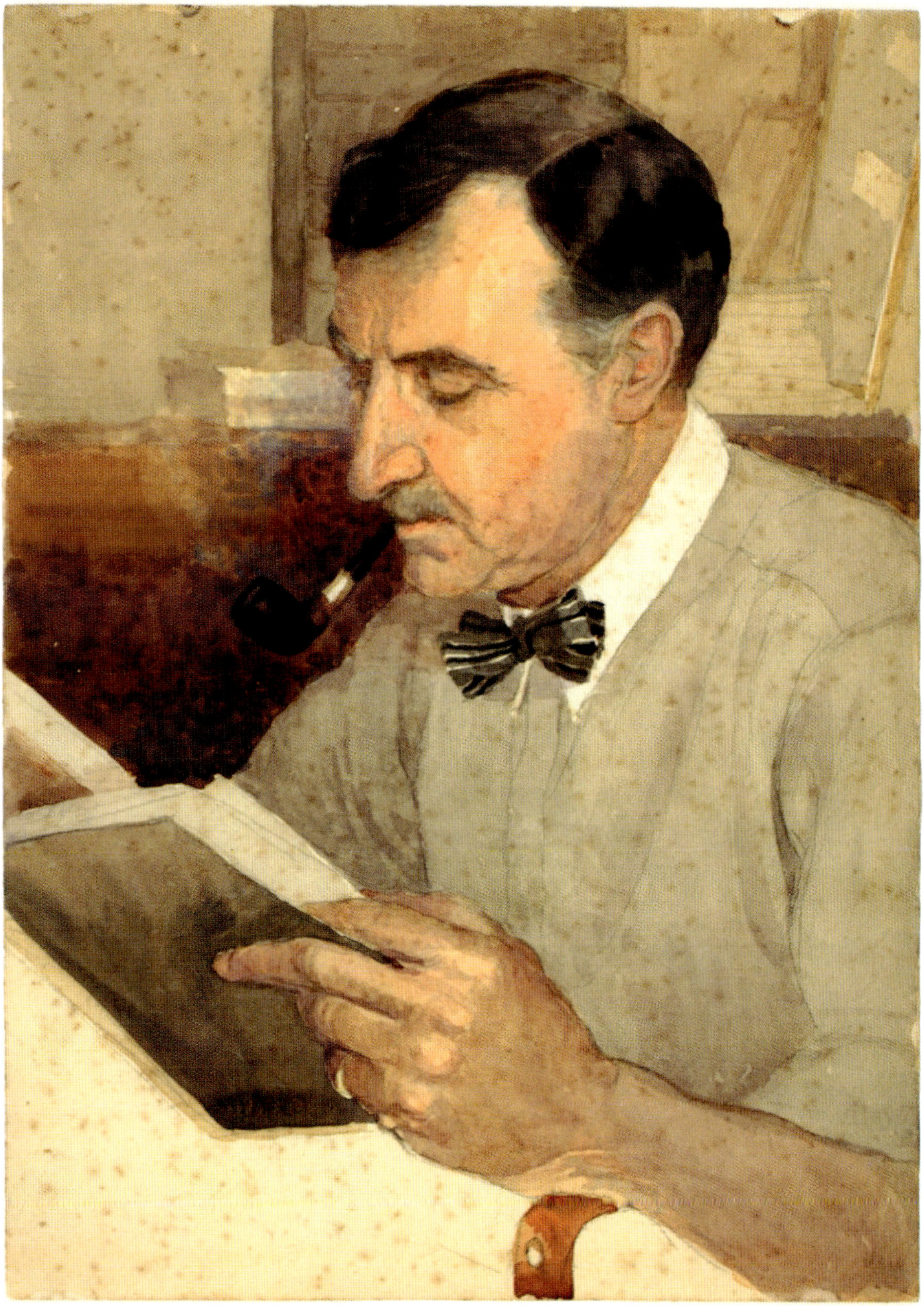

NOT HIS

CHAPTER 15

AUSTRALIA'S BEATRIX POTTER?

It is at the turning point in the life of May Gibbs represented by the publication of her wild-flower baby booklets, that we should turn our eyes back to the childhood years we have invoked in order to see the broader contribution that she made to children's literature.

While colonial expansion made the radical geographical dislocations of May's childhood a not-uncommon experience, what may have helped compensate for such change was a new attitude to children and childhood. Children were no longer seen as dolls or as miniature adults. They were not hidden away in nurseries but were present at family meals and gatherings. Most especially—and May's upbringing certainly illustrated this—their developing characters and interests were taken seriously. This meant that they could be free to lead separate, largely independent lives. For May and her brothers, that meant the freedom to tramp through the Australian bush and swim in its creeks. In short, they had the chance to explore the very environment which their geographical dislocation had offered.

In the imaginative realm as well, these children were also less restricted. Significantly, by the turn of the twentieth century, much children's literature

This watercolour bears an uncanny likeness to JO Kelly—and this could be May accompanying her new husband.

The extended Gibbs family still resided in Perth but many trips were made to Neutral Bay to visit May and her husband.

FACING PAGE: The gumnut adventures continued and was a publishing success rarely seen.

had shed its relation to any wider concerns of life or its self-justification as a source of moral or mystic insight. Perhaps it was simply because adults themselves had become more inclined to playfulness—it has been suggested that they were seeking to perpetuate their own childhoods. What is indisputable is that there was a new sense that life could be more unconfined.

Perhaps for this reason, many of the children's writers in the Edwardian era set their protagonists in an environment that could be described as a lost playground. From Oz in 1900 to Never Land in 1906, and in later creations, this realm became a metaphor for eternal childhood and escapism. And it was during the opening years of the new century that May Gibbs began to envisage an adult role for herself as a creator of children's books.

In January 1901, when Queen Victoria died, jet necklaces were banished along with euphemisms and deference and a high seriousness. The change even extended into the world of children's literature. In one of the most popular children's books of the decade, JM Barrie's *Peter Pan in Kensington Gardens*, there was an extraordinary, even revolutionary, illustration. Arthur Rackham depicted Edward VII saluting the fantastic denizens of the gardens. His royal acknowledgment that they, too, were citizens of his Empire gave an imprimatur to the genre. If the Victorian age championed children's literature as a form in its own right, this illustrative liberty surely set the seal on its legitimacy.

Thereafter, as adults searched for a new mode of behaviour, society seemed to revel in paradoxes. On the one hand, people began talking and thinking, earnestly and frivolously, about sex. At the same time, they celebrated a retreat into animal stories and childlike playfulness. Was some of this due to the fact that many of the new technologies and sciences—automobiles and aeroplanes, sociology and psychology—were also in their infancy? This sense of play was certainly obvious in May's upbringing and early adult years. Her enthusiastic involvement in fancy-dress balls and costume parties was characteristic of the time. Picnics, boating expeditions, party games and elaborate practical jokes were all an extended part of adults playing at forgetting the high seriousness of life. And yet, at the same time, May and other young ladies of her generation required chaperones to accompany them on any overseas trips!

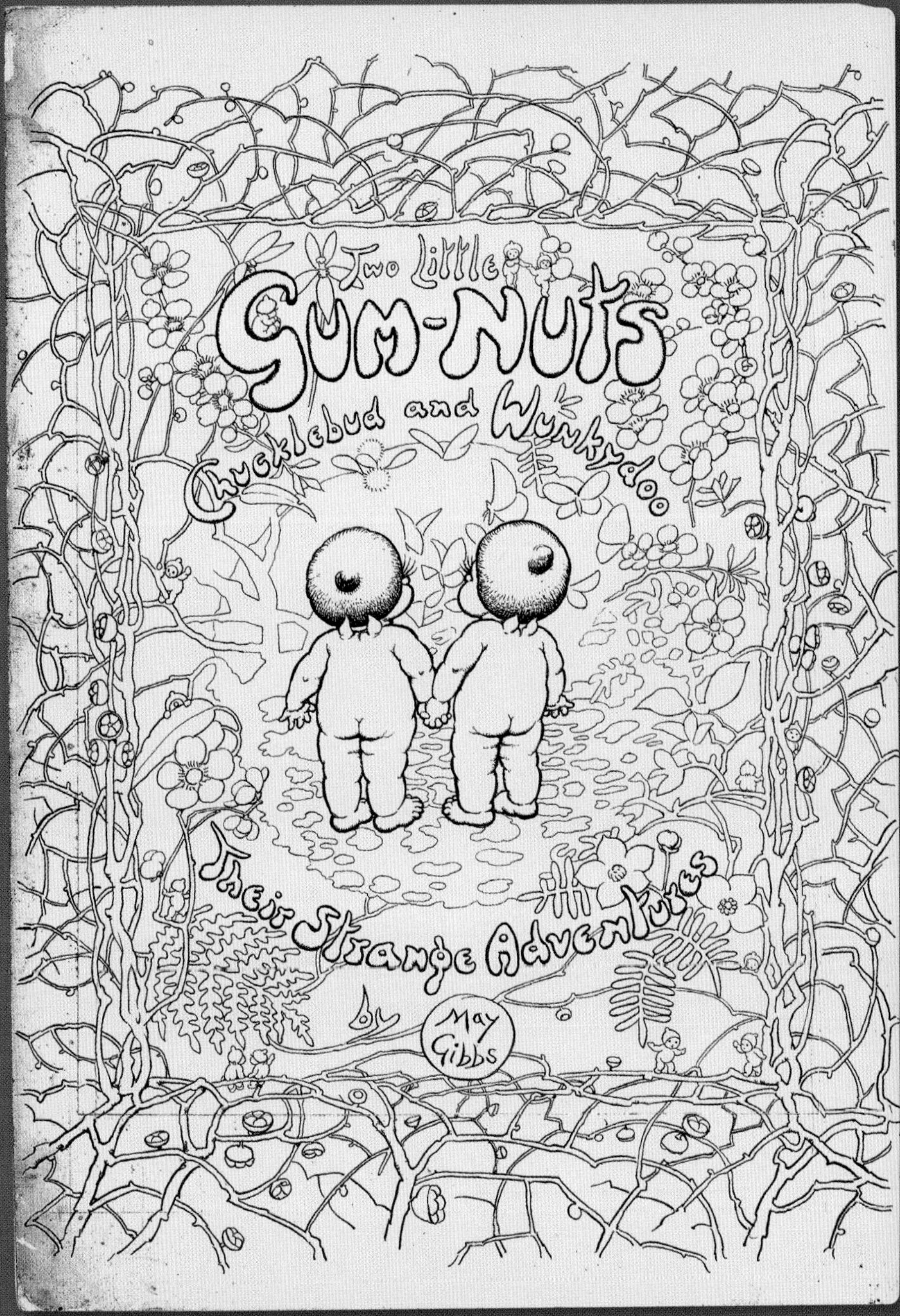
Two Little
Gum-Nuts
Chucklebud and Wunkydoo
Their Strange Adventures
by
May Gibbs

FACING PAGE: The cover illustration for an unpublished book of stories.

These years also ushered in a great age of animal stories—from Kipling's *Just So Stories* in 1902 on to *Doctor Doolittle* in 1920. In these tales, animals were treated as though they were rational and capable of speech, and there was an affirmation of pastoral innocence which encouraged sentiment and anthropomorphism. Kenneth Grahame's 1908 masterpiece *The Wind in the Willows* defined the genre. Its central characters lived in childlike closeness to nature without experiencing true animal savagery or pain.

This was a generation of writers who created make-believe worlds like never before. It has even been suggested by Julia Briggs that this recurring theme was the direct outcome of an adult desire to reform society through the socialist and utopian interests of the era. These writers appealed to an instinct for communion with nature while offering a childlike delight in miniature worlds and rural domesticity. This was complemented by a spate of writing which imagined children constructing their own miniature cities in their nurseries or out of doors, creating them from toys and everyday household objects. These new worlds could then be peopled with fanciful beings who lived in their own alternative societies.

To read May Gibbs' own account of the origins of her miniature world is to see how at one she was with this thinking. 'When I stayed with my cousins in the Bush,' she told *Woman's World* in 1924, 'I amused myself and them by telling stories about the little people I imagined to be there'. These creations 'always took the form of sturdy, common-sense little persons living the same practical busy lives as ants'. May Gibbs spent endless hours observing nature and society, and always travelled with pocket-sized sketchbooks that became diaries in line rather than in word. They were always at hand to capture the defining lineaments, the pose of a figure or the wag of a tail.

So who were May Gibbs' mentors in the world of children's books? In her middle age, May admitted to Mary Marlowe that 'ordinary, conventional fairies with wands and starry crowns never did appeal to her'. She declared that, even in childhood, she had 'rejected the unnatural tinsel and the tawdry spangle in connection with elfland'. More to her taste was the flower-fairy illustration and painting which had become a highly popular and even distinctive genre in the Victorian era, and which would maintain that popularity, under various stylistic guises, until well into the twentieth century. May Gibbs could have derived her attraction to such imagery from a range of sources—from high art to children's book illustration.

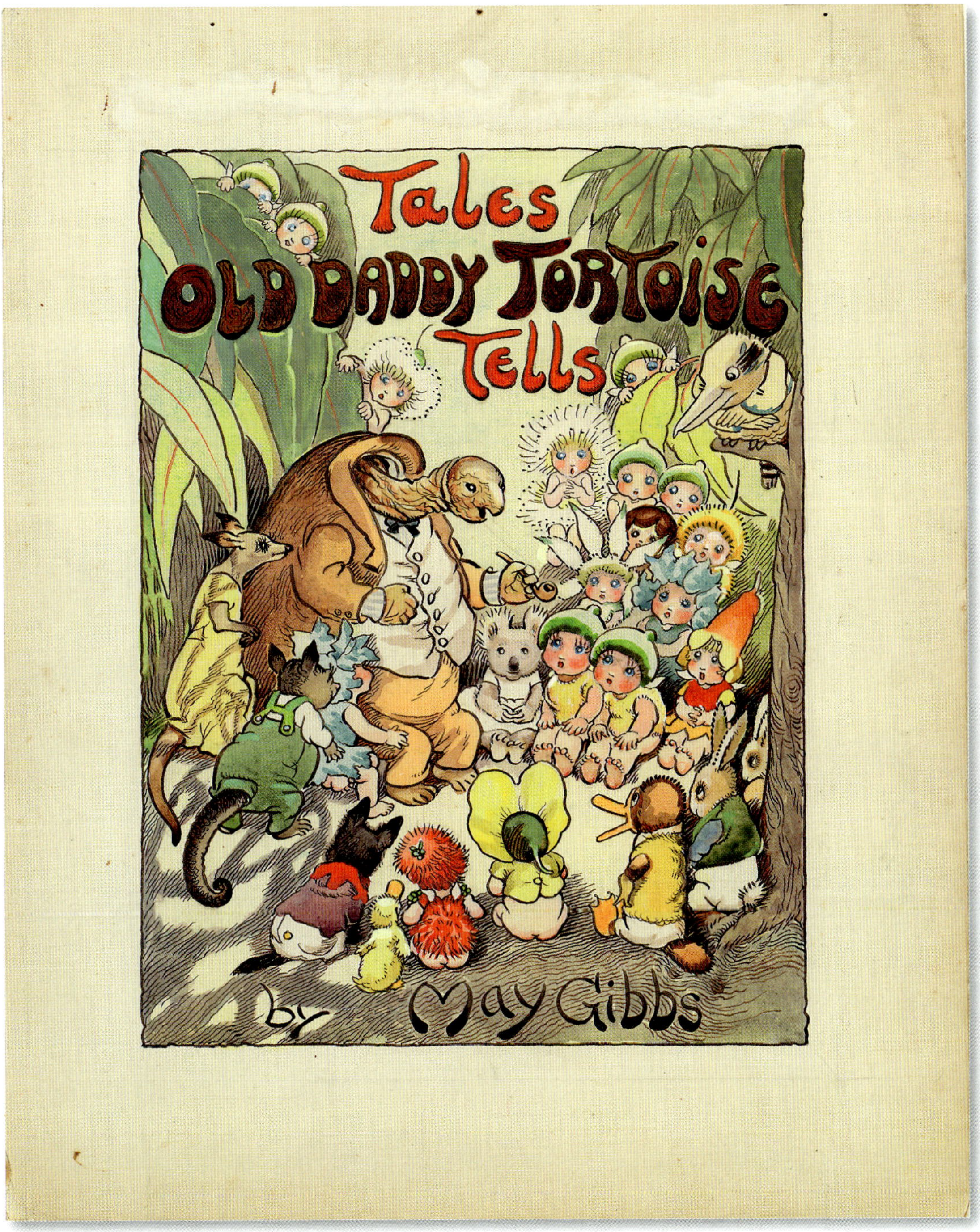
Tales
OLD DADDY TORTOISE
Tells
by
May Gibbs

Costumes and fancy dress were a particularly strong feature of May's work.

Among the host of Victorian book illustrators who were in vogue in the nursery during May's childhood was Walter Crane. Between 1889 and 1906, Crane used classically inspired figures and ornate floral decoration in his illustrations for at least seven major books—from *Flora's Feast* to *Flowers from Shakespeare's Garden*. Perhaps what May took most of all from Crane was his delight and skill in costume design, the way he integrated flowers and characters into a charming amalgam. His flower costumes paraded in all their finery through masques, weddings and feasts.

However, by her own admission May owed her overwhelming allegiance to the work of Crane's contemporary, Randolph Caldecott. It was his less exotic and less academic style, with its sparse decoration and lively characters, which appealed to her rustic upbringing and developing aesthetic. Most importantly, Caldecott drew animals with an easy manner and a comic delight. These were attributes which delighted May throughout her whole life.

An example of Randolph Caldecott's classic illustrations.

In a rare acknowledgment of her sources, May enthused to her publishers about the seminal influence Caldecott had exerted on her: 'I have loved the work & man behind the work since I was a baby'. That affinity carried through into her days of art training in London: 'at the Blackburn School of Black & White … I remember working from some of R. Caldecott's original drawings & feeling greatly excited about it'. It is in this context of British illustrators that the originality and achievement of May Gibbs can best be appreciated. But having cited these predecessors, we are required to ask about those who were her contemporaries.

The work of two other British children's book illustrators is frequently invoked to compare and contrast with that of May Gibbs. They are Margaret Tarrant and Mary Cicely Barker. Tarrant was only just beginning her long association with Harrap in 1913, the year in which May returned to Australia. And it was not until 1923 that Barker published the first of her long series of flower-fairy books, *Flower Fairies of the Spring*. But because May was without any real peer back in Australia, it is within this coterie of illustrators that we can best situate her work.

The five gumnut-baby booklets which May went on to produce between 1916 and 1920 achieved an Australian status that is really only comparable with

FACING PAGE: An unpublished illustration likely to have been produced for a magazine cover.

that of Britain's Beatrix Potter. Some of the parallels between the pair which were specifically evoked almost twenty years ago, merit restatement today:

> Potter's Peter Rabbit and his countryside setting is paralleled by Gibbs' gumnut babies and their bushland world. Initially both Beatrix Potter and May Gibbs favoured modest dimensions for the format of their books and showed a comparable regard for design that made each of their double-page spreads a compact unit. Both used a personal observation of nature to under-pin any flights of fancy—their anthropomorphic creations are not just people in disguise; they display closely observed animal characteristics. In their private lives, coincidentally, both women were also strongly alike. Both found it difficult to break away from a restrictive family circle and establish independent lifestyles and careers, both married late (Potter at forty-seven in 1913 and Gibbs at forty-two in 1919) and both were happy to work in relative isolation. As authors, neither of them spare us the truth about the random perils of the natural world and out of the common objects of their miniature range they created a microcosm of the world. Most significantly, there is a shared felling that the events described continue endlessly below the level of human observation.
>
> Robert Holden

Further parallels in the private lives as well as in the professional careers of these two women can be added. Both had artistic parents who recognised and nurtured their respective daughters' talents, and both girls showed a precocious artistic ability, initially excelling in botanical drawing. Both women had their earliest books rejected by publishers, yet went on to achieve financial independence from their families. And both women used the familiar environments and daily occurrences of their lives to inspire their art and their writing.

In confirmation of the affinity between the two illustrators, there is one final fact to add. Early in their careers, both women were eager to produce books based on the nursery-rhyme format. Potter first proposed such a book to her publishers in 1902, but it was only after her initial phenomenal success, in 1917, that they finally relented and published *Appley Dapply's Nursery Rhymes*. Meanwhile, May Gibbs had been experimenting with the same format. It was as early as 1890, when she was thirteen years old, that she first tried her hand at this format, producing a fifteen-page, handmade version of *Jack and Jill*. This was the year after a double-page of May's drawings had been published in the *W. A. Bulletin*. No doubt this first accolade of published recognition encouraged May to extend herself to a more ambitious project.

Poor Mother

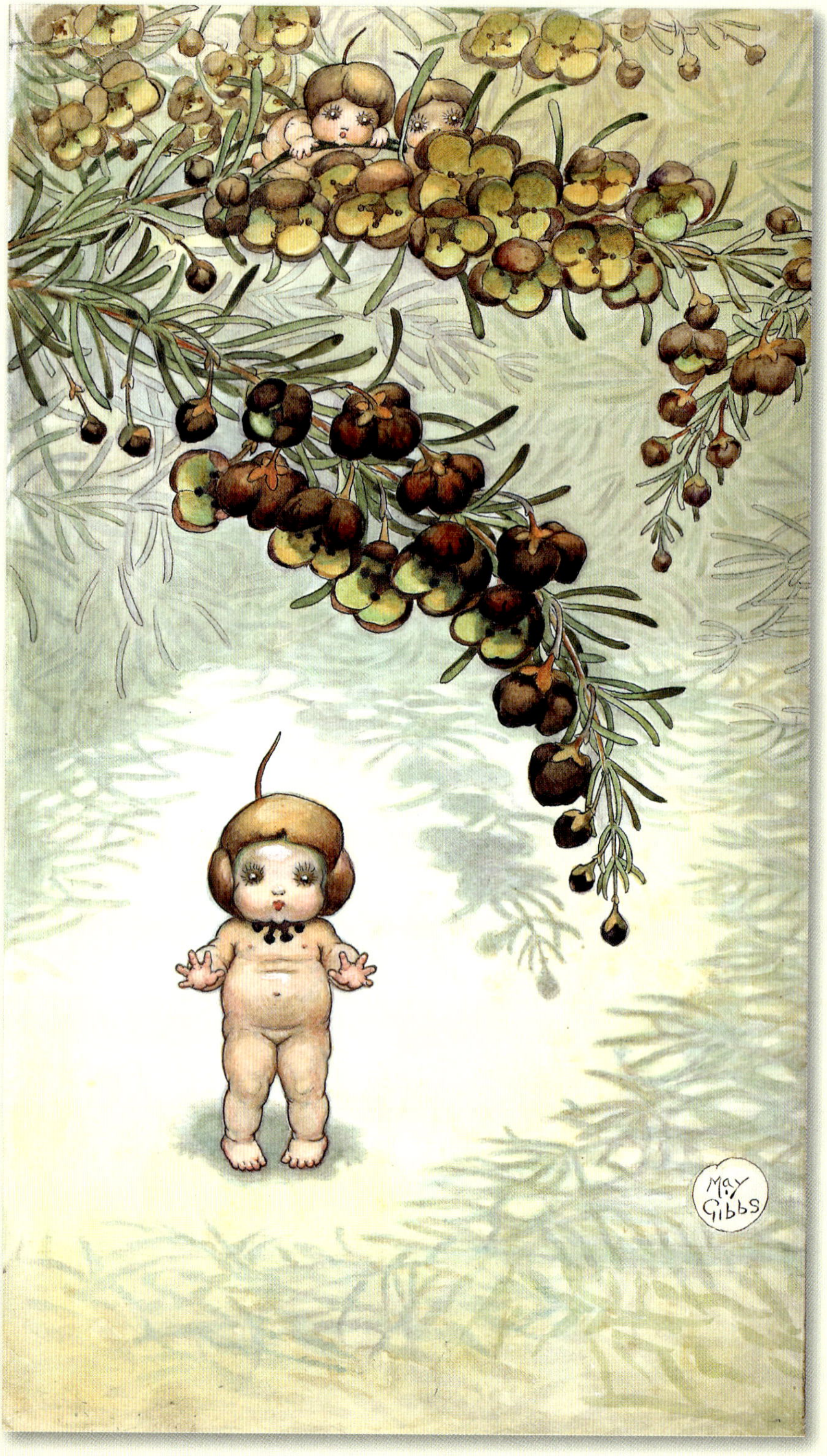
May
Gibbs

Between 1906 and 1908, May compiled a similar handmade book, this one inspired by a cousin. *Win: The Key to All Hearts* was an infinitely more ambitious project: a hand-bound album of fifteen large, oblong, ink and watercolour drawings complete with an illustrated cover. The advances May had made in sophistication and technique were obvious. This time the text was a typescript and the illustrations were highly detailed, finished works. Their spirited style was complemented by the illustrator's obvious delight in depicting costume, all of it enlivened with a clever variety of situations and characters. Typically, however, all the skill lay in the illustrations—the text was weak and hardly did justice to the finished artwork.

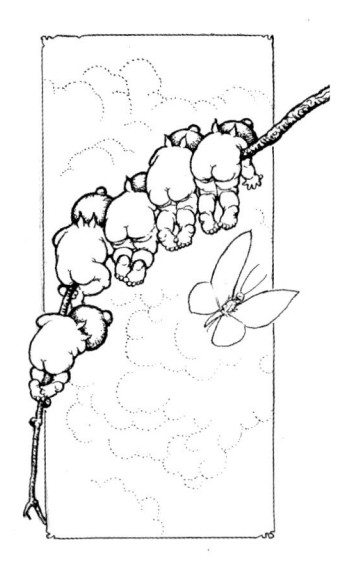

May's final and most ambitious (and, again, unsuccessful) attempt at a format which attracted both her and Beatrix Potter was produced around 1909: *Nursery Rhymes from the Bush*. Unfortunately, the work had an ambiguous audience appeal: as a children's book, its sentiments were too sophisticated; as an adult's book, its large, illustrated format would never have made it a saleable proposition for Australian publishers. Today, the value of these failed publishing attempts is obvious. They allow us an insight into the evolving styles and thought processes May Gibbs explored as she sought to find her own voice and her own individual graphic style.

In 1928, there was an addenda to this shared delight in nursery rhymes. May and her husband James went on one of their many camping trips together in the Australian countryside. They were accompanied by Rene and her husband, Joe Sullivan, whom she had married in 1921. Rene later gave a copy of Potter's *Appley Dapply's Nursery Rhymes* to May, having inscribed it with the words 'with thanks for a jolly holiday'.

Uncovering these early years of May Gibbs has uncovered many affinities with Beatrix Potter. To evaluate May in such company is an appropriate accolade, and it is one that she herself would have welcomed.

FACING PAGE: The front-cover illustration for *Boronia Babies*.

This book opened with an evaluation of a famous poster that May Gibbs created. Thereafter, we saw how her experiences as a propaganda artist for women's suffrage were extended into a series of Australian postcards in 1914. In both spheres, these propaganda works were for a war effort, albeit on different sorts of battle fronts. But they saw their ultimate expression in 1920, the year in which May Gibbs' largest artistic work and her most celebrated and recognisable image was produced. This was the colour lithographic poster which she produced for the New South Wales Department of Public Health to promote the first Baby Week held in the state, from 28 March to 1 April.

This poster was the culmination of all the inspiration and experience of the preceding decade. The propagandist message it voiced was perhaps even more impassioned than that which May had raised for the suffragettes in London a decade earlier. By closing our book with a restatement, and an amplification, of this iconic image after having used it as our opening gambit is to come full circle. And, considering that May's signature by this stage was her well-known name boldly enclosed within a circle, this seems singularly appropriate.

After energising support for the suffragette cause and then enriching Australia's sentiment and pride in their gumnut corps, May Gibbs turned her eyes to a third battle front in 1920. She answered a call to arms in *The Lone Hand* which had been sounded in as rousing and patriotic a voice as anything that had been heard in World War I: 'Is the race that bred the heroes of Gallipoli and Amiens to decline like ancient Rome?'

This was no mere alarmist exaggeration but a sobering reaction to another statistic of the war: Australia had lost 50,000 men and countless more had been maimed and debilitated. 'To make matters infinitely worse,' *The Lone Hand* proclaimed, 'there were probably the same number of fine babies permitted to die in Australia during the period of the war … but without the publicity of casualty lists and honour rolls'. New South Wales was to lead the charge in this new battle with a statewide Baby Week and a Mothercraft and Child Welfare exhibition in Sydney's Town Hall.

There was an urgent need for a 'recruiting' poster, one that would enlist the mothers of Australia as the war front was relocated to the nurseries of their nation. There were new enemies to be faced—'disease, lack of baby care facilities and, above all, ignorance', it was stated in *Voices*—if Australian mothers were to be enlisted as nation builders. The poster May Gibbs created in response to this need was such an instant success that a smaller version was immediately called for to display in ferries and on hoardings— anywhere that might catch the public eye. By the time the major offensive of this campaign was launched at Sydney's Mothercraft exhibition, May's propaganda had conquered all. The exhibition's souvenir program was issued with her image on its cover 'in view of the numerous requests for copies of the stork and kookaburra poster'.

And the popularity of this iconic image did not end there. When the New South Wales Department of Public Health first issued its handbook for mothers in 1931, this image, which had retained its appeal and status for over a decade, was used as the cover illustration. To almost the whole of the following generation of young Australians, it became an abiding presence in their nurseries. Up to 1959, over one million copies in thirty-three editions were printed.

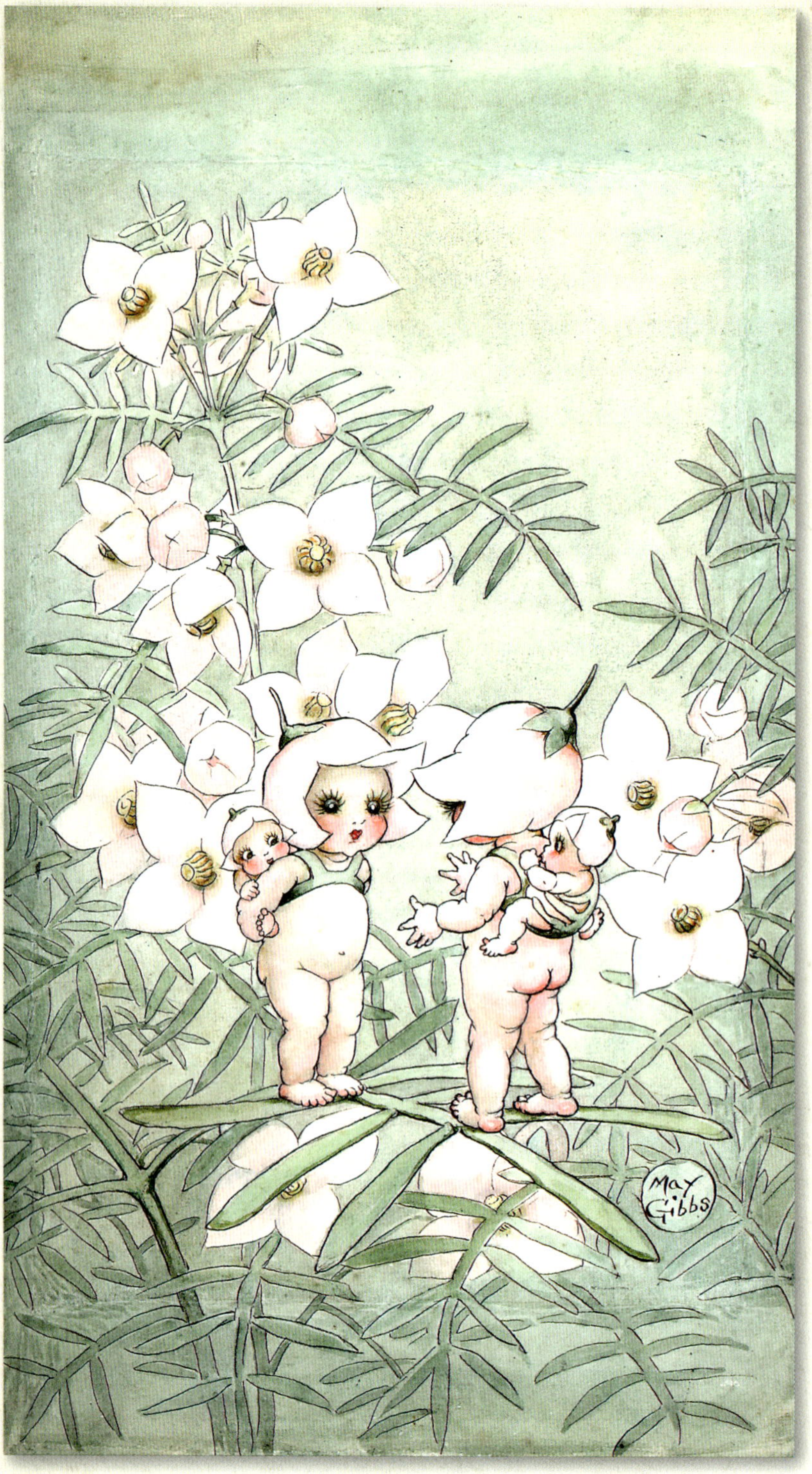
May Gibbs

POSTSCRIPT

Today, almost a century after May Gibbs created the gumnut babies, her popularity is as great as ever. One can only wonder what May would have made of a significant recent accolade—a royal baby being presented with a rare and highly valued first edition of one of her books. In October 2005, on the birth of their first son, Crown Prince Frederik of Denmark and his Australian-born wife, Princess Mary, were given a mint copy of the 1918 printing of *Tales of Snugglepot and Cuddlepie* as an official gift from the people of Australia. This honour was surely the culmination of the acclaim for May Gibbs, which had grown particularly over the previous twenty years. Throughout these years, some highly significant events had corroborated the hold which May Gibbs' fantasy world had achieved on the Australian consciousness.

From December 1984 until January 1985, the first ever major exhibition devoted to May's original illustrations was staged in Sydney's Royal Botanic Gardens. This exhibition, curated by Robert Holden, and containing works lent by the Mitchell Library, attracted a remarkable audience of over 120,000 people. The demand thereafter for further exposure resulted in three similar exhibitions from the same curator: in the Adelaide Botanic Gardens in February 1986, in the Melbourne Botanic Gardens throughout

November and December 1987, and, the culminating event, the Gumnut Town exhibition from April to June 1992, again held in Sydney's Royal Botanic Gardens.

This all added a significant impetus to the campaign to preserve Nutcote, May's home in Sydney's Neutral Bay, which was finally opened to the public on 1 May 1994. The house had been designed and built for May, and she had worked in its dedicated studio from 1925 until her death in 1969. Today, thanks to the indefatigable Nutcote Trust, the property is achieving a status somewhat comparable with Beatrix Potter's Hilltop estate in the English Lake District. In the process, however, it may appear to West Australians that May Gibbs has been unduly claimed by New South Wales. If, indeed, this rivalry did ever exist, then hopefully this new biography rebalances the equation by revealing the hidden picture of May Gibbs' life—that of the many formative years which were spent in Western Australia.

Nevertheless, there is some justification for the eastern state to take some credit for May's achievements. Her arrival in New South Wales in 1913 consolidated her vision, confirmed her unique talents and launched her Australia-wide fame. That state's claim rests on the timing of her arrival, which occurred on the very eve of World War I. Thereafter, in wartime Australia, May's sustained output of patriotic ephemera created something unique. As one contemporary newspaper noted, the 'boys in the trenches' were keenly appreciative of her work. This established her characters in the minds of a highly appreciative audience—an audience that became eager for further gumnut antics, which were soon to follow in more substantial booklets.

It is in this context, one of adult appreciation in wartime, that May Gibbs' covers and postcards should be evaluated and seen as part of a burgeoning appreciation of Australiana generally. In the wider scene, there was the welcome circulation of boomerang-shaped cards by various anonymous artists. These were used to invoke an unmistakable message: wishing the boys a safe return back home. There were gumleaf-shaped cards—some even had actual, fragrant gumleaves pasted onto them. All were evocative reminders of a distant homeland. This was an Australia creating its own proud and distinctive pictorial propaganda—warm, sentimental and startlingly at odds with the image of the knockabout Anzac soldier.

May's gentle appeal was, of course, equally felt by Australian women. One such enthusiast was the noted Australian writer Miles Franklin, who at the time of May's rise to prominence was also achieving international fame. She purchased May's booklets from an Australian bookshop on The Strand in 1919 and, writing to Australia from London, attested to the international spread which May's work had quickly attained. 'The gum nut and gum blossom fairies are adorable', she declared.

Franklin maintained her enthusiasm. The following year, in a full column in the *Sydney Morning Herald*, she amplified her comments, confessing that she had bought complete sets of the gumnut booklets as Christmas presents and that these were for adult friends who were not Australian. It is significant that these friends were also wholehearted in their appreciation of this transplanted Australiana. A year later, Franklin was still praising May's work. She wrote to Angus & Robertson itself to commend Gibbs' ongoing publication, declaring that she 'could find no book ... to approach Snugglepot and Cuddlepie so far as workmanship was concerned, and [that] Miss Gibbs' illustrations are a joy to me'.

Today, May is consistently remembered and honoured for her contribution to the folklore and literature of Australian children. The fact that most of her earliest work, from the 1890s up to the five wild-flower booklets, was primarily addressed to an adult audience has largely been forgotten or misinterpreted. Recently, however, two of the most authoritative surveys of Australian book publishing and illustration tried to reinstate May's broader audience appeal. Anita Callaway reminded us that May's covers for *The Lone Hand* were for a magazine that 'was clearly not directed at children', nor 'were the hand-painted bookmarks ... the series of booklets that followed, nor the profusion of World War I postcards'. An even more adamant opinion was asserted by Martyn Lyons and John Arnold. It held that the 'Gumnut Babies [and its four sequels] were not specifically intended for a child audience but were rather a kind of expanded greeting card, often sent overseas to troops appreciative of redolently Australian scenes'.

And yet, despite all this, the work of May Gibbs seems destined to remain anchored in the realm of classic children's literature. In other words, according to Lyons and Arnold, like 'so many other children's "classics," a child audience took them over within a generation'.

212

Yet there is one last comparison, that emphasises May Gibbs' dual audience appeal: one that situates May's work within the theatrical experience of the earlier life which we have uncovered; one that appreciates and ponders the stage atmosphere of her illustrations, with their 'pantomimic costumes and music-hall head dresses ... rambunctious happenings entirely located in the foreground and innocently enacted by tumbling putti or mock coy chanteuses (depending on one's point of view)'; one that credits this duality of vision by locating these illustrations within the evolving artistic milieu of Sydney in the early twentieth-century war years. This comparison notes that 'May Gibbs and Norman Lindsay were contemporaries and that the innocent world of the naked gumnuts was created at a time when Lindsay was first introducing his buxom, naked courtesans and bacchanalian revellers to an adult audience'.

Surely a new assessment is overdue, one that credits May Gibbs with producing something unique, as Bronwen Handyside has asserted—'the closest thing to a native Australian mythology that white Australia has ever achieved'. This assessment acknowledges that her gumnut babies and their allies (and enemies) have entered the language and imagination of generations of Australians, that they have become synonymous with an Australian sense of identity and self-image.

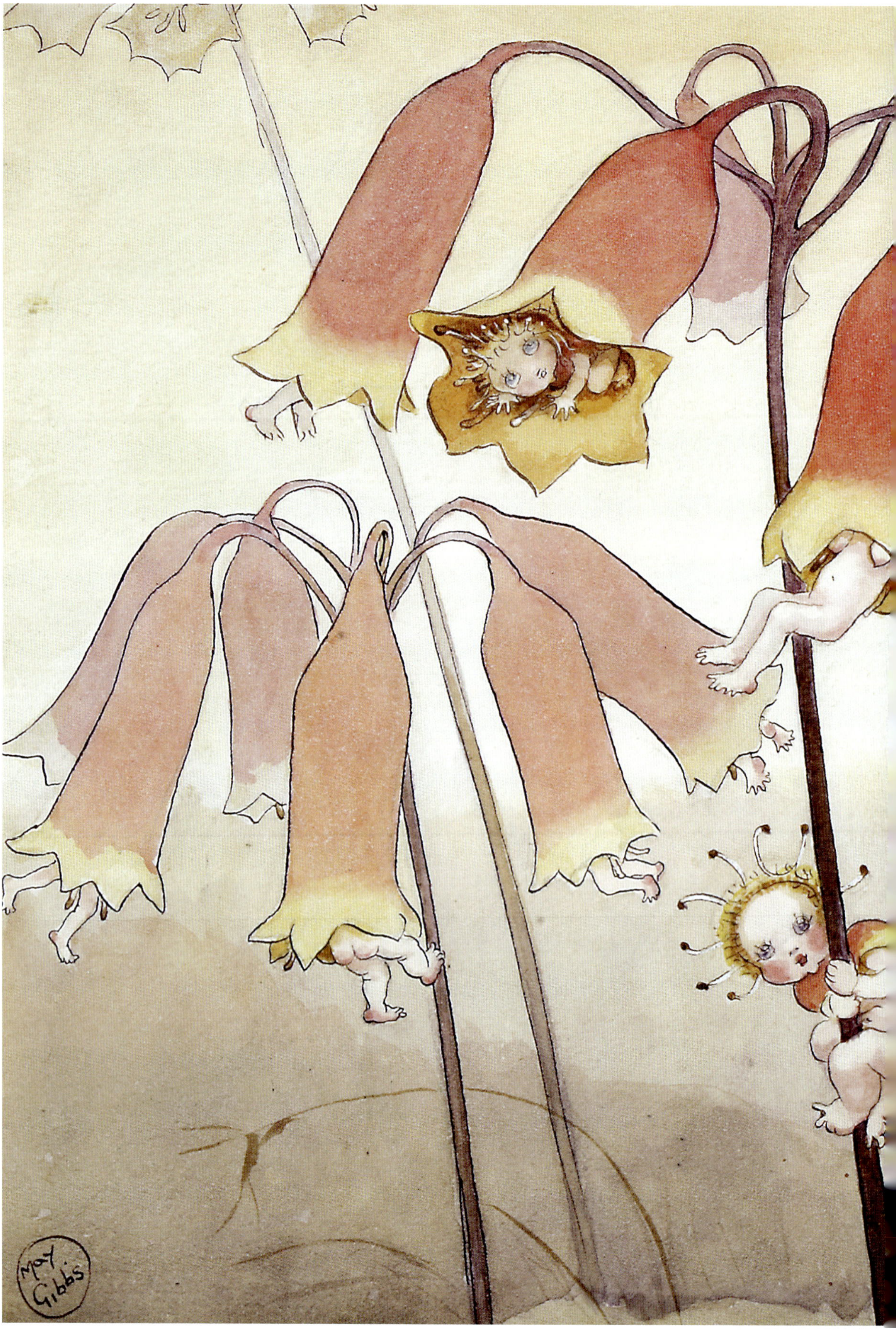
May Gibbs

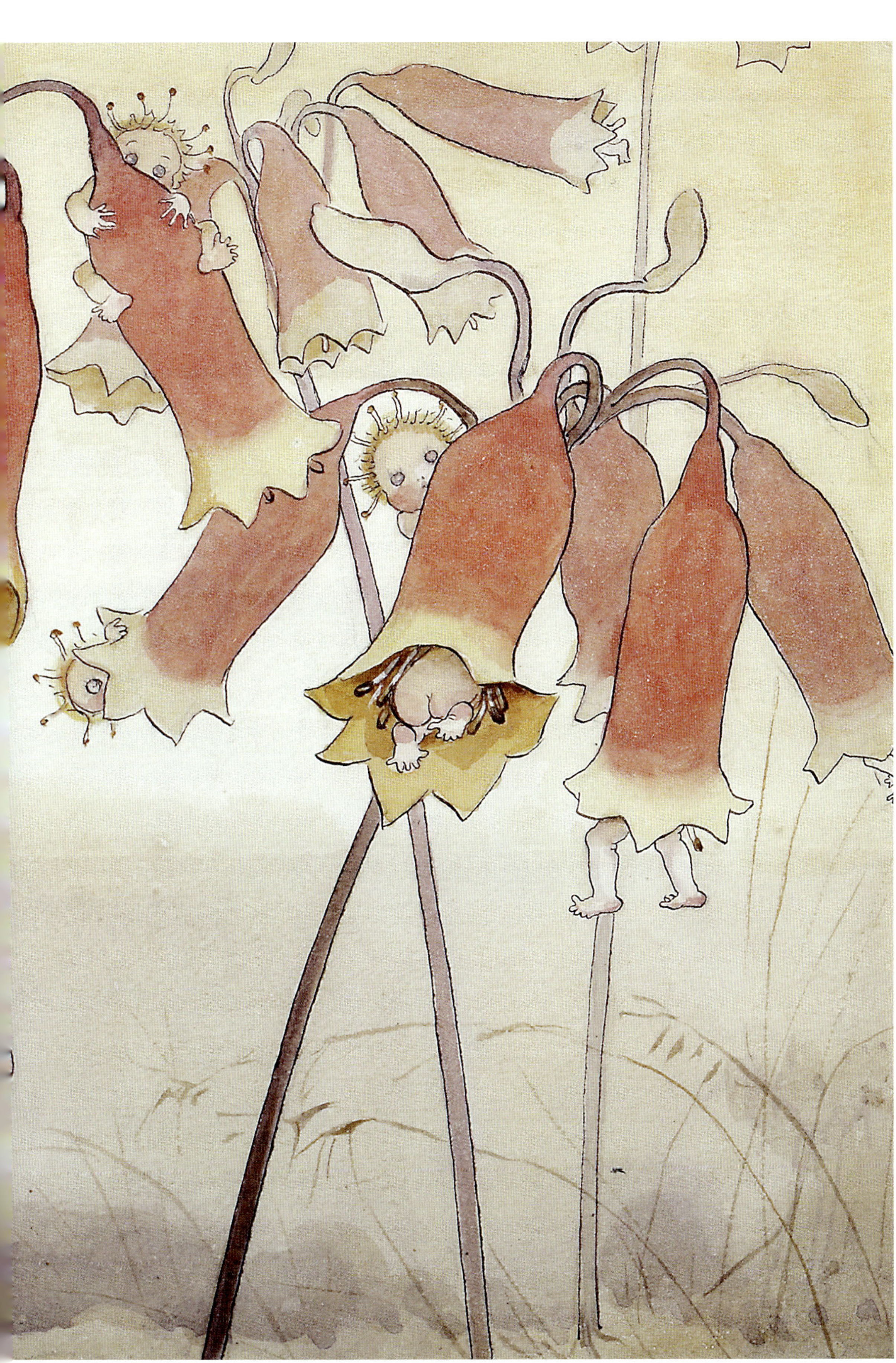

A NOTE FROM ROBERT HOLDEN

I would like to acknowledge the unstinting support which the Nutcote Trust gave to this project, most particularly the sustained interest and informed opinion of Yvonne Hyde, AO. Equally valuable was the assistance of Ian Hoskins, the Local History Librarian at North Sydney's Stanton Library.

As always, colleagues in various libraries have given both professional help and creative support to my research. I especially acknowledge the staff of the Mitchell Library (State Library of New South Wales), the La Trobe Library (State Library of Victoria), the National Library of Australia and the State Libraries of Queensland and Western Australia.

The research of Juliana Bayfield and Jane Brummitt was invaluable, in particular the laborious work of unearthing a wealth of May Gibbs' contributions to newspapers.

My thanks go to Philip Comans and Sean Linkson, who generously invited me into their beachside haven to complete the final chapters in a sublime space.

Finally, I trust that my long friendship with Neil and Marian Shand is complimented by this biography of their 'cousin May'.

A NOTE FROM JANE BRUMMITT

I have been under the spell of May Gibbs all my life.

The captivation owes much to my family connection with her. My father's sister, Josephine Porter, married May's brother, Ivan Gibbs. Ivan was the only one of the Gibbs siblings to have children—Elizabeth May Parker (nee Gibbs) and Ken and John Gibbs. They lived in Perth and I grew up in Adelaide.

As a child I read and reread May's books and chuckled over May's comic strips. I loved her wide-ranging art and sense of humour. She shaped my view of the Australian bush and her Banksia Men terrified me.

In the 1940s, when Josephine and Ivan visited Adelaide, I listened spellbound to their tales of May at Nutcote. Later I stayed with them in Perth and marvelled at works by 'the genius', as they called her.

In 1987 I joined the May Gibbs Foundation when I heard about its goal of saving Nutcote from developers. The catalysts for this brilliant idea were Dr Neil Shand and his wife Marian, and heritage architect John Wood and his wife Helen.

This book's origins grew from an exhibition at the State Library of South Australia in 1991, in support of the South Australian Action Group of the May Gibbs Foundation initiated by Dr Christobel Mattingley. Juliana Bayfield (now Archbold), librarian for the Children's Literature Research Collection, exhibited May's political newspaper cartoons not seen since publication, along with oil paintings, books and postcards held by the library and private individuals. The exhibition proved to be one of the most popular the library had ever mounted and inspired further exhibitions. May's relative by marriage, June Bowman, initiated one at the Glyde Gallery in Perth with the support of John, Sara and Ken Gibbs. Artist and writer, Elizabeth Honey organised another at the Westpac Gallery in Melbourne and when Nutcote was opened to the public in January 1992, May's newspaper cartoons were displayed in Sydney for the first time. In 1997 I began as a volunteer at the State Library of South Australia to further the research Juliana had started. Juliana and I both received generous support from Marcie Muir, bibliographer and authority on both May Gibbs and Australian children's literature.

Without the close friendship and perspectives of my cousins Elizabeth, Ken and John Gibbs, this book would never have materialised. Our mutual aunt, Teresa Porter, also added her memories from the 1940s, and in the extended Gibbs family, Sara, Genevieve, Julie and Bronte Gibbs also provided help.

I appreciate the vast archive and dedicated assistance provided by the Mitchell Library staff. Marian Shand, who assisted in cataloguing the collection, is the relative who knew May best towards the end of her life and was generously hospitable while sharing her insights.

Yvonne Hyde—Nutcote's volunteer archivist, guide, gardener and imaginative editor of the *Nutcote News*—provided invaluable knowledge, support and help. Other friends met through Nutcote include Norma Perry and Marion Shaw and Nan Albinski.

At the Stanton Library in North Sydney staff members were extremely helpful particularly the work of retired librarian Jean Hart.

In Perth at the JS Battye Library of West Australian History, staff member Sue Osmond located the only known copy of May's first published work in its original context.

Help from West Australian relatives and contacts were invaluable. My cousin June Bowman and her husband Brian took me to meet Len Knight, son of Winifred Gibbs. Len showed us the site of the former Harvey River Station. My cousin Theone Pyle located valuable missing details from the Battye library and Dr Michael McCarthy put me in touch with PhD scholar Noreen Riordan. At Heritage House where South Perth's May Gibbs collection is held, curator Dr Christine Sharkey's scholarship and enthusiasm for the work of both May and Herbert Gibbs was inspirational. Towards the final stage of the book Rhee Juhasz and Jenna Lynch at Heritage House made their entire collection available to us. For their support and help with photography I thank Jocelyn Southgate and Kevin and Chris Hussey.

At the Claremont Historical Society, staff and volunteers kindly shared information and Elizabeth Dyer located a diary entry from her relatives, the Bird family, who were friends of the Gibbs. My cousin Margaret Brinsden showed me the Butler's Swamp site, and original wild-flower paintings at the Royal West Australian Historical Society. Staff there were also supportive. Ailsa Smith showed me a letter written by May's father to his artistic friend HC Prinsep in 1908.

At the State Library of South Australia, in addition to Juliana's initiatives, Valerie Sitters provided help through the Royal Geographical Society (South Australia). Other South Australians also helped. Fleur de Laine, a relative on May's mother's side of the family, generously shared her knowledge. Mitcham local historian Maggy Ragless located information about where May first stayed in Adelaide. In Cowell Enid Rehn and Colleen Beinke showed me the site of the Gibbs brothers' farm, and Councillor Bruce Francis who took us to see Ullabidnie Creek, sketched by Herbert Gibbs in 1881. Norwood local historian Beth Brittle and Burnside librarian Andrew Ward helped identify where the Gibbs family had lived in Adelaide.

My deepest thanks goes to my husband Bob. Not only did he wholeheartedly support the saving of Nutcote, but on retiring he supported me and my belief that May's work was much more than a fairytale and deserved to be better known.

ILLUSTRATIONS

i   Wattle babies: May Gibbs. State Library of New South Wales.
ii   Gumnut babies: May Gibbs. State Library of New South Wales.
v   Handkerchief design: May Gibbs. State Library of New South Wales.

INTRODUCTION
vi   Self portrait: May Gibbs c.1917. State Library of New South Wales.
ix   Poster commissioned by the Department of Public Health: May Gibbs 1920. State Library of New South Wales
xi   Flannel flower babies: May Gibbs. State Library of New South Wales.
xii   Portrait of Irene 'Rene' Heames: May Gibbs. State Library of New South Wales.
xiv   Gumnut babies: May Gibbs. State Library of New South Wales.

CHAPTER 1
xvi   Detail of 'Gander Green Lane, Sutton, Surrey': May Gibbs 1900. May and Herbert Gibbs Collection, City of South Perth.
2   Herbert Gibbs 1909. Private Collection.
3   Gumnut babies: May Gibbs. State Library of New South Wales.
4   Gum blossom babies: May Gibbs. State Library of New South Wales.
5   Photograph of Herbert's yacht. Private collection.
6   Gumnut boats: May Gibbs. May and Herbert Gibbs Collection, City of South Perth.
7   'South coast [England] fishing boats, evening': Herbert Gibbs. May and Herbert Gibbs Collection, City of South Perth.
8   Gumnut babies: May Gibbs. State Library of New South Wales.
9   Herbert Gibbs 1918. May and Herbert Gibbs Collection, City of South Perth.
11   'At South Perth': Herbert Gibbs c.1919. May and Herbert Gibbs Collection, City of South Perth.

CHAPTER 2
12   Detail of 'Near the Harvey Station': May Gibbs 1899. May and Herbert Gibbs Collection, City of South Perth.
15   'May Gibbs, Reading Dicken's 'Bleak House'': Herbert Gibbs 1889. May and Herbert Gibbs Collection, City of South Perth.
16   Gum blossom babies: May Gibbs. State Library of New South Wales.
17   Unpublished illustration for *Mimie and Wag*: May Gibbs. State Library of New South Wales.
18   Banksia Man: May Gibbs. State Library of New South Wales.
19   Card: May Gibbs 1886. May and Herbert Gibbs Collection, City of South Perth.
20   Photograph of Herbert and Cecie Gibbs by Henry C. Prinsep 1905. Private collection.
22   Gum blossom babies: May Gibbs. State Library of New South Wales.
23   Illustration: May Gibbs. State Library of New South Wales.
24   'The Dune': Herbert Gibbs. May and Herbert Gibbs Collection, City of South Perth.
25   Portrait of Herbert Gibbs: May Gibbs 1923. State Library of New South Wales.

CHAPTER 3
26   'The Gum Blossom Ballet': May Gibbs. State Library of New South Wales.
28   'Myself': May Gibbs 1903. State Library of New South Wales.
29   Photograph Gibbs family. Private collection.
30   Wild flowers: May Gibbs. State Library of New South Wales.
31   'Studio door: at the Dune' South Perth: Herbert Gibbs c.1925–9. May and Herbert Gibbs Collection, City of South Perth.
32   Wild flowers: May Gibbs. State Library of New South Wales.
33   Wild flowers: May Gibbs. State Library of New South Wales.
34   Illustration: May Gibbs. State Library of New South Wales.
35   Illustration: May Gibbs 1891 and Private collection; Illustration: Kate Greenaway.
36   Boronia Babies: May Gibbs. State Library of New South Wales.
37   Dedication: May Gibbs 1920. Private collection.

CHAPTER 4
38 'May Gibbs in the Gondoliers' by Henry C. Princep 1892. May and Herbert Gibbs Collection, City of South Perth.
40 Photograph of Cecie and Herbert Gibbs at The Dune. Private Collection.
41 Portrait of Cecie Gibbs: May Gibbs 1909. May and Herbert Gibbs Collection, City of South Perth.
42 Detail from illustration: May Gibbs. State Library of New South Wales.
43 (Top) 'Brother, Harold Gibbs with Violin': May Gibbs 1894. May and Herbert Gibbs Collection, City of South Perth. (Below) 'Brother: Ivan Gibbs': May Gibbs 1894. May and Herbert Gibbs Collection, City of South Perth.
44 'Funny little topknot; pen practice on Mother': May Gibbs 1902. May and Herbert Gibbs Collection, City of South Perth.
45 Photograph of May Gibbs 1900. State Library of New South Wales.
46 Watercolour of South Perth: Herbert Gibbs. May and Herbert Gibbs Collection, City of South Perth.
47 Flower babies: May Gibbs. State Library of New South Wales.
48 Wild flowers: May Gibbs. State Library of New South Wales.
50 'At the zoo': May Gibbs 1903, *Spectator*, 20 June 1903, p. 10.
52 'Sketches at the Royal Agricultural Show': May Gibbs. *Western Mail*, 31 October 1908, p.28.
53 Illustration: May Gibbs. State Library of New South Wales.

CHAPTER 5
54 'From Betsie': May Gibbs. State Library of New South Wales.
56 'From life (from mother)': May Gibbs 1898. State Library of New South Wales.
58 Gum blossom babies: May Gibbs. State Library of New South Wales.
59 'Ships': Herbert Gibbs. May and Herbert Gibbs Collection, City of South Perth.
60 Detail of 'Some impressions of the ball': May Gibbs. *Western Mail*, 21 July 1906, p. 23.
61 Photograph of May Gibbs by Henry C. Princep 1906. Private collection.
62 'Shipping in Fremantle harbour': May Gibbs, *Western Mail*, 25 December 1906, p.16.
64 Sketch books: May Gibbs. State Library of New South Wales.
65 Sketch books: May Gibbs. State Library of New South Wales.
66 Postcards: May Gibbs 1909. May and Herbert Gibbs Collection, City of South Perth.
67 Handmade card: May Gibbs. May and Herbert Gibbs Collection, City of South Perth.
69 'In Tipton Sussex': May Gibbs 1905. May and Herbert Gibbs Collection, City of South Perth.
71 Manufacturing Hall, Paris Exhibition 1900.

CHAPTER 6
72 'Chelsea School of Art': May Gibbs 1903. State Library of New South Wales.
74 Illustration: May Gibbs. State Library of New South Wales.
75 'The Society of Gumnut Artists': May Gibbs. State Library of New South Wales.
76 Bon Marche fashion illustration: May Gibbs. *Morning Herald*, 31 October, 1902, p. 2.
77 Alice Hadfield: May Gibbs. State Library of New South Wales.
78 'Sketches from a Perth Sketch Book', *Western Mail* 1906.
79 Details from 'Tennis champions and some others': May Gibbs. *Western Mail* 22 September 1906, p. 23 and 'Some variations of a prominent cricketer and a few other brilliant players': May Gibbs. *Western Mail*, 30 March 1907, p. 28.
81 'The Bonnievale Mining Disaster.': May Gibbs. *Western Mail*, 30 March, 1907, p. 25.
82 Pearling in the Nor West': May Gibbs. *Western Mail*, Christmas number, 25 December 1907, p. 16.
85 Cover of *Little Obelia and Further Adventures of Ragged Blossom Snugglepot & Cuddlepie*: May Gibbs.
86 Gumnut babies: May Gibbs. State Library of New South Wales.
87 Cover of 'The children's corner by Aunt Mary': May Gibbs. *Western Mail*, 25 December 1907.
89 Cover, *Western Mail*, 25 December 1906.
90 Portrait: May Gibbs. State Library of New South Wales.
91 Self-portrait: May Gibbs. State Library of New South Wales.

CHAPTER 7
92 'From life': May Gibbs 1910. State Library of New South Wales.
94 Illustration: May Gibbs. May and Herbert Gibbs Collection, City of South Perth.
95 Illustration: May Gibbs. State Library of New South Wales.
96 Illustration: May Gibbs. State Library of New South Wales.
97 Illustration: May Gibbs 1901. State Library of New South Wales.
98 Postcards: May Gibbs 1911. May and Herbert Gibbs Collection, City of South Perth.

99 Postcard: Herbert Gibbs. May and Herbert Gibbs Collection, City of South Perth.
100 Illustrations: May Gibbs 1901. State Library of New South Wales.
101 Sketchbook and illustrations: May Gibbs. State Library of New South Wales.
102 Illustration from *About Us*: May Gibbs. State Library of New South Wales.
103 Unpublished illustrations: May Gibbs. State Library of New South Wales.

CHAPTER 8
104 Portrait: May Gibbs. State Library of New South Wales.
107 Cover, *The Common Cause*, 4 May 1911.
108 Wattle babies: May Gibbs. State Library of New South Wales.
108 Cover, *The Common Cause*, 13 April 1911.
109 'Locked Out': May Gibbs. May and Herbert Gibbs Collection, City of South Perth.
110 Portrait Irene 'Rene' Heames: May Gibbs. State Library of New South Wales.
112 Photograph of The Coronation March 1911.
113 Poster for The Coronation March 1911.
114 Illustration: May Gibbs. State Library of New South Wales.
116 Illustration for Mimie and Wag: May Gibbs. State Library of New South Wales.
117 Cover and page from *About Us*: May Gibbs. State Library of New South Wales.
118 Wattle babies: May Gibbs. State Library of New South Wales.
119 Illustration: May Gibbs. State Library of New South Wales.
120 Illustration: May Gibbs. State Library of New South Wales.
121 Illustration: May Gibbs. State Library of New South Wales.

CHAPTER 9
122 Design for a cover: May Gibbs. State Library of New South Wales.
124 'Mother, 'Nutcote'': May Gibbs 1928. State Library of New South Wales.
125 Portrait Irene 'Rene' Heames: May Gibbs. State Library of New South Wales.
126 Portrait: May Gibbs. State Library of New South Wales.
127 'The Modern Maid' *Western Mail* 1913, p. 28.
128 Wild flowers: May Gibbs. State Library of New South Wales.
129 Design for *The Lone Hand*: May Gibbs. State Library of New South Wales.
130 Cartoon 'Bib and Bub' and cover artwork for Bib & Bub colouring book: May Gibbs. State Library of New South Wales.
132 Design for a cover of *Sydney Mail*: May Gibbs. State Library of New South Wales.
133 Printed bookmarks: May Gibbs. State Library of New South Wales.

CHAPTER 10
134 Gum blossom babies: May Gibbs. State Library of New South Wales.
136 Cartoon by DH Souter in *The Lone Hand*, September 1911.
137 'Harry Western Artist': May Gibbs. State Library of New South Wales.
138 Cover illustration for *Gem of the Flat*: May Gibbs. State Library of New South Wales.
139 Cover illustration for *Scribbling Sue and Other Stories*: May Gibbs. State Library of New South Wales.
140 Cover, *The Sydney Mail*, 29 April, 1914.
141 Details from 'A post-impressionist's impression of a week-end on the Blue Mountains', *Sydney Mail*, 28 January 1914, p. 6.

CHAPTER 11
142 May Gibbs, 'Australia Day during the War, in Sydney'. May and Herbert Gibbs Collection, City of South Perth.
144 WWI Postcards: May Gibbs. May and Herbert Gibbs Collection, City of South Perth.
145 'Terrible Thought' *Bulletin*, 20 August, 1914, p. 10.
146 Postcard: May Gibbs. May and Herbert Gibbs Collection, City of South Perth.
147 Postcards: May Gibbs. May and Herbert Gibbs Collection, City of South Perth.
148 Calendar: May Gibbs. State Library of New South Wales.
149 Handmade card: May Gibbs. State Library of New South Wales.
150 Postcard: May Gibbs. State Library of New South Wales.
151 Artwork: May Gibbs. May and Herbert Gibbs Collection, City of South Perth.

CHAPTER 12
152 Illustration for 'Are we Downhearted' postcard: May Gibbs. State Library of New South Wales.

154 Series of WWI postcards: May Gibbs. May and Herbert Gibbs Collection, City of South Perth.
155 Series of WWI postcards: May Gibbs. May and Herbert Gibbs Collection, City of South Perth.
157 Postcard, Sister Susies Sewing Shirts for Soldiers: May Gibbs. National Library of Australia.
158 Illustration for Sister Susies Sewing Shirts for Soldiers: May Gibbs. State Library of New South Wales.
160 Cover of *Gumnut Babies*: May Gibbs.
163 Cover of *The Lone Hand*, September 1914.
164 Unfinished illustration: May Gibbs. State Library of New South Wales.
166 Title page of Gumnut Babies: May Gibbs. State Library of New South Wales.
167 Wattle babies: May Gibbs. State Library of New South Wales.CHAPTER 13
168 'Mother Gumnut Watching a Cicadia develop from a Chrysalis': Herbert Gibbs 1923. May and Herbert Gibbs Collection, City of South Perth.
171 Illustration for *The Story of Nuttybub and Nittersing*: May Gibbs.
172 Neutral Bay: Herbert Gibbs 1923. May and Herbert Gibbs Collection, City of South Perth.
173 Illustration: May Gibbs. State Library of New South Wales.
175 Illustration for unpublished book, *Mimie and Wag*: May Gibbs. State Library of New South Wales.
176 Cover of *The Lone Hand*, Christmas 1916.
177 Title page, *Gum Blossom Babies*. State Library of New South Wales.

CHAPTER 14
178 Illustration: May Gibbs. State Library of New South Wales.
180 Gum blossom babies: May Gibbs. State Library of New South Wales.
181 Collage of flower babies: May Gibbs. State Library of New South Wales.
182 Illustrations: May Gibbs. State Library of New South Wales.
183 Gumnut babies: May Gibbs. State Library of New South Wales.
185 Illustrations: May Gibbs. State Library of New South Wales.
186 Illustration: May Gibbs. State Library of New South Wales.
187 Cover illustration: May Gibbs. *Western Mail* 1907.
188 Cover and page for an unpublished book, *Nursery Rhymes from the Bush*: May Gibbs. State Library of New South Wales.
189 Gum blossom babies: May Gibbs. State Library of New South Wales.
190 Flower babies: May Gibbs. State Library of New South Wales.
191 Illustration: May Gibbs. State Library of New South Wales.
192 Boronia babies: May Gibbs. State Library of New South Wales.
193 Portrait of JO Kelly: May Gibbs c. 1928. May and Herbert Gibbs Collection, City of South Perth.

CHAPTER 15
194 'Not His': May Gibbs. State Library of New South Wales.
196 Photograph of Gibbs family. Private Collection.
197 Illustration for *The Little Gum-Nuts Chucklebud and Wunkydoo*: May Gibbs. State Library of New South Wales.
198 Flower babies: May Gibbs. State Library of New South Wales.
199 Cover illustration for an unpublished book: May Gibbs. State Library of New South Wales.
200 Illustration for an unpublished book: May Gibbs. State Library of New South Wales.
201 Illustration by Randolph Caldecott.
202 Gumnut babies: May Gibbs. State Library of New South Wales.
203 'Poor Mother': May Gibbs. State Library of New South Wales.
204 Boronia babies: May Gibbs. State Library of New South Wales.
205 Gumnut babies: May Gibbs. State Library of New South Wales.
206 Flower babies: May Gibbs. State Library of New South Wales.
207 Printed Bookmark and flower babies: May Gibbs.

POSTSCRIPT
208 Flower babies: May Gibbs. State Library of New South Wales.
210 Gumnut babies: May Gibbs. State Library of New South Wales.
211 Flower babies: May Gibbs. State Library of New South Wales.

BIBLIOGRAPHY

MANUSCRIPTS
Bayfield, Juliana & Brummitt, Jane, List of works by May Gibbs reproduced in newspapers
    & periodicals, 1889–1916.
Cowle, Mary (nee Bird), unpublished diary, Battye Library, State Library of Western Australia, MN 1027 ACC 2981A/4.
de Berg, Hazel, oral history tape of May Gibbs, National Library of Australia, NLA 356 (25 May 1968), typescript
    transcription.
Gibbs, Herbert, 'Arrival in South Australia', manuscript c. 1928, May & Herbert Gibbs Art Collection, City of South Perth.
    'Autobiographical notes', Battye Library, State Library of Western Australia, PR 14514.
Gibbs, May, 'Cupid' suite of unpublished illustrations, 1909, Mitchell Library MSS 2048/8, State Library of New South Wales.
——'Cupid' suite of unpublished illustrations, 1910, Mitchell Library MSS 2048/9X, State Library of New South Wales.
——Jack and Jill, unpublished ink and watercolour book, 1890, Nutcote Collection, Neutral Bay, Sydney.
——Letter re. Randolph Caldecott's abiding influence on her work, Mitchell Library MSS 314/3, 73a, State Library of New
    South Wales.
——Man with Cupid, unpublished watercolour, Mitchell Library PXD 738/95 and PXD 764, State Library of New South Wales.
——'Note for book on my life …', undated autobiographical manuscript, Marian & Neil Shand Collection, North Sydney
    Heritage Centre, Stanton Library, A71/4.1.
——Nursery Rhymes from the Bush, unpublished and illustrated manuscript, Mitchell Library PXD 738/97, State Library of New
    South Wales.
——Papers, Mitchell Library MSS 2048/59, State Library of New South Wales (including copyright registration and publishing
    contract).
——Personal Papers, Mitchell Library MSS 2048/67, State Library of New South Wales.
——Scrapbook, Mitchell Library MSS 2048/66, State Library of New South Wales.
——Shipboard diary aboard the Konigin Luise, 1900, Mitchell Library MSS 2048/67, State Library of New South Wales.
——Sketchbook, Mitchell Library PXD 304, folder 17, State Library of New South Wales.
——'That Other Fairytale' and 'This Other Fairytale', unpublished autobiographical fragments, 1960s?, Marian & Neil Shand
    Collection, North Sydney Heritage Centre, Stanton library, A71/2.9 & A71/4.1.
——'Win: The Key to All Hearts', unpublished picture book, 1906–8. Mitchell Library PXD 738/98, State Library of New South
    Wales.
O'Harris, Pixie, A Memory of May Gibbs, c. 1920, Mitchell Library DOC 1661, State Library of New South Wales.

MONOGRAPHS AND ARTICLES
'A Correspondent', Western Mail, 1 October 1904, p. 11.
——Western Mail, 29 October 1911, p. 11.
——Western Mail, 12 November 1904, p. 11.
'A unique flower show', Sydney Morning Herald, 6 December 1911, p. 5.
'A woman's letter', Bulletin, 26 October 1916, p. 18.
'Adrienne', 'Social Notes', West Australian, 30 March 1908, p. 4.
——'A great social gathering', West Australian, 26 June 1908, p. 6.
'Agitation by Symbol', The Common Cause, 15 July 1909, p. 173.
'Amusements', West Australian, 2 November 1899, p. 1.
'Anglo-Australia', British-Australasian, 17 May 1900, p. 735.
'Annual Ball', West Australian, 11 July 1903, p. 9.
'Annual Wild Flower Show', West Australian, 23 September 1897, p. 2.
Armitage, Shelley, Kewpies and Beyond: The World of Rose O'Neill (Jackson, Miss.: University Press of Mississippi, 1994).
'Art Exhibition, The', Western Mail, 14 June 1890, p. 4.
'Artists' Suffrage League, The', The Common Cause, 3 February 1910, p. 599.
Ashton, Julian Rossi, Now Came Still Evening On (Sydney: Angus & Robertson, 1941).
'Australia Day', (Sydney) Daily Telegraph, 30 July 1915, p. 6.

'Australia Day', (Sydney) *Daily Telegraph*, 31 July 1915, p. 11.
'Australian Exhibition of Art and Work', *West Australian*, 9 January 1908, p. 4.
'Australian Soldier's Gift Book', *Sydney Morning Herald*, 6 December 1916, p. 6.
Australian Wild Flower Show, Sydney Town Hall, September 3–5, exhibition catalogue (Sydney: [Girl's Realm Guild of NSW, 1914]).
'Baby Week', *Sydney Morning Herald*, 29 March 1920, p. 6.
Barrington, Molly, 'The Brownies of the Bush', *Sydney Mail*, 10 December 1913, p. 15.
'Books for Children', (Perth) *Western Women*, 1 March 1915, p. 25.
Briggs, Julia, 'Transitions, 1890–1914', in Peter Hunt (ed.), *Children's Literature: An Illustrated History* (Oxford: Oxford University Press, 1995).
British Official Catalogue, Paris Exhibition, 1900 (London: [Great Britain Royal Commission, 1900]).
Broome, Lady, *Colonial Memories* (London: Smith, Elder & Co., 1904).
Bulletin, advertisement, 11 December 1897, p. 12.
Bullock, Ian and Richard Pankhurst (eds), *Sylvia Pankhurst: From Artist to Anti-Fascist* (New York: St. Martin's Press, 1992).
Butler, Lady, *Letters to Guy* (London: Macmillan & Co., 1885).
'Cake fair at South Perth', *West Australian*, 25 April 1898, p. 4.
Callaway, Anita, 'May Gibbs', in Joan Kerr (ed.), *Heritage: The National Women's Art Book* ([Sydney]: G + B Arts International Ltd., 1995).
Catalogue of the Western Australian Court at the Paris Exhibition 1900 (Paris: Paul Dupont, 1900).
Chapman, Jean, 'Cecilia May Gibbs, 1877–1969', *Orana*, 25 (2), May 1989, pp. 55–6.
'Children's Fancy Dress Ball, The', *West Australian*, 29 August 1891, p. 2.
'Christmas Flowers', *Sydney Morning Herald*, 16 December 1914, p. 5.
Cole, Percival R, 'Social Life in a Sydney School', illustrated by May Gibbs, *Sydney Mail*, 25 June 1913, pp. 26–7.
'Concert by Mrs. Rogers' Pupils', *West Australian*, 22 May 1890, p. 3.
'Concert in Perth', *West Australian*, 19 August 1889, p. 3.
Crawford, Elizabeth, *The Women's Suffrage Movement: A Reference Guide 1866–1928* (London: Routledge, 2001).
Cunnington, Susan, *Georgian England (1714–1820)* illustrated by May Gibbs (London: George Harrap, 1913).
'Dorcas Society, The', *West Australian*, 8 July 1889, p. 3.
'Dress at the S. P. C. A. Ball', *West Australian*, 19 July 1897, p. 3.
'Dresses, The', *West Australian*, 30 December 1907, p. 6.
'Eastern Suburbs, The'', *South Australian Register*, 28 September 1882, p. 6.
'Educational', *West Australian*, 16 September 1887, p. 4.
Eipper, Chris, 'Snuggles, Cuddles and Sexuality', *Australian Journal of Anthropology*, 14 (3), 2003, pp. 336–51.
'Entertainments', *West Australian*, 11 August 1908, p. 6.
'Entertainments', *Western Mail*, 8 May 1909, p. 33.
'First Australian Baby Week', *The Lone Hand*, 2 March 1920, p. 13.
Franklin, Miles, 'Not Honey–Nectar!', *Sydney Morning Herald*, 20 November 1920, p. 7.
'Fremantle Spring Fete', *West Australian*, 6 October 1893, p. 3.
'Friday March 30, 1900', *Sydney Morning Herald*, 30 March 1900, p. 4.
Gibbs, May, 'The Birth of the Gumnut Babies', *Woman's World*, November 1924, p. 629.
——'Parson Dick of Pinginup', *Western Mail*, 13 June 1908, p. 48.
'Gondoliers, The', *West Australian*, 27 June 1892, p. 6.
Goodman, Helen, exhibition catalogue, *The Art of Rose O'Neill* (Chadds Ford, PA: Brandywine River Museum, 1989).
Graham, Edith, *A Little Bush Poppy* (Melbourne: Lothian, [1915]).
Grey, George, *Journals of Two Expeditions of Discovery in North-West and Western Australia*, (London: T. & W. Boone, 1841), 2 vols.
Grover, Montague, 'Australians in London', *Argus*, 9 April 1904, p. 5.
Guide to the Contents of the Western Australian Museum and Art Gallery (Perth: West Australian Museum & Art Gallery Committee, 1900).
Hamilton, Cicely, *Life Errant* (London: J. M. Dent, 1935).
——*Marriage as a Trade* (New York: Moffat, Yard & Co., 1909).
Handyside, Bronwen, 'A tribute to May Gibbs', *Lip*, (2) no. 2, 1977, pp. 36–8.
'Herr Francik's Concert', *West Australian*, 24 August 1894, p. 7.
Holden, Robert, *A Golden Age: Visions of Fantasy* (Sydney: Angus & Robertson, 1992).
——*Cover Up: The Art of Magazine Covers in Australia* (Sydney: Hodder & Stoughton, 1995).

——'Teaching Our Poorer Citizens the Alphabet of Art', Voices, (3) no. 4, summer 1993/4, pp. 20–8.
Illustrated Catalogue of the First Annual Exhibition in Oil-&-Water-Colours ([Perth: Wilgie Sketching Club], 1890).
'In the streets', (Sydney) Daily Telegraph, 31 July 1915, p. 11.
'Introduction', Art in Australia, no. 4, 1918, Art Gallery of New South Wales exhibition note.
James, Winifred, Bachelor Betty (London: A. Constable & Co., 1907).
'Japanese Fair, The', West Australian, 4 December 1890, p. 3.
'Juveniles' Ball, The', West Australian, 3 August 1891, p. 2.
'Karrakatia Club, The', West Australian, 5 August 1895, p. 5.
Lane, Margaret, The Tale of Beatrix Potter (London: Warne & Co., 1946).
Lang, Jean, Pathway to Magic: The Story of May Gibbs in Western Australia (Perth: Challenge Bank, 1991).
'Lawn Tennis', West Australian, 6 December 1922, p. 7.
'Letters from the Front', Advertiser, 23 July 1915, p. 9.
Lilley, Beatrice, 'Bib and Bub–and May Gibbs', Woman, 20 January 1947, p. 21.
Linder, Leslie, The Journal of Beatrix Potter, from 1881 to 1897, transcribed from her code writing (London: Warne, 1966).
Lindley-Cowen, L (ed.), The West Australian Settler's Guide and Farmer's Handbook, Part 1 (Perth: Bureau of Agriculture, 1897).
Lindsay, Norman, 'The Transplanted Artist', Home, 2 (4), December 1921, pp. 18–19, 91–2, 94, 96–7.
Lyons, Martyn and John Arnold (eds), A History of the Book in Australia 1891—1945 (St Lucia, Queensland: University of Queensland Press, 2001).
Mack, Amy, Bush Days (Sydney: Angus & Robertson, 1911).
——Scribbling Sue and Other Stories, illustrated by May Gibbs (Sydney: Angus & Robertson, [1914]).
Mackness, Constance, Gem of the Flat, illustrated by May Gibbs.(Sydney: Angus & Robertson, [1914]).
'Mme. Charvin's war concert', Sydney Morning Herald, 11 October 1915, p. 4.
Madame Charvin's War Concert, program, Town Hall, Sydney, 9 October 1915 ([Sydney: Madame Charvin (Yvonne Leverrier) 1915]) (copy in May Gibbs' scrapbook, Mitchell Library MSS 2048/66, State Library of New South Wales).
Marlowe, Mary, 'Mother of the Gum Nut Babies: May Gibbs at home', Woman's World, 1 December 1922, p. 13.
'May Gibbs' Way, The', (Rockhampton) Daily Record, 1 March 1919, p. 4.
May, Phil, Phil May's Sketch Book: Fifty Cartoons (London: Chatto & Windus, 1897).
'Mining disaster at Bonnievale', West Australian, 10 January 1906, p. 7.
'Miss May Gibbs: Her Creative Work', (Sydney) Sun, 5 September 1915, p. 18.
'Miss May Gibbs, Queen of the Gum-nuts', (Sydney) Sun, 11 March 1917, p. 14.
Moore, William, 'Australian Literature and Art', United Empire, 4 (2), February 1913, p. 140.
——'Careers for Australasian Girls IX: What the artist's life offers', New Idea, 6 (13), December 1907, pp. 848–9.
——'The National Galleries of Queensland and West Australia', Studio, 68 (282), September 1916, pp. 216–24.
Muir, Marcie and Robert Holden, The Fairy World of Ida Rentoul Outhwaite (Sydney: Craftsman House, 1985).
'Musical "At Home" at Government House', West Australian, 27 August 1892, p. 6.
National Art Gallery of New South Wales Loan Exhibition, catalogue (Sydney: National Art Gallery of New South Wales, 1918).
'News and notes', West Australian, 11 August 1894, p. 4.
——West Australian, 6 May 1897, p. 4.
——West Australian, 30 November 1897, p. 4.
'Notes and news', West Australian, 10 June 1890, p. 2.
'O. B. I. Concert', West Australian, 15 August 1908, p. 9.
O'Conor, Juliet, 'Chimney Pots to Gumnuts: May Gibbs' About Us', Dromkeen Society Bulletin, September 2007, pp. 5–6.
'Of Interest to Women', Sydney Mail, 28 April 1915, p. 32.
Pankhurst, Sylvia, 'Sylvia Pankhurst', in Margot Oxford (ed.), Myself When Young, by Famous Women of To-Day (London: Frederick Muller, 1938), pp. 259–312.
'Paris Exhibition Commission', West Australian, 11 December 1899, p. 5.
'Paris International Exhibition, The', West Australian, 4 August 1900, p. 10.
'Perth, Monday, October 9, 1905', West Australian, 9 October 1905, p. 6.
'Perth Musical Union', West Australian, 25 July 1888, p. 3.
'Perth Musical Union, The', West Australian, 3 October 1889, p. 3.
'Perth Musical Union, The', West Australian, 19 December 1889, p. 6.
'Perth Wild Flower Show, The', West Australian, 13 October 1892, p. 2.

'Perth Wild Flower Show, The', *West Australian*, 6 October 1893, p. 6.
Pesman, Ros, *Duty Free: Australian Women Abroad* (Melbourne: Oxford University Press, 1996).
Potter, Beatrix, *Appley Dapply's Nursery Rhymes* (London: F. Warne, n.d.), inscribed by Rene Heames Sullivan to May Gibbs, 1928, private collection.
'Pure Foods', illustrated by May Gibbs, *Sydney Mail*, 25 June 1913, pp. 5–7.
'Queen of the Gum-Nuts: Bush Lore Portrayed', *Sunday Sun*, 11 March 1917, p. 14.
'Queen Victoria Home for Consumptives', *Sydney Morning Herald*, 16 August 1899, p. 8.
'Recital by a celebrated violinist', (Albany) *Australian Advertiser*, 10 August 1892, [p. 3].
'Rescue of Varischetti', *Sydney Morning Herald*, 29 March 1907, p. 6.
Review of the Westralia Gift Book, *Advertiser*, 22 August 1916, p. 9.
Ridley, MA (ed.), *A Journey to Western Australia 1886–7 on the S. S. Australind: Diary of Ishmael Rogers* ([Perth: MA Ridley, 196-?]).
Rivett-Carnac, Marion, *Fairies, Elves and Flower Babies*, illustrated by Marion Wallace-Dunlop (London: Duckworth, 1899).
Roe, Jill (ed.), *My Congenials: Miles Franklin & Friends in London* (Sydney: Angus & Robertson, 1993), 2 vols.
——*Stella Miles Franklin* (Sydney: Harper Collins, 2008).
[Rosman, Alice Grant], 'The Travels of Economical Emily', *Everylady's Journal*, 6 August 1911, pp. 136–7.
——'The Travels of Economical Emily', *Everylady's Journal*, 6 September 1911, pp. 200–1.
——'The Travels of Economical Emily', *Everylady's Journal*, 6 November 1911, pp. 328–9.
——'The Travels of Economical Emily', *Everylady's Journal*, 6 January 1912, 8, p. 11.
——'The Travels of Economical Emily', *Everylady's Journal*, 6 February 1912, pp. 78–9.
Rosman, Alice Grant, 'Girls Who Go to London Town: How Australian Aspirants Fare', *Everylady's Journal*, 6 February 1913, pp. 74–5, 122.
——'Girls Who Go to London Town: How Australian Aspirants Fare', *Everylady's Journal*, 6 April 1913, pp. 202–3, 250.
——'Girls Who Go to London Town: How Australian Aspirants Fare', *Everylady's Journal*, 6 June 1913, pp. 330–31.
——'Girls Who Go to London Town: How Australian Aspirants Fare', *Everylady's Journal*, 6 August 1913, pp. 458–9.
——'Girls Who Go to London Town: How Australian Aspirants Fare', *Everylady's Journal*, 6 September 1913, pp. 521–2.
——'Girls Who Go to London Town: How Australian Aspirants Fare', *Everylady's Journal*, 6 October 1913, pp. 604–5.
Ross, Estelle, *Barons and Kings (1215–1485)*, illustrated by May Gibbs & Stephen Reid (London: George Harrap, 1912).
'S. P. C. A. Ball', *Morning Herald*, 13 July 1906, p. 6.
'S. P. C. A. Annual Ball, The', *West Australian*, 17 July 1908, p. 2.
'S. P. C. A. Ball, The', *Western Mail*, 21 July 1906, p. 15.
'S. P. C. A. Ball, The', *West Australian*, 17 July 1908, p. 2.
Scott, Myra, *How Australia Led the Way: Dora Meeson and British Suffrage* (Canberra: Commonwealth Office of the Status of Women, 2003).
Seddon, George, *Swan Song: Reflections on Perth and Western Australia 1956—1995* (Nedlands: University of Western Australia, 1995).
Sharkey, Chris, *May and Herbert Gibbs* (South Perth: May Gibbs Trust, 2000).
——exhibition catalogue, *Mostly May Gibbs* (South Perth: City of South Perth, 2001).
——*The Cultural Context of Federation: The Gibbs & South Perth Connection 1890–1910* (South Perth: City of South Perth, 2002).
——and Pendle, Phillip, *The People, the Places* (South Perth: May Gibbs Trust, 2000).
'Shipping', *West Australian*, 7 December 1903, p. 6.
'Shipping', *West Australian*, 8 December 1903, p. 6.
'Sir T. F. Buxton's visit', *West Australian*, 4 May 1898, p. 6.
Snell, Ted, *Cinderella on the Beach* (Nedlands: University of Western Australia Press, 1991).
'Socks of Poor Material', *Argus*, 5 March 1915, p. 7.
'Social', *Sydney Morning Herald*, 1 November 1913, p. 6.
'Social Notes', *West Australian*, 18 October 1898, p. 7.
'Social Notes', *West Australian*, 10 March 1906, p. 13.
'Society of Arts', *Western Mail*, 1 January 1897, [p. 24].
'Society of Arts & Crafts', *Sydney Morning Herald*, 15 December 1914, p. 10.
'Society of Arts & Crafts', *Sydney Morning Herald*, 25 October 1916, p. 5.
South Australia: A Brief Account of its Progress and Resources (Adelaide: Government Printer, 1881).
'South Perth Mechanics' Institute', *West Australian*, 22 May 1899, p. 5.
'South Perth Mechanics' Institute Opening Ceremony', *West Australian*, 8 August 1899, p. 7.

'Spirit of the Bush, The', *Theatre Magazine*, 1 January 1917, p. 4.
Stevens, Bertram and George Mackaness (eds), *The Children's Treasury of Australian Verse* (Sydney: Angus & Robertson, [1913]).
'This is the Day', (Sydney) *Daily Telegraph*, 30 July 1915, p. 6.
Tracy, Beatrix, 'London', *British-Australasian*, 30 June 1910, p. 43.
Turner, Ethel, 'The Magic Button', serial in eight weekly parts, illustrated by May Gibbs, *Sydney Mail*, 10 December 1913–28 January 1914.
Twopeny, Richard, *Town Life in Australia* (London: E. Stock, 1883).
'Vandorian', 'A Woman's Letter', *Bulletin*, 26 October 1916, p. 18.
'Vigilans et Audax', *West Australian*, 21 May 1888, [p. 2].
'Vigilans et Audax', *West Australian*, 7 June 1890, p. 2.
Vivienne, May, *Travels in Western Australia* (London: William Heinemann, 1901).
Vote, The, report of the debate between GK Chesterton and Cicely Hamilton, (3) 15, April 1911, p. 295.
'W. A. Exhibition of Women's Work', *West Australian*, 15 August 1907, p. 2.
'W. A. Exhibition of Women's Work', *Western Mail*, 17 August 1907, p. 20.
'W. A. Society of Arts', *West Australian*, 19 December 1899, p. 4.
Wallace-Dunlop, M and M Rivett-Carnac, *Fairies, Elves and Flower-Babies* (London: Duckworth & Co., 1899).
Walsh, Maureen, *May Gibbs: Mother of the Gumnuts* (Sydney: Angus & Robertson, 1994).
'Wants', *West Australian*, 22 November 1886, p. 3.
'West Australian Contingent', *West Australian*, 6 November 1899, p. 6.
'West Australian Society of Arts', *West Australian*, 24 May 1902, p. 44.
West Australian Society of Arts Eighth Exhibition, catalogue (Perth: The Society, 1902).
Western Australia: A Short Sketch of the Climate, Products, Population and Prospects of the Colony ([London: C. Bethell & Co., et al., 1884?]).
'West Procession, The', *Votes for Women*, (3) new series no. 124, 22 July 1910, p. 705.
Westralia Gift Book to Aid Y. M. C. A. Military Work and Returned Nurses Fund, The, by Writers and Artists of Western Australia (Perth: V. K. Jones, 1916).
Wheeler, Maude, 'The Lights O' London', *Truth*, 28 April 1901, p. 8.
'When Suzie Went Steerage', *The New Idea*, 6 March 1911, pp. 217–18.
——'When Suzie Went Steerage', *The New Idea*, 6 April 1911, pp. 305–6.
——'When Suzie Went Steerage', *The New Idea*, 6 May 1911, pp. 399–401.
——'When Suzie Went Steerage', *Everylady's Journal*, 6 June 1911, pp. 12–13.
'Wild Flower Show, The', *West Australian*, 14 October 1892, p. 2.
'Wild Flower Show, The', *West Australian*, 24 August 1894, p. 7.
'Wild Flower Show, The', *Sydney Morning Herald*, 25 September 1912, p. 5.
Wilmot-Buxton, E.M., *The struggle with the crown (1603–1715)*, illustrated by May Gibbs (London: George Harrap, 1912).
'With the collectors', *Sydney Morning Herald*, 31 July 1915, p. 13.
Woodward, Bernard, 'The Wilgie Sketching Club', *West Australian*, 11 December 1889, p. 3.
Woollacott, Angela, *To Try Her Fortune in London: Australian Women, Colonialism and Modernity* (Oxford: Oxford University Press, 2001).

INDEX

Ackerman, Jessie 57
Adelaide 10, 13
Advertiser 162
Angus & Robertson 128, 138–139, 180, 182
Anzacs 145, 154–156, 162, 166
   Anzac Day 179
Argus 60
Armitage, Shelley 184
Arrival in South Australia 8
Art in Australia 182
Artists' Suffrage League 111, 112
Art Gallery of New South Wales 182
Ashton, Julian
   Now Came Still Evening On 32
Astley, Francis Palmer 3
Austral Club 60
Australasian Artists' Dinners 60
Australasian Exhibition of Art and Work 84
Australia Day 154, 161
Australian and New Zealand Women Voters' Committee 111
Australian Comforts Fund 154
Australian Soldiers' Gift Book 162
Australian Women's National League 154
Australian Women's Service Corps 154

Baby Week 206
Banksia Men 18
Barker, Mary Cicely 201
Barrie, JM
   Peter Pan in Kensington Gardens 196
Barrington, Molly 135
Baskerville, Margaret 63
Baynton, Barbara 63
Best, Amy 86
Bird, Mary 19
Bishops Girls' College 22, 24, 86
Blob 51, 76
Bloomsbury group 105
Boer War 47
bookmarks 133, 146–150, 179
Bon Marche 47–49, 186
Briggs, Julia 198
British Australasian 60, 70, 95
British immigrants 8, 22

Broome, Lady Anne
   Letters to Guy 32
   Colonial Memories 46
Bourne, Una 63
Bull, John 49
Bulletin xiii, 120, 128, 145, 146, 166, 184
Bunbury 14, 18
Bush Days 170

Caldecott, Ralph xiv, 189, 201
Castles, Amy 63
Centennial Exhibition 32
Chapman, Jean 141
Chelsea Polytechnic Institute 74, 77, 115
Cherniavski, Leo, Jan and Mischel 91
Chesterton, GK 106–107
Christian Commonwealth, The 107
Christmas bell babies 146, 149
Cinderella 157
Claremont 19
colonies 6, 14, 45
Common Cause, The 106–107, 111
Cook, Joseph 143
Cope & Nicol Art School 73
copyright 179
Cowell 8
Crane, Walter 182, 201
Crawford, Elizabeth 111
Creeth, Mildred 49
Crossley, Ada 63
cupid 118, 149, 184–192

Daily Mail 100
Daily Record 180
Daily Telegraph 156
Davison, Emily 131
Dawn, The 57
De Berg, Hazel 190
Dennis, CJ 180, 189
Dickens, Charles 149
Doctor Dolittle 198
Dot and the Kangaroo 121, 169
Dr Stork viii, ix, 206–207
Dune, The 20, 24, **24**, 29, **30**, **40**

Dunlop, Marion Wallace 115

Emery, Eliza 1
Everylady's Journal 118
Eyre Peninsula 10

Fabian Society 60
Fashion Fancies 186
First Australasian Exhibition of Women's Work, The 84
flannel-flower babies xi, 146, 149
Forrest, Sir John 24, 46, 51–52
Forrest, Lady Margaret 30, 35–37, 46–49, 49
Francik, Herr Adalbert 43, 45
Franklin Harbour 8
Franklin, Miles xiii, xiv, 184
Fry, Roger 105
Fuller, Florence 24

Gadfly, The 3
Gaiety Theatre Company 40
Gallipoli 154–156, 162, 179, 206
Gander Green Lane, Surrey xvi, 1
Gem of the Flat **138**, 139
Gibbs, Cecilia 'Cocia' 1–10, 13–19, **20**, 21–24, 27–29, **29**, 30, 36–37, **40**, **41**, **44**, 45, 47–49, 67, 77, 80, 95, **124**, 125, 133
Gibbs, Cecilia May
   adolescence 27–46
   art school 55, 57, 73–74, 77
   autobiography viii, 4, 73
   awards 32, 36–37, 74, 84, 86
   bookmarks 131–133, **133**, 179
   books 19, 83–84, 96, 115–116, 118, 138–141, **160**, 161–162, 166, **166**, **167**, 170, 200, 201–205, 211
      About Us 115, **117**
      Chucklebud and Wunkydoo **197**
      Further Adventures of Bib and Bub, The 37
      Gum-nut Babies **160**, 177, 180–182
      Gum-Blossom Babies 177, **177**, 180
      Jack and Jill (unpublished) 202

229

Little Obelia 83, **85**
Little Ragged Blossom 37, **75**
Mimie and Wag (unpublished) 17, 116, **116**
Nursery Rhymes from the Bush 188, **189**, 205
Tales of Snugglepot and Cuddlepie, The 19, **26**, 27, 37, 170
Wattle Blossom Babies 118
wild-flower baby booklets 180, 182, 195
Win: The Key to All Hearts (unpublished) 205
birth viii, 1, 4
botanical art 16, 32–37, **33**, **48**, 49, 64, 74, 173, **208**
cards 19, **19**, **148**–150
calendars 126, 146–149, **148**, 150, **151**, 166
cartoons **50**, 51–52, 76–80, **78**, **80**, **127**, 128, **130**, 141, **145**, 190
childhood 6–11, 14–24, 195
costumes 175, 214
education 16–18, 22–24, 40
England, visits to 64–74, 76–77, 88, 93–118
Mamie 20, 116
marriage 123, 190–192
newspaper/magazine work 35, 51–52, 60, 62, 76, **76**, 77–83, **81**, 82, 86, 87, 88, **89**, 91, 99, 102, 106–112, **106**, **107**, 128–131, **129**, **132**, 135–138, **140**, 141, 145, 163, **176**, 179, 186, **187**, 210
performer 8, **38**, 40–45, 52
portraits xii, 90, 104, 110, 122, 124, **125**, 193
portraits of May **15**, **38**, **45**, **61**, **142**, 168
self portraits vi, 28, 60, **109**, **191**, **194**
postcards **66**, 98, 118, 126, **144**, 146, **146**, 147, 150, 154, 155, 157, **157**, 161–166, **162**, 174, 210
poster, Department of Health vii, **ix**, 206–207
publishers 96–99, 116, 180
writing 88, 188
'Parson Dick of Pinginup' 88
That (or This) Other Fairytale (unpublished) viii, 4, 73
Gibbs, Ellen (nee Holden) 16
Gibbs, George (uncle) 3–19
Gibbs, Harold Emery (brother) 22, **43**, 77
Gibbs, Herbert (father) 3–4, **5**, 6–10, 13–19, **20**, 21–24, **25**, 27–29, **29**, 30, 36–37, **40**, 46, 77, 133

Cottesloe Beach 3
North Beach 3
Gibbs, Herbert 'Bertie' (brother) 4, 8, 10
Gibbs, Ivan (brother) 8, 10, 40, 43, **43**, 79, **79**, 143
Gibbs, William (grandfather) 1–3
Gondoliers, The **39**, 43
Graham, Edith
A Little Bush Poppy 161, 174
Grahame, Kenneth
Wind in the Willows, The 198
Greenaway, Kate 35
Grey, George 16
Grover, Montague 60
Gumnut babies 35, 118, 131–133, 135, 157, 161, 174–177, 180–184, 201
Gum-Blossom Babies 174–177, 180, 184
Gum Blossom Ballet 19
Gye, Hal 182, 188–190
Sentimental Bloke, The 189

Hadfield, Alice (cousin) 77, **77**
Hadfield, Emily (aunt) 77
Hamilton, Cicely 106–108, 123, 125, 190
Life Errant 125
Marriage as a Trade 108
Pageant of Great Women 106
Harrap, George G 96, 99
Georgian England 96
Struggle with the Crown, The 96
Harvey River 12–19
Harvey River Cattle Station 14–19
Heames, Irene 'Rene' xiii, 107, **110**, 112, **125**, 125, 133, 145, 149, 170, 205
HMAS *Sydney* 145
Holden, Winifred 16
Holman, Ada 63
Home, The 136
Hopkins, Livingston 21
Hughes, Frank 81

Irvine, Robert
Bubbles, His Book 120
Isle of Wight 17, 74

Jacka, Lieutenant-Corporal Albert 154
James, Winifred
Bachelor Betty 63
Just So Stories 198

Karrakatta Women's Club 29
Kelly, James Ossoli (JO) 192, 205
Kennedy, Daisy 63
Kewpie 184–186
King Edward VII 95, 196

Knightsbridge 14
Konigin Luise 64, 145

Lake Claremont 19
Lambert, George W 120
Lane, Margaret
The Tale of Beatrix Potter xiv
Lang, Jean
Pathway to Magic x
Lawson, Louisa 57
Leason, Percy 128, 182
Lind, Ruby 111
Linder, Leslie xiv
Lindsay, Norman 118, 182
Lindsay, Rose 63
Linton, James WR 46
London 57–74, 77, 93–118
London School of Economics 60
Lone Hand, The 126, 128, 135, 170, 206
Long, Jean x

Mack, Amy 170, 173
Scribbling Sue and Other Stories **139**–141
Mackness, Constance
Gem of the Flat **138**, 139
Mamie and Wag 116
Manchester School of Art 115
Mansfield, Katherine 63
Marlowe, Mary 198
May, Phil 21, 51
May Queen, The 40
McEwan, Ian
Atonement xv
Meeson, Dora 63, 111, 112
Melba, Dame Nellie 58, 63, 70
Melbourne International Exhibition 32
mining boom 45–46, 80
Miss A Spoon 189
Mitchell Library 190
Moore, Carrie 63
Moore, William 84, 93, 118, 166
Morning Herald, The 76, 79, 99
Mother Craft and Child Welfare exhibition 206
Mr A Dish 189
Mrs Kookaburra vii
Murray Street 24

Nanson, Janet 24
National Library of Australia viii, 22, 138, 146, 190
National Union of Women's Suffrage Societies 106

New South Wales Department of Health
   206–207
Norwood 13–14
Nutcote 84, 169, 210
O'Connor, Kathleen 63–64
O'Conor, Juliet 116
O'Harris, Pixie 150
O'Neill, Rose 184

Pankhurst, Emmeline 100, 106, 112, 115
Pankhurst, Sylvia 100, 112–115
Paris Exhibition 49, 70
pearling 83–84,
Pedley, Ethel 121, 169, 170
Persic 93
Perth x, 19, 24, 27, 30, 43, 45, 74, 84,
   86, 125
   Amateur Operatic Society 29, 43
   Art gallery 86
   Cup 86
   Grammar School 24
   Musical Union 30
   Sailing Club 3
   Wild Flower Show 36–37
Pioneer Club 60
'Possum, The 21
Potter, Beatrix xiv, 51, 96, 201–205
   Appley Dapply's Nursery Rhymes 202,
   205
Preston, Margaret 63
Prichard, Katharine Susannah 63
Prinsep, Henry Charles 21, 29, 43
Proctor, Thea 63
Psyche 3

'Queen of the gum-nuts' x
Queen Victoria 47, 196
   Diamond Jubilee 46, 64, 70

Rackham, Arthur 196
Red Cross 145, 157, 161
Rentoul Outhwaite, Ida 88–91, 121,
   186
Richardson, Henry Handel (Ethel) 63
Robinson, Sir William 43
Roe, Jill
   Stella Miles Franklin xiv
Rogers, Daisy (cousin) 39, 67–68
Rogers, Emily (cousin) 4
Rogers, Fanny (aunt) 22
   Mrs Rogers & Daughters 39–40
   Mulgrave House 39
Rogers, Ishmael & Jennett (grandparents)
   1, 4
Rogers, Ishmael (uncle) 22, 39

Rowan, Ellis 30–32, 35–37
Royal Academy of Art 70, 95, 112
Royal Agricultural Show 68
Royal College of Art 3
Royal Colonial Institute 95
Royal Society for the Welfare of Mothers
   and Babies viii

Scott, Myra 111
Scott, Rose 184
Scribbling Sue and Other Stories **139**,
   139–141
Seddon, George
   Swan Song x
   The Birth of Snugglepot xiii
Selfridges 118
Selk, Bobbie 79
Sharkey, Chris
   May and Herbert Gibbs x
Sigma 24
Sister Susies Sewing Shirts for Soldiers
   156–162
Slade School of Art 3, 4, 112
SMS *Emden* 145
Snell, Ted
   Cinderella on the Beach 40
Social Kodak, The 76
Society for the Prevention of Cruelty to
   Animals (SPCA) 86
Society of Women Painters 138
Souter, David Henry 136
   Bubbles, His Book 120
South Australia 6, 8, 57
South Australian 14
*South Australia: a brief account of its
   progress and resources* 6
South Australian Register 10, 13
South Perth 46, 49, 51–52, 80
Spectator, The 51
Spinster Villa 189
SS *Afric* 76
SS *Australind* 22
SS *Chimborazo* 6
SS *Hesperus* 8
Stirling, Captain James 14
Streeton, Arthur 153–154
Studio 166
Suffrage Atelier 112
suffragettes 100, 105–115, 125, 131
Sun, The 133, 161, 166, 173, 177
Surrey 1, 4, 68
Sydney Mail 131, 135, 138, 141, 170
Sydney Morning Herald 81, 120, 148,
   156, 170, 173, 174
Sydney Wild Flower Show 173

Tarrant, Margaret 201
Theatre Magazine 131
Tracey, Beatrix 58
Turner, Ethel 131, 135
Twopeny (Nowell), Richard
   Town Life in Australia 24

Vareschetti, Modesto 81
Venn, Henry W 71
Victoria & Albert Museum 95–96
Victoria Cross 154
Vivienne, May 49
Voices 206
Vote, The 108
Votes for Women 105

W.A. Bulletin 21, 24, 35, 202
Walsh, Maureen 10, 108, 125
Wattle Day 118
West Australian 16, 18, 21, 30, 32, 36,
   40, 43, 46, 49, 71, 80, 86, 99, 126
West Australian Society of Arts 49, 74
Western Mail 24, 35, 52, 57, 64, 68, 77,
   80, 83, 84, 86, 88, 102, 128, 186
Western Australia 14, 27, 32, 35, 45,
   57, 64
   gold discoveries 27, 45
   Government House 21, 29, 43, 86, 99,
   148
   Paris Exhibition Commission 49, 70–71
*Western Australia Settler's Guide and
   Farmer's Handbook* 14, 16
Western Women 141
Westralia Gift Book, The 162
Whitfield, Jessie 120
   Spirit of the Bushfire 120
wild flowers 16, 32
Wildlife Preservation Society of Australia
   170
Wilgie Sketching Club 29, 35–36
Williams, Frederick Matthews 46
Wimbledon 77, 143
Woman's Christian Temperance Union 57
Woman's Franchise League 57
Woman's Voice 57
Woman's World xiii, 198
Women's Coronation Procession 111
Women's Social and Political Union 100,
   115
women's suffrage 29, 55–57, 100–115,
   205
Wood, Charles W 95, 116
Woodward, Bernard 24, 29
World War I 120, 143, 153–166, 206,
   210

231

THE AUTHORS

ROBERT HOLDEN has had a distinguished career as a librarian, curator, writer and book reviewer. Although his work has ranged across a broad spectrum of interests, he is particularly known for his pioneering research on Australian children's book illustration. Apart from three exhibitions which celebrated the work of May Gibbs, his most notable triumph in this field was the mammoth 1988 exhibition devoted to a century of Australian children's book illustration. He was invited to curate this exhibition, which showed at the biennial international children's book fair in Bologna, Italy, then moved to the Australian Embassy in Paris and thereafter to the Victoria & Albert Museum in London.

He has been awarded a Senior Fellowship by the Literature Board of the Australia Council, had a book optioned by Paramount Studios and been one of the Mitchell Library's History Fellows. This is his thirtieth book.

JANE BRUMMITT'S lifelong passion for May's work was fostered by her aunt, Josephine Porter, the wife of May's brother Ivan. From her mother's family, Jane's great aunt Kitty Broadhurst became a suffragette during the period when May supported the British campaign as a caricaturist. These connections combined with her background as a primary school teacher and teacher librarian fired Jane's enthusiasm to help save May's Sydney home, Nutcote. Insights gained through that battle were the catalyst for this book and Jane is donating her royalties to its ongoing preservation.

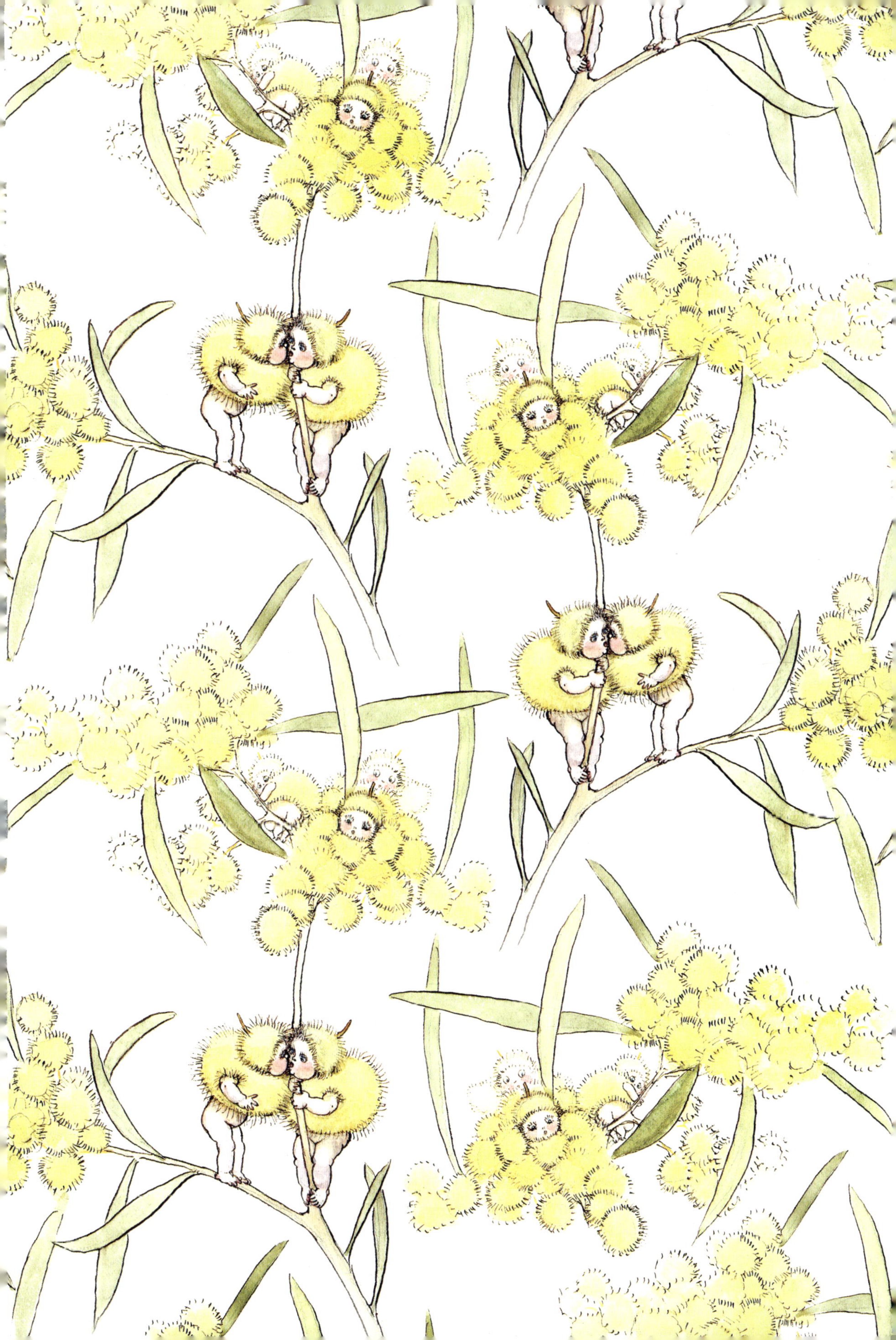

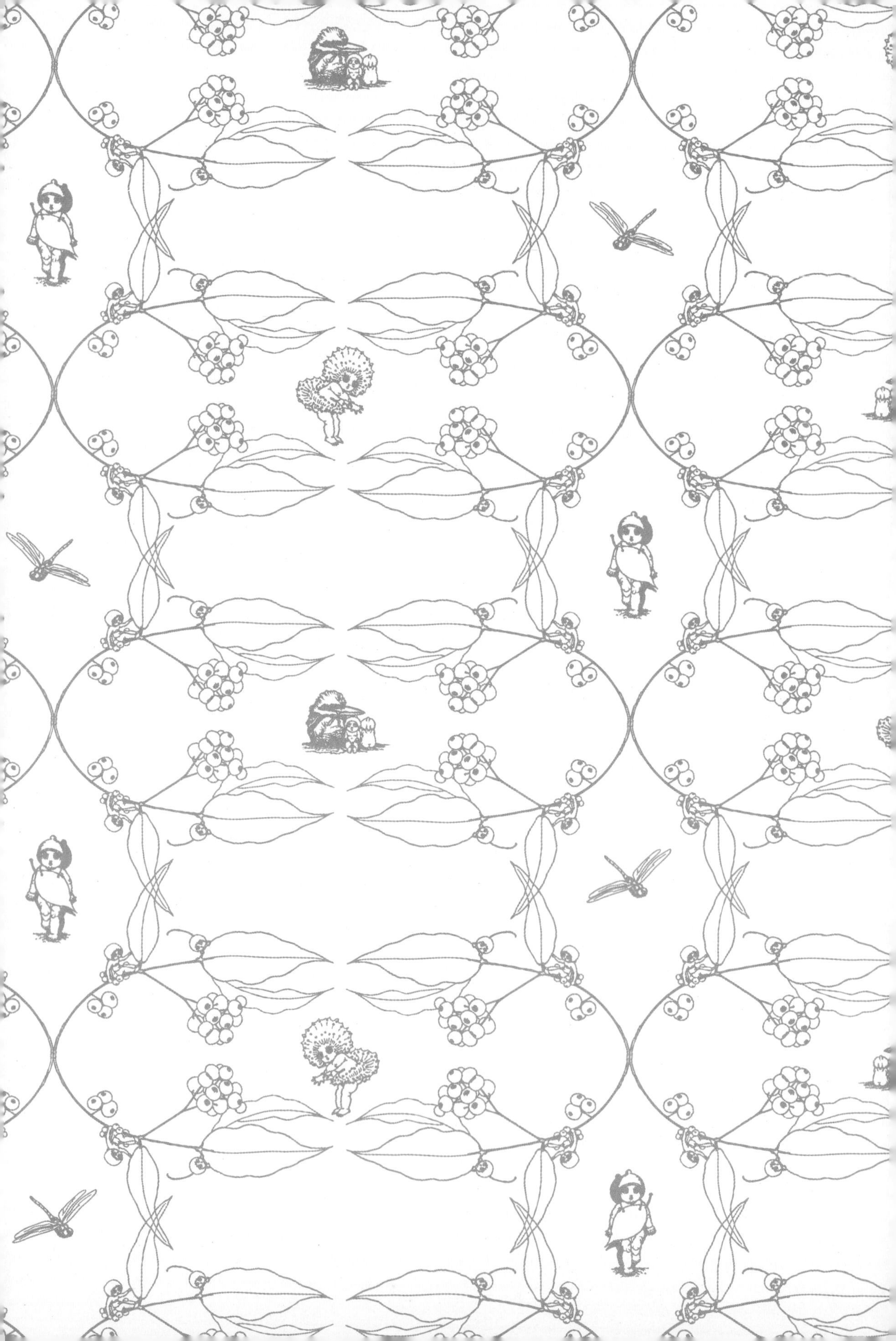